HITLER'S
VIOLENT YOUTH
HOW TRENCH WARFARE AND
STREET FIGHTING MOULDED HITLER

HITLER'S
VIOLENT YOUTH
HOW TRENCH WARFARE AND
STREET FIGHTING MOULDED HITLER

BOB CARRUTHERS

Pen & Sword
MILITARY

This edition published in 2015 by

Pen & Sword Military
An imprint of
Pen & Sword Books Ltd
47 Church Street
Barnsley
South Yorkshire
S70 2AS

ISBN: 9781473833517

A CIP catalogue record for this book is available from the British Library.

Printed and bound in England
By CPI Group (UK) Ltd, Croydon, CR0 4YY

Pen & Sword Books Ltd incorporates the imprints of Pen & Sword Aviation, Pen & Sword Family History, Pen & Sword Maritime, Pen & Sword Military, Pen & Sword Discovery, Pen & Sword Politics, Pen & Sword Atlas, Pen & Sword Archaeology, Wharncliffe Local History, Wharncliffe True Crime, Wharncliffe Transport, Pen & Sword Select, Pen & Sword Military Classics, Leo Cooper, The Praetorian Press, Claymore Press, Remember When, Seaforth Publishing and Frontline Publishing

For a complete list of Pen & Sword titles please contact
PEN & SWORD BOOKS LIMITED
47 Church Street, Barnsley, South Yorkshire, S70 2AS, England
E-mail: enquiries@pen-and-sword.co.uk
Website: www.pen-and-sword.co.uk

CONTENTS

INTRODUCTION

A S A RESULT of the terrible tragedy which befell the Jewish people of Europe, the name Adolf Hitler will forever be synonymous with the creed of extreme anti-Semitism. Due to the inhuman scale of the suffering endured by the Jewish population, genocide is commonly assumed to have been his primary goal and the overriding concern of Adolf Hitler. However, the sobering truth is that, although anti-Semitism was a potent factor in the mix of ideas that shaped Hitler's *weltanschauung* (or world view), it was not the key to his life's work. From his own account as published in the pages of '*Mein Kampf*' we can be certain that, in his own eyes at least, Hitler's life's work was in fact the accomplishment of his pan-German nationalist vision. From a surprisingly early age this political goal was his overwhelming priority and we can be certain that nationalism was the key stimulus on the formation of Hitler's political outlook. Nonetheless, it is the terrible human cost of the Hitlerian regime which continues to demand an explanation today. How did a civilised nation, so much like our own in so many respects, allow itself to be dragged into such an abyss of barbarism?

The answer lies with this peculiar and enigmatic individual. Hitler was a mass of paradoxical contrasts. He was an extremist in every sense of the word and there is no doubt he was extremely gifted in the art of oratory and could command the adoration of a nation; yet he was also naive, boorish, nervous and gauche. He possessed a genius when it came to grand concepts and presentation, and he knew how to excite the passions of an entire nation and to galvanise organisations into action, yet he was utterly incapable of empathising with his fellow human beings. Human rights were an alien concept for Adolf Hitler, yet ironically he was a genuine aesthete who, within his own narrow bounds, lived for opera, music, art and architecture. However, it is notable that none of the liberal values, which colour the arts, were allowed to permeate his world. He espoused only the most conservative and radical solutions to political and social issues.

The most marked trait of Hitler in power was his belief that every strategic or political issue could only be settled by precipitate military action. Hitler had developed this mind-set in the trenches of the Great War and the vicious rough and tumble of the beer halls, and the street fighting of the twenties and thirties added the finishing touch. Despite the fact that these early experiences are absolutely essential to understanding the motivations which led Adolf Hitler to do what he did, historians all too often overlook these vital formative experiences. During the early part of the twentieth century millions of young men had been exposed to a world of violence in the trenches of France and Belgium. However, the Great War marked the young Adolf Hitler in a fundamental and far-reaching manner that is all too readily disregarded. Hitler was an extraordinarily driven individual who was already an ideologue before he reached the trenches, and his embryonic political aspirations were further nurtured in the mud of Flanders. It was here that his life-long love of militarism and his instinctive willingness to take risks was matched by an inherent joy in the process of violence. Hitler perceived the dismal business of making war not as a destructive activity, but as an instrument of social progress and his experience in the trenches did nothing to persuade him away from that view.

From his involvement in the Great War Hitler emerged more convinced than ever that every problem, regardless of the odds to be overcome, could be solved by a sudden and decisive act. In his fledgling political career he fully embraced that philosophy and as a result, he was to come unstuck in the Munich Beer Hall Putsch of November 1923, being imprisoned in a fortress for his pains. However Hitler remained undaunted and, from the night of the long knives onwards, he achieved a string of political and military victories created by a cocktail of brinkmanship, surprise, treachery and violence. His gambler's instinct was rewarded by such an unbroken string of success stretching from the Sudetenland to the gates of Moscow that he came to believe that, no matter how disproportionate the odds stacked against Germany, they could always be overcome by unexpected and decisive action backed by an iron resolve. This unshakable belief was to lead Germany down the path to ruin, dishonour and ignominy.

Despite the fact that Hitler could produce immense energy he was also extremely lazy and unfocused. This trait manifested itself in the fact that he was generally willing to abrogate responsibility for large areas of government policy. He also had the unfortunate habit of delegating the same responsibility to multiple and competing functionaries. In this haphazard way he would let matters take care of themselves. Hitler viewed the apparatus of the state and its functionaries (for which he used the catch-all term the 'Reich') as an organic mechanism which would deliver solutions to many of the issues of the day. For Adolf Hitler the 'Reich' was indeed a machine which needed no operator. It is shocking to realise that the awful human catastrophe inflicted upon the Jews was not even his paramount concern, but unhappily this is indeed the case.

This new book revisits this important area of study by combining the revised and updated findings of two earlier books which were previously published as separate volumes. Those volumes were 'Private Hitler's War' which dealt with his military experiences in the Great War and 'Hitler's Demons' which dealt with the social and political factors influencing his development. In retrospect it was a mistake to separate the military experience from the civilian social influences operating on Adolf Hitler. In order to produce a more coherent portrait of the disparate factors at work on Hitler, I have revised and combined those two separate strands into one work. This single volume hopefully encapsulates all of the most important issues affecting Hitler's formative years and brings them together in a single volume. In order to let the historical record speak I have relied extensively on lengthy quotations from Hitler's own version of events as published by him in the pages of 'Mein Kampf'. I have used the 1937 translation by James Murphy as this edition was published in the UK by Hutchison and Co Ltd. and as such was the only officially sanctioned version which was widely available during the Nazi era.

'Mein Kampf' is routinely dismissed as unreadable and this was certainly the case in contemporary circles where many Nazi functionaries, including Göring, privately joked that they had never read the thing. Italian Fascist dictator and Nazi ally, Benito Mussolini, was famously critical, stating that the book was '…a boring tome that I have never been able to read'. He also remarked that Hitler's beliefs, as expressed in the book, were '…little more than commonplace clichés'. For students of history, politics and general readers with an interest in the period that is certainly not the case. While it is true that large sections of political exposition are rambling and turgid, they do nonetheless repay the reader with an insight into the workings of the mind of Adolf Hitler. The book also contains highly accessible elements of autobiography which are intriguing as they afford us the ultimate primary source glimpse into the private world of Adolf Hitler. On balance I'm sure most readers would side with Winston Churchill who stated, shortly after Hitler's ascension to power, that no other book deserved more intensive scrutiny.

I still believe that Churchill was right. 'Mein Kampf' should not be dismissed as readily as is so often the case. With Hitler in power Germany and its dominions became the grim powerhouse which, in the pages of 'Mein Kampf', he had promised it would be. From 1933 onwards Germany was a place where a social and economic revolution was being built upon injustice, oppression, racism, arbitrary imprisonment, forced labour and extra-judicial death sentences. The warnings of the horrors to come had been plain for all to see since 1924. Hitler ruled over a world in which cruel and unjust excesses were commonplace and all of this had been foretold and clearly elucidated in the pages of 'Mein Kampf'.

We should never lose sight of the fact that Hitler was a masterful politician writing for political purposes. We should obviously approach his words with extreme caution, but they should nonetheless be studied and carefully considered, and where there is no reason to do otherwise, we should be prepared to give the autobiographical sections some weight. This is especially the case where Hitler's account can be cross referenced with other accounts by the likes of Kubizek and Hanisch.

'Mein Kampf', if taken at face value, certainly seems to back up the point of view that pan-German nationalism was at the very heart of

Hitler's thinking. As such it forms a key part of the functionalist versus intentionalist debate. The Intentionalists insist, with considerable force behind their argument, that the infamous passage stating that if 12,000-15,000 Jews were gassed, then 'the sacrifice of millions of soldiers would not have been in vain' proves quite clearly that Hitler had a master plan for the genocide of the Jewish people from the outset. Functionalist historians reject this assertion, noting that the passage does not call for the destruction of the entire Jewish people and they also stress that, although 'Mein Kampf' is suffused with an extreme anti-Semitism, it is the only time in the entire book that Hitler ever explicitly refers to the murder of Jews. It should be noted that he also advocated the murder of journalists who didn't conform exactly to Hitler's perception of the national interest. Given that 'Mein Kampf' is 720 pages long, Functionalist historians caution that it may be placing too much stress on that one sentence. Regardless of which school of thought we fall into, what certainly comes over loud and clear from the pages of 'Mein Kampf' is Hitler's willingness to advocate violent and inhumane solutions to political issues and to publicly articulate mass murder as an answer. Promoting the idea of murdering 15,000 perceived trouble-makers may not amount to advocating the murder of an entire race, but it is sufficiently deluded to merit the conclusion that the writer may have engineered and sanctioned the subsequent events.

My own view hesitantly accords with the Functionalist historians, the evidence points towards the fact that Hitler had, with the introduction of the Nuremberg laws in 1935, effectively overcome his Jewish enemies; and from that point onwards his expansionist agenda was his main focus. The other deciding factor, for me, is the fact that the actual programme of mass murder did not begin until 1941. At that point Hitler was no longer Hitler the politician, as from then on he was completely absorbed by his role as Commander in Chief of the Armed Forces. However, I am certainly open to persuasion, and it is certainly problematic for me, and I suspect many others, to credit the notion that the absence of any documentation fully supports the idea that Hitler had no detailed knowledge of the genocidal programme. Nonetheless, that is the situation we are faced with and unbelievably there is not a shred of hard evidence of the existence of a coherent master plan, there are no directives, no orders, no budgets and no records. Many Functionalists have supported the view that the memorandum written by Heinrich Himmler to Hitler, on 25 May 1940, containing proposals regarding the 'Final Solution to the Jewish Question,' (proposals which Hitler accepted) proves that there was no master plan for genocide stemming back to the 1920s. In the memorandum, Himmler famously rejected a programme of state sanctioned murder on the grounds that one must reject 'the Bolshevik method of physical extermination of a people out of inner conviction as un-German and impossible'. Himmler went on to state that something similar to the 'Madagascar Plan' should be the preferred 'territorial solution' to the 'Jewish question'. However, owing to the declining military situation, the strength of the Royal Navy and the power struggles being waged within the unwieldy German bureaucracy, the policy of expulsion was no longer viable. By January 1942, the Wansee conference, attended by senior members of the bureaucracy, under the direction of Heydrich took the first step on the road which was to lead to systematic mass murder of the Jews. The idea that millions would be worked to death was overtly sanctioned and formed the thin edge of the wedge.

In support of their arguments that the bureaucracy was the driving force behind the programme of genocide, Functionalist historians have also noted that in 'Mein Kampf' the only anti-Semitic policies are the Twenty-Five Point Platform of the Nazi Party (adopted in February 1920). This manifesto demanded that only 'Aryan' Germans be allowed to publish newspapers and own department stores, placed a ban on Jewish immigration, advocated the expulsion of all *Ostjuden* (Eastern Jews; i.e. Jews from Eastern Europe who had arrived in Germany since 1914) and stripped all German Jews of their German citizenship. Although these demands do reflect a hateful anti-Semitism, they do not amount to a programme for genocide. Beyond that, some historians have claimed that although Hitler was clearly imbued with anti-Semitism, his degree of anti-Semitic hatred contained in 'Mein Kampf' is no greater or less than that contained in the writings and speeches of earlier *völkisch* leaders such as Wilhelm Marr, Georg Ritter von Schönerer, Houston Stewart Chamberlain and Karl Lueger, all of whom routinely called Jews a 'disease' and 'vermin'.

Unusually for a book of this nature, I have chosen to rely heavily on the memoirs of Reinhardt Hanisch, a companion of Hitler's from his days in the Vienna men's hostel and his one time business partner. Some authorities in the past have rejected the Hanisch monograph as unreliable. Increasingly however historians have come to reassess Hanisch and in the process have come to accept the voracity of much of what you are about to read here. It is now widely accepted that Hanisch is essentially an accurate, if somewhat self-serving source. Until recent years, and the rehabilitation of Hanisch, scholars and general readers seeking a primary insight into the early life of Adolf Hitler have had to be content with the recollections of his boyhood friend Kubizek, author of 'The Young Hitler I Knew'. There have been suggestions that Kubizek's book was ghost written, but even if that were to be the case there is no doubt that the events described actually transpired. The current body of opinion is that both of these sources are generally accurate accounts of life with Hitler.

Similarly the testimonies of most of Hitler's wartime comrades are generally accepted as being accurate and the key accounts have been included here. One recent source which has come to light is Alexander Moritz Frey's account of his war time experiences with Hitler and their subsequent encounters in Munich. Moritz Frey was a bitter opponent of Hitler and some aspects of his account, such as bumping into a visibly agitated Hitler on the night before the Beer Hall Putsch, seems to be highly unlikely, other parts however do ring true. The other key source I have allowed to speak at length is another Hitler antagonist in the form of Otto Strasser who, in 1940, wrote a deeply partisan account of his dealings with Hitler, which is quoted at length here.

I trust that you will find the ideas expressed in this book compelling and persuasive. However, the debates stemming from the events of the last century continue to unfold today and it is important to keep an open mind.

There really is no final answer and the judgement of each individual reader is as valid as the next. What really matters is the sum of the knowledge we accumulate in addressing these inexplicable events and our willingness to explore the past in a genuine spirit of openness. Thank you for buying this book, I sincerely hope it repays your investment in time and money.

BOB CARRUTHERS

- CHAPTER 1 -

FROM SCHICKLGRUBER TO HITLER

THE ROOTS OF the family tree which produced Adolf Hitler are confused and rather tangled, as a result the task of providing a clear and unambiguous account of Hitler's antecedents is anything but straightforward. We do know for certain that Adolf Hitler was the fourth child of the marriage which took place in January 1885 between the twice widowed Austrian customs official Alois Hitler (formerly known as Alois Schicklgruber) and his pregnant housekeeper Klara Pölzl. However lurking in the shadows behind these bare facts there were obviously some dark family secrets. There were unresolved doubts concerning the true identity of Hitler's paternal grandfather and the true nature of the familial relationship between his parents was highly circumspect. Throughout his life Adolf Hitler was notoriously reluctant to expand upon his own genealogy. This was embarrassing for a politician around whom was built a cult of personality hitherto unparalleled in world history. Hitler's party politics centred on the questions of nationality and race, and it was inevitable therefore that his own family background would at some stage be exposed to close public scrutiny. When that time duly arrived, it was to prove an uncomfortable experience indeed for Adolf Hitler.

At the age of thirty four, while held prisoner in Landsberg prison, Hitler sat down to begin the task of recording his life and political philosophy in the pages of 'Mein Kampf'.[1] He was aware of 'the diligent scrutiny' with which his opponents were prying into his early life. The autobiographical sections of 'Mein Kampf' should, in theory, provide us

---

1. Hitler is often recorded as having dictated the whole work to Rudolf Hess. He in fact began the work on a borrowed typewriter some time before the arrival of Hess. See Timothy Ryback 'Hitler's Private Library'.

with a frank description of Hitler's private life from the writer's point of view; but these passages need to be handled with extreme caution as they were obviously written for mass consumption by a master politician.

The autobiographical sections of *'Mein Kampf'* are clearly designed to present a sanitised version of his early family life and it is important to observe that there is absolutely no mention whatsoever of the strange and notable occurrence of the switch of his father's surname from Schicklgruber to Hitler. In the pages of *'Mein Kampf'*, Hitler in fact made only two limited, and apparently contradictory, statements concerning the whole early life of his father which are limited to just two grossly misleading lines. Initially Alois was described in the following terms: 'He was the son of a poor cottager, and while still a boy he grew restless and left home.' Later, in describing his own visit to Vienna, Hitler states that Alois 'was the poor son of a village shoemaker'. Hitler knew full well there was much more the waiting world would like to know concerning the story of Alois Schicklgruber, but he deliberately chose to give the world only these two highly questionable snippets which were obviously designed to gloss over the uncomfortable and dubious background concerning the real truth about his father's early life.

By the time he came to write *'Mein Kampf'*, Hitler was already living his life in the public eye and there was good reason for the obfuscation concerning his own father's family background. The exact detail surrounding the early life of Alois Hitler had the potential to be highly embarrassing to a man with nationalist political aspirations. Hitler could not hide the fact that he was descended from unsophisticated rustic stock, this was not in itself controversial, and in political terms it could even be viewed as an advantage. However, the problems for Hitler went beyond the fact that there was uncertainty concerning the true identity of his grandfather on his father's side. The painful reality for Adolf Hitler was that he lived in the shadow of a document created in 1876, which legally recognised him as the product of a union between second cousins. This was ready-made political ammunition for Hitler's opponents, and with rumours rife that his parents may in fact have been uncle and niece, it was inevitable innuendo and allegations concerning incest and inbreeding would come to haunt the footsteps of Adolf Hitler.

The problems for Hitler stemmed from his father's side of the family tree, the roots of which can be traced back to the village of Strones in the Waldvertiel district of Austria. Today it is no longer possible to carry out any first hand research into Alois' background in either Strones or in nearby Döllersheim, for the simple reason that both places no longer exist. In the wake of the *Anschluss* of 1938, and disregarding the fact that his paternal grandmother was buried there in a grave honoured by the local Nazi party, Adolf Hitler permitted Strones to be totally destroyed. The official line was that it had been incorporated into the adjoining military training facility of Döllersheim following an expansion of the army base. Given Hitler's disinclination to save the village, it is difficult to conclude otherwise than that the decision was connected to the fact that Alois had been born there and the male side of Hitler's family roots lay exposed in Strones.

As long as the place existed, an obvious avenue into the exploration of the Hitler family history would remain open to investigation by unfriendly factions. As the Hitler myth grew and prospered, a burgeoning Hitler industry had already appeared in Strones and in Döllersheim where, in 1938, the main square was re-named as Alois Hitler Place. Hitler family trees and plaques soon appeared in prominent places but the local community had its own collective memory and the local gossip might be accessible to all who cared to ask a few leading questions. The destruction of the village was all the more sinister for the fact that it had been located on the extreme perimeter of the Döllersheim military facility. This historic site could easily have been spared; but the lack of personal intervention from Adolf Hitler ensured that Strones was flattened and all traces wiped from the face of the earth.

The *Wehrmacht* helped to do a thorough job in exorcising Strones from the map and any archaeological evidence has been well and truly obliterated. Speculation that Hitler was behind these developments was increased by additional incriminating evidence. The village residents were not re-settled in a single new location, but were instead scattered to widely spread new homes. The village and the community therefore both vanished from history taking with them the opportunity for hostile forces to pry into one avenue which provided first hand evidence of the true origins of Hitler's father and the male side of his family. The net result is that the surrounding debate concerning the true paternal origins of the *Führer* rages on to this day.

It is, of course, possible that Hitler had no knowledge of the family history on his father's side. This was certainly the case according to his sister Paula who, in 1945, gave a forthright explanation during the first of her interviews with the US Army:[2]

'Only the relatives on our mother's side were close to us. The Schmieds and the Koppensteins are our dear relatives, especially a cousin Schmied who married a Koppenstein. I knew no one of my father's family. My sister Angela and I often said: "Father must have had some relatives, but we don't even know them."'

If his own information and family contacts were as sketchy as Paula would have us believe, and there is no reason why we shouldn't, we can understand why Hitler was understandably nervous concerning the growing speculation surrounding his own family tree. He finally took, what he must have considered to be, positive action on 29 February 1932, when he retained the distinguished Viennese genealogist Karl Friedreich von Frank to research his family tree in return for the substantial sum of 300 Marks. The work was presented to Hitler in April 1932, and Hitler was initially so pleased he wrote von Frank a letter of congratulation on 25 June 1932.[3]

Unfortunately Hitler's mood of appreciation would not last long. It transpired that the scholar had made an error resulting in the appearance in Hitler's family tree of the decidedly Jewish sounding name of Salomon. By 16 June 1932, a letter appeared in the *Neue Zürcher Zeitung* drawing

---

2. Paula Hitler was interviewed twice by the US Army. The first interview was conducted by George Allen of Headquarters Staff 101st airborne division 101st CIC Detachment on 12 July 1945. The second interview was conducted by agent designated as C-1o and took place on 6 June 1946.

3. See Brigette Hamman 'Hitler's Vienna' for a fuller exposition of the events surrounding Hitler's family tree.

attention to this fact and making the claim that Hitler and his followers would not accept the name of Salomon as an ethnic German name.[4] A revised and corrected family tree was issued by von Frank in 1933, but by then the damage had been done and anything else from that point onwards smacked of a cover up. For once, Hitler was not playing fast and loose with the truth and, in this particular instance, he for once had the facts on his side. In a further effort to nail the rumours Hitler switched genealogists. He employed Rudolf Koppensteiner who came with the added advantage of an in-depth knowledge of the Waldviertel and a familial connection.[5] Koppensteiner too produced an accurate family tree which did not feature the name Salomon, but the rumours persisted nonetheless and in 1938, in a typical fit of pique Hitler simply forbade the publication of any further family trees concerning his own ancestry. He was particularly concerned that the flourishing Hitler heritage industry which had grown up around Döllersheim and Strones should be curtailed. In November 1938, the *Gauleiter* of the Lower Danube District informed his subordinate that the *Führer* had forbidden the display of family trees and memorial plaques designed to serve the memory of the *Führer's* ancestors.[6]

The continuing doubts over the true identity of his parental grandfather led to the inevitable speculation that Hitler was hiding something, and in the febrile political climate of the thirties, this could only mean he had Jewish blood. This rumour was prevalent in the thirties and was encouraged by foreign press which frequently printed sensationalist stories concerning Hitler's family background. Most famous was a Daily Mail article which purportedly traced the grave of

---

4. This was not necessarily the case. Pfiefer von Salomon was a leading figure of the NSDAP.

5. Paula Hitler: 'He did not care for our relatives either. Only the relatives on our mother's side were close to us. The Schmieds and the Koppensteins are our dear relatives, especially a cousin Schmied who married a Koppenstein. I knew no one of my father's family. My sister Angela and I often said: "Father must have had some relatives, but we don't even know them." I myself have a family sense. I like my relatives from the Waldviertel, the Schmieds and the Koppensteins. I usually wrote my brother a birthday letter, and then he wrote a short note, and sent a package. This would contain Spanish ham, flour, sugar, or something like that, that had been given to him for his birthday.'

6. Ibid.

Hitler's grandfather to a Jewish cemetery in Budapest. In the post war era further fuel was added to the fire by the now discredited writings of Josef Greiner,[7] who claimed to have been a close associate of Hitler. After the war the Jewish dimension was given more substance by Hans Frank, the former Nazi Governor of Poland who, while awaiting his execution, swore that Hitler had knowledge that his father had been conceived while his grandmother was serving in the household of a Jewish family called Frankenreiter who were then resident in Graz. This story has long since been discredited on the obvious grounds that there was no Jewish family called Frankenreiter living in Graz in the 1830s, in fact there were no Jews whatsoever living in the town until the 1860s. Until then, Jews had not been permitted to live in Graz or indeed the whole of the province of Styria.

It is no surprise therefore that, in the pages of 'Mein Kampf', Hitler was particularly coy concerning the background of his own father, the man who had originally been named Alois Schicklgruber. Strangely, Alois had carried on life under his original surname until he stood on the brink of middle age then, in 1876, just four years before the birth of Adolf Hitler the thirty-nine year old Alois had abruptly changed his surname from the rustic Schicklgruber to the more workmanlike Hitler. In nineteenth century Austria literacy was by no means universal and a wide variety of spellings were applied to his new surname. There has been speculation that the name may have its origins in the common Czech name Hidlar. The consensus however is that Hitler was simply an alternate of spelling of the German word Hüttler meaning small-holder. In an age where standards of learning were low and literacy was far from universal misspellings were very common and mattered as little as they did in Shakespeare's England. During the nineteenth century the name was widely rendered as Hütler, Hüttler, Hüettler, Hiedler and Heitler. From the evidence of Hitler's own family tree it does not appear to have been uncommon even for siblings to have used different spelling variations of the same surname. The particular variant which resulted in

---

7. Josef Greiner 'Das Ende des Hitler – Mythos'.

the 'Hitler' spelling appeared for the first time in the fifteenth century but prior to 1876, when Alois first began using the name it had fallen into disuse.

Regardless of the exact form of the name, the decision to change Alois' surname was to prove a momentous decision with far reaching and totally unforeseen consequences. Had Alois not taken the fateful decision to change his name, the National Socialist movement may well have been still-born. It has become a cliché, but it is almost inconceivable that the *Führer* could have risen to such strong prominence on the back of adoring crowds chanting *'Heil Schicklgruber!'*

The thorny question of the true identity of Hitler's genetic grandfather has never been satisfactorily resolved. Not surprisingly, it later assumed great importance in a party obsessed by racial identity. In addition to the two studies into his genealogical background which Hitler himself commissioned, there were also a number of clandestine investigations into his background by Nazi party functionaries and, on at least two occasions, by the Gestapo. It is ironic that a man who presided over a party which set so much stock on the 'purity' of racial bloodlines should have such a questionable cloud over his own pedigree. 'People of the same blood should be in the same Reich', was one of the key lines in the opening statements of *'Mein Kampf'* and, of course, this was the party which insisted that members of the SS should be able to prove pure 'Aryan' blood lines stretching back over three previous generations. For Hitler's opponents the potentially incestuous nature of the relationship between Alois and Klara Hitler was political dynamite. It opened up all of the obvious opportunities for satire concerning inbreeding and the curious ways of unsophisticated country folk. For Hitler there were even darker rumours to contend with. The local speculation was that Alois and Klara, Hitler's parents, were both actually descended from Johan Nepomuk Hüettler and were in fact uncle and niece. This unattractive conjecture could not have been helped by Hitler's mother's lifelong habit of referring to her husband as 'uncle'. Nor could it have escaped attention that, prior to their marriage, Alois had always referred to his future wife as his 'niece'.

Hitler knew that when the young Alois had left his rural home to move to Vienna and try to build a new life, at the age of just thirteen, Alois had experienced extreme economic hardship at first hand. The young Adolf no doubt had the benefit of these experiences recounted to him many times and was therefore well aware of how difficult life had been for his father. Hitler seems to have recalled every detail of the story and made a point of respectfully recording his father's early trials and hardships in 'Mein Kampf':

'When he was barely thirteen years old he buckled on his satchel and set forth from his native woodland parish. Despite the dissuasion of villagers who could speak from "experience", he went to Vienna to learn a trade there. This was in the fiftieth year of the last century (1850). It was a sore trial, that of deciding to leave home and face the unknown, with three gulden in his pocket. By then the boy of thirteen was a lad of seventeen and had passed his apprenticeship examination as a craftsman but he was not content. Quite the contrary. The persistent economic depression of that period and the constant want and misery strengthened his resolution to give up working at a trade and strive for 'something higher'. As a boy it had seemed to him that the position of the parish priest in his native village was the highest in the scale of human attainment; but now that the big city had enlarged his outlook the young man looked up to the dignity of a State official as the highest of all.'

Alois obviously was a man who drew strength from adversity and his decision to strive to become a customs officer was pursued with total dedication. Alois' unstinting efforts eventually resulted in a solid and respectable career as a minor customs official as Hitler dutifully recorded in 'Mein Kampf':

'In this little town on the Inn, hallowed by the memory of a German martyr, a town that was Bavarian by blood but under the rule of the Austrian State, my parents were domiciled towards the end of the last century. My father was a civil servant who fulfilled his duties very conscientiously.'

Reinhold Hanisch, a later acquaintance of Hitler's, recorded how

Hitler had told him with some pride of his father's work on a celebrated case. Apparently Hitler's father had distinguished himself a number of times by his work as a customs official. An example was the case of a certain man in Vienna who received parcels of cigars from Germany. Alois was struck by the inferior quality of these cigars, and at the examination of one of the packages a cigar broke. A diamond fell out, and so a smuggler was discovered.[8]

Episodes such as this can only have served to enhance the reputation of Alois Hitler, however there was unfinished business with the Customs Service as far as Alois was concerned. Alois had gone as far as he could, his limited academic record dictated that further promotion was impossible. Progress beyond a certain level was simply not allowed to those without the necessary qualifications. Alois had certainly studied very hard and passed all of the internal examinations, but he had been blocked in his efforts to advance further in his career by the unalterable fact that he lacked the necessary paper qualifications which would have opened the door to further advancement and promotion. In his later years Alois was satisfied that he had achieved most of his life's goals. He had progressed as far as the rules allowed him to and Alois was a great respecter of rules. The Customs service had provided the family with a comfortable lifestyle and Alois expected the young Adolf to diligently respect his wishes and follow a career into the civil service. Naturally Alois was keen to see that his son did not repeat his own mistakes and he was anxious that the young Adolf should make the best of his educational opportunities, however the young Adolf was already proving himself to be a willful and stubborn character, not at all pliant to his father's wishes. Alois therefore attempted to coerce the youngster into studying hard by the only means he knew, which was violence. As a boy, Hitler was to endure numerous and frequent thrashings.

After the war, Hitler's sister Paula was twice interrogated by the US Army and on 12 July 1945, she gave a brief account of his early

---

8. Hanisch, Reinhold 'I Was Hitler's Buddy'. The New Republic first published in three weekly parts on April 5, 12 and 19 1939.

life which backs up the view that Hitler had to endure an inordinate amount of physical beating at the hand of his violent father.

'Since I was so much younger than my brother he never considered me a playmate. He played a leading role among his early companions. His favourite game was cops and robbers, and that sort of thing. He had a lot of companions. I could not say what took place in their games, as I was never present. Adolf as a child always came home too late. He got a spanking every night for not coming home on time.'[9]

Paula was very much a dark horse in the Hitler story. It has been conjectured that she may have been educationally sub-normal. She never married, did not join the Nazi party and shunned the limelight. She was seven years younger than Hitler and played a relatively minor role in his youth, he referred to her as 'the kid'. After the Second World War, Paula lived a quiet unobtrusive life in Bertchesgaden, under the pseudonym Paula Wolf. She was something of a disappointment for her US interrogators as she able to throw very little light on either Hitler or the regime he led. The painstaking efforts of her interrogators produced virtually nothing which was of real value at the first interview. In order to ensure that this was indeed the case, Paula was interrogated again on 6 June 1946. Once again she could provide virtually no meaningful intelligence on the inner workings of the Third Reich, she again could furnish information only on the simple domestic world that she recalled from her childhood. It is important to note however that the subject of Alois and the beatings he meted out to the young Adolf again reared its ugly head.

'It was especially my brother Adolf, who challenged my father to extreme harshness and who got his sound thrashing every day. He was a scrubby little rogue, and all attempts of his father to thrash him for his rudeness and to cause him to love the profession of an official of the estate were in vain. How often on the other hand did my mother

---

9. Paula Hitler was interviewed twice by the US Army the first interview was conducted by George Allen of Headquarters Staff 101st airborne division 101st CIC Detachment on 12 July 1945. The second interview was conducted by agent designated as C-1o and took place on 6 June 1946.

caress him and try to succeed with her kindness, where the father could not succeed with harshness!'

In total contrast to Alois, Hitler's mother Klara is generally held to have possessed a compassionate nature. She was inclined to be adoring and indulgent when it came to her son. This is not surprising as she had already experienced the unbearable pain of losing four children and Adolf was at times a sickly child. It is entirely understandable therefore that Klara doted on her children and her stepchildren, although one dissenting voice came from Alois Junior, who bitterly recalled that she favoured Adolf by taking his side in any dispute. Although the passages in *'Mein Kampf'* concerning Alois may have been somewhat coloured for public consumption and do not reveal the whole truth about the man, however concerning Klara we have absolutely no reason to doubt the voracity of the passages of *'Mein Kampf'*. Hitler was absolutely devoted to his mother and loved her totally and absolutely unconditionally. For her part she reciprocated his love to the point of immoderation. In the pages of *'Mein Kampf'*, Hitler clearly recalled the devotion of Klara to her family:

'My mother looked after the household and lovingly devoted herself to the care of her children. From that period I have not retained very much in my memory; because after a few years my father had to leave that frontier town which I had come to love so much and take up a new post farther down the Inn valley, at Passau, therefore actually in Germany itself.'

Hitler's view of his home life was mirrored by Paula's own recollection of life in the Hitler household. When pushed by her interrogators Paula Hitler resorted to expanding on the domestic life of her family. It is interesting to note that even a loving daughter still considered her father's attitude to be extremely severe. Alois certainly left his mark on all who came into contact with him:

'The married life of my parents was a very happy one, in spite of their very unlike characters. My father, who was of great harshness in the education of his children and who only spoiled me as the pet of the family, was the absolute type of the old Austrian official,

conservative and loyal to his emperor to the skin. My mother,
however, was a very soft and tender person, the compensatory element
between the almost too harsh father and the very lively children who
perhaps were somewhat difficult to train. If there were ever quarrel
or difference of opinion between my parents it was always on account
of the children.'

In 1892, the Hitler family moved from Braunau to Passau. The Austrian customs house was on the German side of the border and for three years Hitler enjoyed a brief but nonetheless formative glimpse of life in Kaiser Wilhelm's Empire. The three year stay in Germany itself appears to have had a profound impact on the young Adolf at a crucial stage in his development. The Bavarian accent and Bavarian way of life left their indelible mark and Hitler thrived in his new environment. The German idyll was destined to be cut short however as Alois was soon promoted and recalled to a post in the interior of Austria. Hitler ruefully recorded this disappointing event in the pages of *'Mein Kampf':*

'In those days it was the usual lot of an Austrian civil servant to
be transferred periodically from one post to another. Not long after
coming to Passau my father was transferred to Linz.'

Alois arrived in Linz in 1894, and acquired a small farm at Hadfeld near Fischlam, a small agricultural community near Lambach, which was situated some thirty miles from Linz itself. The family moved from Passau to Linz to join him in April 1895, and the children were once again re-united with the over-bearing Alois. From that time onwards Hitler regarded the city of Linz as his home city. Hitler began his school career at the tiny primary school in Fischlam and was soon making good progress which continued over the next two years. While Hitler continued to absorb these new experiences Alois was coming to the end of his working life and took retirement at the age of fifty-eight and settled down to a new career as a farmer working the Hadfeld smallholding. It was to prove an unhappy switch. By 1897, the farm was proving to be too much for Alois who sold up and moved the family to Lambach. Accordingly Hitler switched to the slightly larger school at Lambach where he continued to make good progress academically.

Alois was very keen for his son to follow in his own footsteps and become a civil servant. Accordingly he placed a great deal of pressure on the young boy to conform to these wishes and apply himself at school. Unfortunately the young Adolf was about to unveil a stubborn side to his character as he later recorded in 'Mein Kampf':

'It was at this period that I first began to have ideals of my own. I spent a good deal of time scampering about in the open, on the long road from school, and mixing up with some of the roughest of the boys, which caused my mother many anxious moments. All this tended to make me something quite the reverse of a stay-at-home. I gave scarcely any serious thought to the question of choosing a vocation in life; but I was certainly quite out of sympathy with the kind of career which my father had followed. I think that an inborn talent for speaking now began to develop and take shape during the more or less strenuous arguments which I used to have with my comrades. I had become a juvenile ringleader who learned well and easily at school but was rather difficult to manage.'

Astonishingly, given the man he was to become, the young Adolf seems to have seriously considered the possibility of becoming a parish priest. Hitler was aware that his father had considered the church a worthy calling and this may well have prompted Hitler's thoughts in this direction. Given all that we now know about Adolf Hitler this astounding revelation seems unlikely, but it was plainly recorded for posterity in the pages of 'Mein Kampf'. Unlike many of the claims which are hotly debated, there is no apparent reason to doubt the fact that the young man at some stage genuinely harboured this ambition however fleetingly:

'In my free time I practised singing in the choir of the monastery church at Lambach, and thus it happened that I was placed in a very favourable position to be emotionally impressed again and again by the magnificent splendour of ecclesiastical ceremonial. What could be more natural for me than to look upon the Abbot as representing the highest human ideal worth striving for, just as the position of the humble village priest had appeared to my father in his own boyhood days? At least, that was my idea for a while.'

Hitler's early infatuation with the church appears to have left at least some residual echoes. He had no enthusiasm for the more esoteric neo-religions backed by Himmler, Rosenberg and Goebbels. This was spotted by his opponents as a potential Achilles heel. Much later in his life Hitler's brief flirtation with the church was revisited on 6 November 1936, when a meeting took place between Cardinal Michael Faulhaber and Hitler. The passage outlining Hitler's early faith was something which the Catholic Church was able to latch on to like a laser beam. Clinging on to the perceived remains of Hitler's religious faith, Faulhaber was able to begin the Machiavellian process of driving a wedge between Hitler and the senior figures of his party. During the course of the meeting Faulhaber attempted to have Alfred Rosenberg's fiercely anti-Christian book 'The Myth of the 20th Century' banned and replaced with a church friendly volume 'The Foundations of National Socialism' written by Bishop Alois Hudal. Hitler prevaricated and acknowledged to Faulhaber:

'I have always informed my party chiefs that I have no desire to play the role of the religious reformer ...I will not do so.'[10]

In the largely Catholic community of Lambach the highly respectable position of village priest was an aspirational role and one which his father certainly admired. One might have expected Alois to encourage his son in his new found enthusiasm for the church, but the two appear to have differed strongly over Adolf's suitability for life in the church. Alois must have sensed that the church was an entirely unsuitable vocation for the headstrong and argumentative Adolf. Alois considered that Adolf had natural intelligence and retreated to his familiar refrain that Adolf should therefore aspire to a career in the civil service. Hitler could not understand Alois' continuing infatuation with the civil service and according to 'Mein Kampf' seems to have made his point strongly and often:

'But the juvenile disputes I had with my father did not lead him to appreciate his son's oratorical gifts in such a way as to see in them

---

10. See Ryback, Timothy 'Hitler's Private Library' for a fuller exposition.

a favourable promise for such a career, and so he naturally could not understand the boyish ideas I had in my head at that time. This contradiction in my character made him feel somewhat anxious.'

The young Adolf seems to have maintained his interest in a career in the church only a short time before it faded, to be replaced with other thoughts of art, politics and militarism:

'As a matter of fact, that transitory yearning after such a vocation soon gave way to hopes that were better suited to my temperament.'

In November 1898, the family moved again, this time the switch was to Leonding, a village located on the outskirts of Linz. The Hitler house was a fairly substantial dwelling which was an outward symbol of the middle class status to which Alois had aspired. The location was idyllic on a rural lane just across the way from the village church and with the local Gasthaus Weisinger conveniently suited at the bottom of the hill. The location suited Alois but, as he began his secondary education, the young Adolf Hitler was faced with the long walk into Linz, taking a full hour to school and back each day. Although Hitler had performed well in his *Volkschules* (or primary schools) the transition to secondary education was to prove a huge problem for the young man. His progress at *Realschule* in Linz was very disappointing and was compounded by a series of disagreements with his father.

Hitler junior was by now convinced that he was destined to become a great artist and he was becoming more and more disinterested in formal education. As he began to lose interest academically the poor results began to set alarm bells ringing. In the pages of *'Mein Kampf'*, Hitler attempted to disguise his lack of academic progress with the highly suspect claim that it was all a deliberate ploy on his part. With the shamelessness which marks him out as a member of the political class Hitler, in all seriousness, proclaimed to the world that his lack of academic success was actually part of a carefully conceived master plan to thwart his father's ambitions for him to pursue a career as a civil servant:

'My father forbade me to entertain any hopes of taking up the art of painting as a profession. I went a step further and declared that I

would not study anything else. With such declarations the situation became still more strained, so that the old gentleman irrevocably decided to assert his parental authority at all costs. That led me to adopt an attitude of circumspect silence, but I put my threat into execution. I thought that, once it became clear to my father that I was making no progress at the Realschule, for weal or for woe, he would be forced to allow me to follow the happy career I had dreamed of.

I do not know whether I calculated rightly or not. Certainly my failure to make progress became quite visible in the school. I studied just the subjects that appealed to me, especially those which I thought might be of advantage to me later on as a painter. What did not appear to have any importance from this point of view, or what did not otherwise appeal to me favourably, I completely sabotaged. My school reports of that time were always in the extremes of good or bad, according to the subject and the interest it had for me. In one column my qualification read 'very good' or 'excellent'. In another it read 'average' or even 'below average'. By far my best subjects were geography and, even more so, general history. These were my two favourite subjects, and I led the class in them.'

Hitler's father kept up the pressure on the young Adolf to achieve, but judging from his surviving school reports it does not appear that Adolf Hitler was academically able. He certainly was not considered worthy of a classical education by his father. Alois felt that Hitler should concentrate on practical subjects which pointed Hitler away from the Gymnasium, the type of school which would offer the possibility of a University place in favour of the *Realschule* which offered a route towards more technical qualifications. With drawing, geography and history on the curriculum there was certainly a greater focus on the few subject areas which did interest the young Adolf:

'Considering my character as a whole, and especially my temperament, my father decided that the classical subjects studied at the Lyceum were not suited to my natural talents. He thought that the Realschule would suit me better.'

The subjects studied by students attending *Realschule* were more practical in application and were designed to produce engineers rather than artists. Alois was a very practical man and he placed little value on a classical education. One point of agreement which was reached between Alois and Adolf was on the subject of Hitler's artistic talents:

'My obvious talent for drawing confirmed him in that view; for in his opinion drawing was a subject too much neglected in the Austrian Gymnasium. Probably also the memory of the hard road which he himself had travelled contributed to make him look upon classical studies as unpractical and accordingly to set little value on them.'

There was no doubt that Hitler had a real talent for drawing, but in other subjects such as mathematics he was clearly out of his depth. The first signs that Hitler was struggling academically soon began to reveal themselves. The *Realschule* at Linz was much more of a trial for Hitler, he missed the comfort of the small village schools of his childhood. In 1924, Professor Huemer, who was Hitler's form master for three years at Linz *Realschule*, was called upon to give evidence as to Hitler's character at the Treason Trial following the unsuccessful Munich Putsch of November 1923. The professor, despite the fact that he supported Hitler's aims, was only able to testify in negative terms saying:

'Hitler was certainly gifted, although only for particular subjects, but he lacked self-control and, to say the least, he was considered argumentative, autocratic, self-opinionated and bad tempered. He was unable to submit to school discipline. Nor was he industrious; otherwise, gifted as he was, he would have achieved much better results.'[11]

According to Kubizek part of the reason for Hitler's taciturn nature at school was the fact that he was shunned by the other schoolboys who by and large came from well-to-do inner city families and took delight in ridiculing Hitler as a country peasant. This contributed to the fact that Hitler formed no friendships at school. Isolated and angry

---

11. Heumer was actually appearing as a defence witness.

as he now was, Hitler was no longer the class leader, as he had been at Fischlam and Leonding, and clearly he had difficulties concentrating. His marks soon suffered accordingly which can only have served to enrage the notoriously short-tempered Alois.

Alois was an autocratic father in a sense of the word which might be difficult for most 21st Century readers to comprehend. During the course of her second interrogation, Hitler's sister Paula revealed just how dogmatic and intransigent Alois could be on the subject of how his children should live their lives when she described to her interrogator Alois' attitude towards whether or not Hitler's half sister Angela should be allowed to marry:

> 'Of my other brothers and sisters I especially remember my stepsister Angela as a beautiful girl. Also she was watched by my father very harshly. He was examining every suitor with the strict demand that only a civil servant was allowed to marry her. Actually in 1903, she married the Revenue officer Leo Raubal in Linz, who died very young in 1910.'

Alois' unbending attitude towards Angela's choice of husband was mirrored in his attitude to Adolf and his choice of career. However much Hitler sought to argue or play up, Alois was still strongly of the opinion that his son should ultimately become a civil servant. It was a conviction which Alois would take with him to his grave and it was the foundation of a chasm between Alois and Adolf. The clear impression of this fundamental dispute between father and son was to stay with Hitler who recorded his thoughts in Landsberg prison some 25 years later:

> 'At the back of his mind he had the idea that his son also should become an official of the Government. Indeed he had decided on that career for me. The difficulties through which he had to struggle in making his own career led him to overestimate what he had achieved, because this was exclusively the result of his own indefatigable industry and energy. The characteristic pride of the self-made man urged him towards the idea that his son should follow the same calling and if possible rise to a higher position in it. Moreover, this idea was strengthened by the consideration that the results of his

own life's industry had placed him in a position to facilitate his son's advancement in the same career.'

At 10 A.M. on the morning of 3 January 1903, Alois, as punctual as ever, dropped in for his morning drink at his local pub the Gasthaus Weisinger (sometimes referred to as Gasthaus Steifler), when he suddenly collapsed and died, probably of a sudden haemorrhage in the lungs. This came as a devastating, emotional and financial blow to the family. For Adolf, who was just fourteen, it was a mixed blessing, the threat of domestic violence was over and more importantly he was suddenly released from the pressure which had been on him to find a job working for the civil service. He was now free to pursue his preferred choice of study, that of art. Hitler's doting mother was always ready to indulge his every whim. With Alois gone, Hitler appears to have convinced his mother that the hour long walk to school was too much for his delicate constitution and, despite the expense he was allowed to take up lodgings in Linz itself. Hitler spent term time in the residence of Frau Sekira. This fresh extravagance was presumably justified on the grounds that it would benefit his schooling. The results suggested otherwise and Hitler only just scraped into the third form after being forced to sit a remedial exam.

In 1905, Klara followed in her son's footsteps and moved the small family unit into Linz. They took up residence at Humboldtstrasse 31 set on a busy thoroughfare in a less affluent part of the inner city. The flat was located in an unassuming apartment block which still survives to this day. In the small apartment there was a shared room for Klara and Paula and a very small room for the young Adolf. Despite the ordinariness of his surroundings Hitler fell in love with Linz and later developed grandiose plans to completely redevelop the city. In the meantime there were other matters to concern the young man. School life was proving as difficult as ever and the need to produce results was clearly becoming a trial, but there was one aspect of life in Linz which delighted and captivated the young Adolf. Linz had its own opera house and it was in Linz that Hitler discovered grand opera. It was a beginning of a life-long love affair with opera and with the work of Wagner in particular.

Hitler recorded his thrilling discovery of Wagner from a performance of Lohengrin which Hitler saw for the first time at the age of twelve. He later recalled this important moment with crystal clarity in the pages of 'Mein Kampf':

'A precocious revolutionary in politics I was no less a precocious revolutionary in art. At that time the provincial capital of Upper Austria had a theatre which, relatively speaking, was not bad. Almost everything was played there. When I was twelve years old I saw William Tell performed. That was my first experience of the theatre. Some months later I attended a performance of Lohengrin, the first opera I had ever heard. I was fascinated at once. My youthful enthusiasm for the Bayreuth Master knew no limits. Again and again I was drawn to hear his operas; and today I consider it a great piece of luck that these modest productions in the little provincial city prepared the way and made it possible for me to appreciate the better productions later on.'

- CHAPTER 2 -
HITLER AND GERMAN NATIONALISM

I N ADDITION TO the convoluted social and domestic factors which played their part in determining the man Adolf Hitler would become, there were also a wide range of historical, geographical, political and social factors which influenced the young man and his thinking. The external influences which played upon the young Adolf Hitler had their roots deep in the complex tapestry of German and Austrian history.

Braunau, the small town on the river Inn which was the site of Hitler's birth in 1889, was then part of the Hapsburg Empire of Austria-Hungary. However Braunau am Inn was located in the extreme west of the Hapsburg Empire very close to the German border and at various times in history had been in fact part of Bavaria. The region was known in Hitler's day by its Austrian name as the *Innviertel*. However the hilly and wooded area of the Inn river valley area had formerly been better known by the Bavarian name of *Innbaiern* during the time when it belonged to Bavaria. In 1777, the region was ceded to Austria, however in 1809, during the Napoleonic Wars it was returned to Bavaria and became once more the Innbaiern, but this was to prove a short-lived interlude and in 1816, the region was ceded to Austria again and reverted to the Austrian name of *Innviertel*. Hitler described the *Innviertel* as 'Bavarian by blood but under the rule of the Austrian State.'[12]

Regardless of which political boundary applied at any given time, the area was predominantly ethnic German in character and the vast majority of the population were German speakers who were naturally inclined to consider themselves part of the greater German Reich. The word Reich is a term very frequently used by Hitler, but the word as understood by

---

12. *'Mein Kampf'*: Murphy trans 1938, Coda Books Electronic Edition 2011.

him requires some careful exploration. It is a German form of the Latin word *Regnum*, but it does not necessarily mean Kingdom, Empire or Republic. In German, it is a sort of basic word that may apply to any form of constitution. James Murphy, the first official translator of '*Mein Kampf*', suggested that perhaps the English word 'Realm' would be the best translation as it suggests a harmonious region populated by willing subjects belonging to a commonly accepted grouping. August Kubizek later recalled how much Hitler relied upon this word when all others failed and he was left grasping for the requisite vocabulary to adequately frame his political ideas.

It should be noted though that the word Empire can, of course, be used interchangeably to refer to the periods when the Reich was literally an Empire. The forerunner of the first German Empire was the Holy Roman Empire which Charlemagne founded in A.D. 800. Charlemagne was King of the Franks, a group of Germanic tribes that subsequently became Romanized. In the tenth century Charlemagne's Empire passed into German hands when Otto I (936-973) became Emperor.

In '*Mein Kampf*', Hitler often refers to the Austrian area of the German Reich by the archaic term as the *Ostmark* (Eastern Frontier), by this he meant the frontier land that was initially founded by Charlemagne as the eastern bulwark of his new empire. The *Ostmark* was originally inhabited principally by Germano-Celtic tribes called the Bajuvari. By Hitler's time the *Ostmark* had indeed served for centuries as the eastern border of Western Christendom against invasion in the endless wars against the Turks. Formally known as the Holy Roman Empire of the German Nation, the Empire (or First Reich as it was later called) continued to exist under German emperors until Napoleon overran and dismembered all of the German territories during the first decade of the nineteenth century. Finally, yielding to personal pressure from Napoleon, on 6 August 1806, the last Emperor Francis II formally resigned the German crown, and the First Reich passed into history.

In consequence of its central position Austria has constantly been the scene of a never-ending procession of military encounters which have left their terrible marks on the long suffering population. Empires had come and gone, borders were redefined and populations were divided. The recurring turmoil of the Napoleonic wars was no exception and had also left its own bloody stain on the area in which Hitler was born and grew up. These historical echoes contributed further to the formation of Hitler's political view of the world which eventually coalesced into his rabid strain of ultra-nationalism.

Hitler was painfully aware that from 1792 to 1814, the French Revolutionary Armies had overrun Germany. In 1805, the Bavarian Elector was made King of Bavaria by Napoleon and was compelled to support Napoleon in all his future campaigns with a force of 30,000 men. Bavaria had effectively become the absolute vassal of the French. This was 'The Time of Germany's Deepest Humiliation', which in the pages of 'Mein Kampf' is referred to again and again by Hitler. Hitler took the phrase from an 1806 pamphlet entitled 'Germany's Deepest Humiliation' which was originally published in southern Germany. Among those who helped to circulate the pamphlet was the Nürnberg bookseller, Johannes Philipp Palm. Unfortunately Palm was denounced to the French by a Bavarian police agent. At his trial he bravely refused to disclose the name of the author. On Napoleon's personal orders, Palm was shot at Braunau-on-the-Inn on 26 August 1806. At the time of Palm's death Braunau was officially part of Bavaria, a situation which, had it endured, may have satisfied some of Hitler's political frustrations. Unfortunately, the Innveirtel had been ceded back to Austria in 1816. A monument erected to Palm on the site of his execution was one of the first public objects that made a great impression on Hitler as a little boy and was duly recorded in the pages of 'Mein Kampf':

> 'Over a hundred years ago this sequestered spot was the scene of a tragic calamity which affected the whole German nation and will be remembered for ever, at least in the annals of German history. At the time of our Fatherland's deepest humiliation a bookseller, Johannes Palm, uncompromising nationalist and enemy of the French, was put to death here because he had the misfortune to have loved Germany well. He obstinately refused to disclose the names of his associates, or rather the principals who were chiefly responsible for the affair.'

As he grew up, Hitler began to take an interest in militarism. This unfortunate interest was spurred on by a chance discovery of Heinrich Gerling's two volume illustrated history of the Franco Prussian War, which Hitler's father appears to have collected as illustrated periodicals which had then been bound into book form, and the young Hitler soon discovered these in his father's library. They were to become his favourite reading. Hitler understood the military aspects of the campaign and obviously embraced the concept of military duty. Unfortunately Hitler was one if those individuals who could not distinguish between the abstract idea of war as a glorious endeavour and the appalling reality of war as a destroyer of lives. The terrible human price of war is not always apparent from the pages of a military history book, but most readers can easily conceptualise the awful human cost of war. Hitler however, was incapable of seeing the wider picture, throughout his life he viewed war as a noble pursuit. It is almost impossible to rationalise the fact, but Hitler loathed being at peace. In the pages of *'Mein Kampf'* he described how, as a boy, he rued the fact that he was born at a time of peace and actually wished to see a state of war declared. This short passage is often overlooked, but it offers a chilling insight into the mind of a man who was not content to be at peace and who considered war to be a good and necessary thing. It is this bizarre passage which is one of the key defining extracts from the whole rambling opus:

'During the boisterous years of my youth nothing used to damp my wild spirits so much as to think that I was born at a time when the world had manifestly decided not to erect any more temples of fame except in honour of business people and State officials. The tempest of historical achievements seemed to have permanently subsided, so much so that the future appeared to be irrevocably delivered over to what was called peaceful competition between the nations… Why could I not have been born a hundred years ago? I used to ask myself. Somewhere about the time of the Wars of Liberation, when a man was still of some value even though he had no 'business'. Thus I used to think it an ill-deserved stroke of bad luck that I had arrived too late on this terrestrial globe, and I felt chagrined at the idea that my

life would have to run its course along peaceful and orderly lines. As a boy I was anything but a pacifist and all attempts to make me so turned out futile.'

A mature adult can normally recognise the fact that, in reality, warfare is brutal, barbaric and harrowing. There is nothing redeeming or uplifting about the whole dismal process. The events of even the smallest war have catastrophic and traumatic consequences for individuals and societies. Maimed children, shattered lives, mental anguish, disease, starvation and despair are the reality behind the façade of the smart uniforms and ordered parades. Hitler however was oblivious to the mental, physical and emotional damage which blights the lives of those unfortunate to find themselves visited by war. This inability to appreciate the wider consequences of militarism and empathise with its victims is all the more puzzling in the light of the fact that Hitler had served in the trenches for almost the whole course of the Great War. He had witnessed suffering on an unimaginable scale yet he remained blind to the human consequences. Hitler it seems shared the ability, common to so many politicians, to rationalise unacceptable and unlawful actions with the simple platitude that 'the end justifies the means'. His inability to empathise with the misfortune which war visited on his fellow human beings was the defining flaw in Hitler's psychological make-up. His childhood desire to live in a world visited by military conflict speaks volumes and lay at the root of everything else which follows. It is depressing to realise how much misery flowed from this one chance discovery in his father's library:

'Browsing through my father's books, I chanced to come across some publications that dealt with military subjects. One of these publications was a popular history of the Franco-German War of 1870-71. It consisted of two volumes of an illustrated periodical dating from those years. These became my favourite reading. In a little while that great and heroic conflict began to take first place in my mind. And from that time onwards I became more and more enthusiastic about everything that was in any way connected with war or military affairs.'

The military aspects of the Franco-Prussian campaign were easy enough for Hitler to comprehend, but the political and historical background soon began to raise other questions in the mind of the young Adolf Hitler. There were a number of dangerous conclusions which could readily be drawn from the young Hitler's meditations upon the traumatic events of 1870-71.

Bismark had succeeded in his political aims by the application of force. His victories had brought huge benefits to Germany and had been bought at relatively little cost. Hitler's passionate interest would have embraced these conclusions. The study of the Franco-Prussian war soon led Hitler's inquiring mind to delve into a study of the reasons behind it. Unfortunately it was this formative foray which formed the first tiny steps on the road to a career in politics. Hitler's early infatuation with the Franco-Prussian war soon roused ominous questions in the young man's fevered mind concerning German nationhood and nationalism which were to have disastrous consequences for humanity in the twentieth century:

> 'But this story of the Franco-German War had a special significance for me on other grounds also. For the first time, and as yet only in quite a vague way, the question began to present itself: Is there a difference – and if there be, what is it – between the Germans who fought that war and the other Germans? Why did not Austria also take part in it? Why did not my father and all the others fight in that struggle? Are we not the same as the other Germans? Do we not all belong together? That was the first time that this problem began to agitate my small brain.'

By the time of Hitler's birth in 1889, Austria was still under the rule of the venerable House of Habsburg and now formed part of the Austro-Hungarian Empire. The august Emperor Franz Josef I had been on the throne since 1848. He presided over a steadily declining empire and Bismark had been eager to bring German Austria into the Second Reich which was founded in 1871, but even he was unable to overcome the political obstacles in order to achieve this ambition. The Austria which Hitler knew was governed as part of a relatively new state which had been created as a result of the *Ausgleich* or Compromise of 1867. The Austro-Prussian War of 1866 had proved to be the final factor in the road to the *Ausgleich* and the hasty decision to restructure the Austrian Empire to include two separate spheres was taken in the wake of the embarrassing defeat which Austria had suffered at the hands of the Prussians during the brief 'war of the brothers' in 1886. Austria had also lost the ability to exercise a continued influence in a unified Germany and she also had to give up any remaining claims in Italy. The deflated Austrian state needed to redefine itself in order to maintain unity in the face of the explosion of nationalist sentiment.

Under this unwieldy and ill-fated arrangement the Austrian Habsburgs agreed to share power with a separate Hungarian government. The cumbersome Dual Monarchy arrangement was designed to function as a union between the crowns of the Austrian Empire and the Kingdom of Hungary, which were united under Emperor Franz Josef, who ruled as both Emperor and King. This scheme divided the territory of the former Austrian Empire into two spheres of political control. The Compromise established the framework of the new government in which the Cisleithanian (Austrian) and Transleithanian (Hungarian) regions of the state were governed by separate Parliaments and Prime Ministers with joint responsibility for some key ministries such as defence. The Habsburg dynasty effectively ruled through the office of Emperor of Austria over the western and northern half of the country, the territory that was formerly the Empire of Austria, and as the ruling monarch of the Kingdom of Hungary, presided over the remainder of the territory which enjoyed self-government and representation in joint affairs principally in the sphere of foreign relations and defence. The Dual Monarchy had two capitals which were Vienna for the Austrian sphere and Budapest for Hungarian sphere. Austria-Hungary was then geographically the second largest country in Europe after the Russian Empire, and the third most populous after Russia and the newly born Second German Empire established by Bismark in 1871. It is history's misfortune that Hitler was born into an area which inherited this tortured historical legacy. Geographically the *Ostmark* was almost identical with the German part of Austria. The political future of the region was unclear and there was a great deal of unhappiness with the current situation. Adolf Hitler was deeply influenced by these resonances and he constantly harked back to the imagined glories of the First Reich and yearned to see this area re-united with the Second German Reich under Kaiser Wilhelm II.

Hitler was acutely aware of the frustrating history of the pan-German nationalist movement but it was not just Hitler who was unhappy with the present state of affairs. For many citizens the Austro-Hungarian Empire produced a glaring mismatch between the ruling monarchy and the aspirations of the population in much of the territory over which they ruled. The vast majority of the population in the west of the Hapsburg Empire considered themselves German in political, national, racial and linguistic terms. Although only around one third of the population of the Empire as a whole were ethnic Germans they wielded a disproportionate amount of political and economic power and naturally sought to preserve the status quo. They were bitterly opposed to what they considered to be the growing Slavic influences on the Habsburgs and many, particularly among the younger generation were pan-German in outlook and actively sought the re-union of Austria with the German Empire. Between the ages of eleven and fourteen Hitler became obsessed with the cause of German nationalism and in the pages of 'Mein Kampf' he expanded at length upon these influences:

'And thus it was that at a comparatively early age I took part in the struggle which the nationalities were waging against one another in the old Austria. When meetings were held for the South Mark German League and the School League we wore cornflowers and black-red-gold colours to express our loyalty. We greeted one another with "Heil!" and instead of the Austrian anthem we sang our own Deutschland Uber Alles, despite warnings and penalties. Thus the youth were educated politically at a time when the citizens of a so-called national State for the most part knew little of their own nationality except the language. Of course, I did not belong to the hedgers. Within a little while I had become an ardent 'German

National', which has a different meaning from the party significance attached to that phrase today.'

The various factions at work were not clear cut and they often split families in two, the Hitler household was one such example. Alois understood the concept of duty, he had sworn an oath to serve and was fiercely loyal to his Emperor Franz Josef and in consequence was a supporter of the Habsburgs. The young Adolf owed no such allegiance and was resolutely pan-German in outlook. He earnestly yearned for re-unification with the state which was presided over by Kaiser Wilhelm II and passionately wanted to see Germany and Austria united. By the time he was fourteen the dream of a single pan-German nation had fully taken root as an ambition in Hitler's mind. It was a dream which Hitler would spend a large part of his adult life seeking to make into a reality. Long before he finally achieved his goal he recorded his life long aspiration in 'Mein Kampf':

'It has turned out fortunate for me today that destiny appointed Braunau-on-the-Inn to be my birthplace. For that little town is situated just on the frontier between those two States the reunion of which seems, at least to us of the younger generation, a task to which we should devote our lives and in the pursuit of which every possible means should be employed. And so this little frontier town appeared to me as the symbol of a great task.'

The unwieldy arrangements of the compromise were difficult to deliver in practice and throughout the late eighteenth century, there were increasing tensions between the German and Slav populations in the Empire. Eventually the ripples of discontent reached the German domiciled city of Linz. The spirit of German nationalism dominated the Linz Realschule and in Hitler's day the younger generation were particularly sympathetic to the idea that Austria's German population was under threat from the Slav, Magyar and Italian factions which formed part of the Austria-Hungarian Empire. Linz was entirely German in character but there was continual trouble and ferment just to the north in neighbouring Bohemia where the German population of Prague faced discrimination. Soon there was even unrest in Linz too.

A few hundred Czechs had always lived there, and had gone about their business as quiet and modest workmen and artisans. In the 1890s the ordered peace of Linz society was shattered by the actions of a Czech Capuchin monk, named Jurasek. He founded a Sokol Club, preached fierce pro-Slav rhetoric in St. Martin's Church in Czech, and collected money for the building of a Czech school. According to Hitler this caused a great outrage in the town and some of the more concerned Nationalists began to conjecture that this was in fact the forerunner of a mass Czech invasion of Linz. If Hitler is to be believed, the result of their vocal campaign was that, almost unanimously, the German population of Linz joined in the Nationalist struggle against the erosion of German values and influence.

Hitler records that those teachers of the *Realschule*, who were nationalists, led the struggle. Dr. Leopold Pötsch, the history teacher who did so much to inspire Hitler, was also an active politician. As a member of the Town Council he was one of the leading lights of the Nationalist Party. He hated the Hapsburg multi-racial state and the enthusiastic young Nationalists followed his lead.

In joining the popular crusade which clamoured for the reunification of Austria with Germany, Hitler was identifying himself as a supporter of the Bavarian influenced *Grossdeutschland* faction. Hitler, along with many others, subscribed to the idea that he was a member of a pan-national Germanic race which was not limited by national borders and comprised elements of the populations of Germany, France, Italy, Czechoslovakia, Poland, Lithuania and, of course, Austria.

The *Grossdeutschland* concept followed a typically Bavarian and liberal philosophy under which the criteria for defining a German national embraced the widest possible definition. Qualification as an ethnic German as far as the *Grossdeutschland* faction was concerned was based on a vague set of standards embracing a blurred notion of common heritage, culture and language. The opposition to the *Grossdeutschland Lösung* came in the form of the Prussian-backed *Kleindeutsche Lösung* or lesser German solution. The Prussian aristocracy and plutocracy favoured a strict definition of nationality – and citizenship-based strictly defined national borders. The unwritten political sub text was that integration with a wider pan-German population endangered the sense of order and control which the Prussian ruling classes valued so highly.

The *Grossdeutschland* movement formed a part of a more general nation building process witnessed throughout Europe in the 19th and 20th centuries which witnessed the birth of nation-states like Germany. The desire for the creation of a pan-German national state which integrated the German speaking territories including Austria, was viewed by many as an attempt to balance the power of the authoritarian Prussian monarchy within Germany by the introduction of the counter weight provided by the more liberally-minded southern German states. Following the events of 1848, the issue was finally resolved in favour of the *Kleindeutsche Lösung*, but Germany remained culturally divided between a Protestant, Prussian-dominated north and a Catholic south and south-west dominated by Bavaria. The German nationalists in Austria shared a deep sense of frustration at their exclusion from the Second Reich.

Hitler's dream of a reunification between Germany and Austria had long been shared by many others and a number of attempts had been made to achieve this by force of arms. In the 19th century, there had been a concerted effort to realise the *Grossdeutschland* dream and form a unified Germany including Austria. This last great attempt had taken place in 1848, when pan-German liberals and nationalists united in armed revolution and formed the Frankfurt Parliament. Richard Wagner, Hitler's great hero, was also a revolutionary in the ranks of the 1848 rebellion. This National Assembly demanded the unification of all German populated lands into one German state, however, the Frankfurt Parliament proved to be the high water mark for the *Grossdeutschland* faction. It was successfully opposed by the Prussian dominated bloc which championed the more controllable *Kleindeutschland Losüng* and effectively excluded Austria from the Second German Empire.

In the latter half of the nineteenth century there were constant rumblings and talk of further foment, but for the young Adolf Hitler and millions like him the *Grossdeutschland* vision was to remain an elusive goal, a forlorn hope for the liberal and catholic forces as regional, religious and monarchical rivalries between Prussia and Austria all conspired to prevent a unification from taking place. Divisions were heightened by the short Austro-Prussian war of 1866.

With the foundation of Bismark's Second German Empire in 1871, the Second Empire was born, but even the great political master could not extend the boundaries to include Austria. Following Bismark's triumph, the *Kleindeutschland* solution favoured by Prussian conservatives gained complete ascendancy. For the German Empire and Otto von Bismarck, the cultural and religious differences between a protestant and conservative philosophy and the catholic liberalism of the south were just too great a hurdle to cross. They conspired to assure the permanent exclusion of Austria from the Second Empire. This unpalatable state of affairs was to prove an unbearable burden to Adolf Hitler and others like him and he and the adherents of the *Grossdeutschland* concept still clung to their vision of reunification. Hitler recorded his frustration in the pages of '*Mein Kampf*':

> '*I was forced to accept the fact, though with a secret envy, that not all Germans had the good luck to belong to Bismarck's Empire. This was something that I could not understand.*'

It was to take the twisted political genius of Adolf Hitler to make the *Grossdeutschland* dream a reality. In 1924, when he wrote these words, surely even Hitler could not have dreamt that in just fourteen short years the *Anschluss* of 1938 would achieve the historic goal which had eluded even the great Bismark himself.

At the time he wrote '*Mein Kampf*', Adolf Hitler, incarcerated in Landsberg prison, still shared the deep rooted frustrations of the *Grossdeutschland* faction and his desire for reunification shaped his political views for the next fourteen years.

The political and social wounds of the pan-German nationalists ran much deeper still. During the long wilderness years from 1848 to 1938, the frustrated ideals of the nationalists came to be reflected under the wide canopy of the *völkisch* movement. This loose assortment of political and mystic initiatives had its roots deep in a brand of romantic nationalism which took root in the nineteenth century and really flared into life after World War One. It was this brand of *völkisch* tinged nationalism which was to prove the prime motivating factor in the mélange of influences which initially formed Hitler's idiosyncratic world view and philosophy.

Hitler is now synonymous with the monstrous crimes inspired by his anti-Semitism, but it is sobering to realise that this was not his principal agenda. Anti-Semitism, although a strong motivating factor, always ranked second to his ethnic national aspirations. It is important to recognise that Hitler's peculiar brand of *völkisch* ultra-nationalism was his primary motivation from a comparatively early age. Nationalism predated and always overshadowed the anti-Semitic elements of Hitler's political agenda.

Interviewed by Leon Goldensöhn, the US Army psychologist at Nuremberg in 1946, many senior Nazis declared their own belief that anti-Semitism was a side issue which Hitler would abandon once it had outlived its usefulness.[13] Ethnic nationalism was the key driving force which drew the young Hitler to embark upon the long road which would lead to the blight of National Socialism and it was ethnic nationalism which was the key stone on which the whole evil edifice of National Socialism was founded. It was some years later before the anti-Semitic agenda was added to Hitler's personal political credo. Initially only nationalism mattered to Hitler and by the time he was fifteen his unique interpretation was at the very core of Hitler's *weltanschauung* (or world view), and was duly recorded for posterity in the pages of *'Mein Kampf'*:

'I developed very rapidly in the nationalist direction, and by the time I was 15 years old I had come to understand the distinction between dynastic patriotism and nationalism based on the concept of folk, or people, my inclination being entirely in favour of the latter.'

By his own testimony Hitler was a fully formed *völkisch* nationalist from an early age. The development of Hitler's anti-Semitic agenda took place over a much longer period of time. It evolved in stages and

---

13. Leon Goldensöhn: The Nuremberg Interviews, p.116. Pimlico 2006.

coalesced between 1908 and 1919, under the influence of events in Vienna, the trenches of the Great War and in new friendships formed in Munich. We know from Kubizek that in the Hitler household Alois despised overt anti-Semitism and considered the matter uncouth and vulgar. In its early stages anti-Semitism was stimulated, in part at least, by the young Hitler's interest in the *völkisch* movement. It was this early infatuation which started Hitler down the path that would lead to the addition of an anti-Semitic barb to the social Darwinist politics of ethnic nationalism and ultimately merge into the National Socialist philosophy which would come to destroy the lives of millions.

The German word *'völkisch'* is often erroneously translated as 'folkish' which gives entirely the wrong connotations. There is no easy equivalent of this word in the English language. The word *völkisch* has very little connection with the slightly whimsical word 'folk' as we commonly use it to express our concept of 'folklore' or 'folk music'. For those on the left of the political spectrum the word *volk* represented the equivalent of 'proletariat'. For those on the right, the word came to mean 'race' and, under the national Socialists, evolved into an altogether more sinister set of beliefs. The *völkisch* movement embraced a very wide suite of ideas which combined the arcane and esoteric aspects of occultism alongside fragments of genuine archaeology to produce a vague philosophy based around revived religions and the veneration of the ancient Germanic race. In right wing circles, the *völkisch* movement was accompanied by a virulent type of anti-Semitism which was inextricably tied to ethnic nationalism. The *völkisch* ideas were also cloaked in a layer of gothic romanticism shroud which added a glamour and allure. Mysterious Nordic runes were rediscovered and imbued with quasi-magical powers. Horoscopes were taken seriously by sober-minded German citizens who would formerly have discounted them as nonsense. The theories of Helena Petrovna Blavatsky a self-professed psychic and mystic, and a founder of the Theosophical Society, were also highly influential in *völkisch* circles. Her outlandish ideas on how the Aryan race had evolved from a lost race which had perished with Atlantis were given wide credence.

The *völkisch* movement therefore attracted dreamers of every description fed on a strong yearning for an imagined past in which Wagner's heroes and the gods of Norse mythology assumed real life status. The myths and invented gibberish soon became inextricably mixed with genuine historical figures from the Dark Ages. To top it all the *völkisch* movement embraced the idea that the Germanic peoples were descended from a superior Nordic race known as the Aryans. The notion of this noble race of prehistoric supermen was so widely touted in *völkisch* circles that their existence had become an unquestioned and universally accepted reality. The myth of the Aryan race was readily accepted and was by 1905, so familiar it had become a self evident truth. The fact that there was absolutely no archeological evidence whatsoever which even hinted at the existence of an Aryan race was simply ignored in favour of a slew of false claims, unsupportable hypotheses and 'folk memories' designed to circumvent the lack of real evidence for the existence of the Aryans.

In the early years of the twentieth century this confused mélange formed the basis of a new set of pseudo religious beliefs which saw the return of esoteric summer and winter solstice ceremonies to the spiritual landscape of Germany. Later in life Hitler roundly rejected the *völkisch* beliefs as occult mumbo jumbo and in 'Mein Kampf' he made a pointed attack on the mystics who gathered round the *völkisch* mast head. However, at least some of these ideas which were genuinely rooted in German history would have many resonances for Adolf Hitler and as a young man some *völkisch* concepts clearly had an influence on his early politics. Hitler's enthusiasm for history and its effect on his later development is recorded in the pages of 'Mein Kampf' in which Hitler recorded his gratitude towards Dr Leopold Pötsch his old history teacher in Linz:

> *'It was still more fortunate that this professor was able not only to illustrate the past by examples from the present, but from the past he was also able to draw a lesson for the present. He understood better than any other the everyday problems that were then agitating our minds. The national fervour which we felt in our own small way*

*was utilised by him as an instrument of our education, in as much
as he often appealed to our national sense of honour; for in that way
he maintained order and held our attention much more easily than
he could have done by any other means. It was because I had such
a professor that history became my favourite subject. As a natural
consequence, but without the conscious connivance of my professor,
I then and there became a young rebel. But who could have studied
German history under such a teacher and not become an enemy of
that State whose rulers exercised such a disastrous influence on the
destinies of the German nation?'*

Völkisch ideas ranged from the relatively sober reverence for the
Teutons which Hitler experienced and enjoyed during history lessons at
Realschule in Linz through to the lunatic mysticism of re-invented pagan
religions based on *Wotanism* which Hitler openly despised.

As early as 24 February 1893, Guido von List was delivering the first
of his many lectures on the ancient cult of Wotan and its priesthood
to the *völkisch* fringe group, *Verein Deutsche Geschichte*. Guido based
his lecture around the claim that the cult of *Wotanism* was the national
religion of the Teutons before it was destroyed by Christianity. The
evidence for this 'lost' religion was based on 'oral tradition' and was
soon revived to form the basis of a political mythology which was widely
embraced in *völkisch* circles. Other words, phrases and concepts which
would later come to form the cornerstones of the National Socialist
creed were also beginning to emerge around the time that Hitler
was studying at *Realschule* in Linz. In May 1894, a tombstone relief
depicting a figure which was described as an 'Aryan' nobleman treading
on an unidentifiable beast was excavated from the cloister flagstones at
Heiligenkreuz. Adolf Josef Lanz in his first published work, interpreted
this relief as an allegorical depiction of the eternal struggle between the
forces of good and evil. It was Lanz who was principally responsible
for developing his ideas into a new religion, glorifying the blue-eyed,
blond-haired 'Aryans' as the forces for good striving against the various
dark skinned races – the *untermenschen* who were characterised as
irredeemably evil.

Hitler is likely to have encountered and imbibed various *völkisch* concepts, touching on Germanic mythology and mysticism from his time at Lambach choir school onwards. It was certainly the case that the former abbot Father *Hagn* (Hook) had, as early as 1868, ordered the *Hakenkreuz* (hooked cross) to be carved on the Lambach Abbey entrance way. Although this is likely to have been a harmless pun on the abbot's name, it is highly likely that this would have been Hitler's first encounter with the symbol which widely adopted *völkisch* movement. It should be noted that Hitler did not at any time refer to this design as a 'swastika', to him it was always referred to by its German name *Hakenkreuz* or 'hooked cross'. The word swastika is of Indian origin and played no part in Hitler's world, it was first put into Hitler's mouth by translators of *'Mein Kampf'*, beginning with James Murphy.

Hitler undoubtedly assimilated some influences from the *völkisch* movements generally, but their influence on him has often been over-stated. Nonetheless his Munich bookseller, Elsa Schmidt-Falk testified that she had sold Hitler a copy of Guido von List's *Deutsch Mythologishe Ladschaftbilde*[14] ('Images of German Mythological Landscapes') and Kubizek suggests that Hitler carried around List's 'The Secrets of the Runes' which was published in 1908. That book contains List's thoughts on the dangers of Freemasons, Jews and non-Aryan races – concepts which were to become all too familiar when regurgitated by Hitler in the 1920s.

By 1924, Hitler, it appears from his writings in *'Mein Kampf'*, had experienced some kind of epiphany and as a result had roundly turned on the exponents of *völkisch* theory. There can be little doubt that his attacks were aimed at von List, Lanz and their ilk. Despite being a youthful adherent to arcane *völkisch* ideas the mature Hitler clearly recorded his feelings of antipathy towards these diverse *völkisch* groups at characteristic length in the pages of *'Mein Kampf'*. The champions of the *völkisch* movement were dismissed as 'all those dreamers who live in the past and all the lovers of bombastic nomenclature.'

---

14. Hamann: 'Hitler's Vienna' p. 212.

We have no reason to doubt the fact that by 1924, Hitler held genuine feelings of antipathy towards the more esoteric ideas which he is often erroneously accused of having championed. It would appear that Heinrich Himmler was the real driving force behind the adoption of the more obscure and often downright lunatic ideas which were officially sanctioned during the Nazi era. This had little to do with Hitler and was championed by his indulgence of Himmler who in turn was able to support genuine odd balls such Karl Maria Wiligut.[15] However, it is clear beyond doubt that, during his youth, at least some of the early *völkisch* influences rubbed off on Hitler and that those influences stayed with him at least on a subliminal level throughout his life. His love of runes and historical references betrays the lasting influence on him. Speaking in Munich in 1920, for example, Hitler expanded at length upon the Aryans of the north:

'A race of giants in strength and health, grown in ethnic purity…
we know that Egypt reached its high cultural level on account of
Aryan immigrants, as did Persia and Greece. The immigrants were
blonde, blue-eyed Aryans!'[16]

The passage above was in fact lifted almost straight from List's book, *The Names of Germania's Tribes* where the idea first appeared, and we can therefore be certain it was certainly not dreamt up independently by Hitler.

---

15. Heather Pringle: 'The Master Plan', p.46. Harper Perennial.
16. Hamann: 'Hitler's Vienna' p. 211.

- CHAPTER 3 -
LINZ AND STEYR

BY 1905, HITLER had reached the age of fifteen and stood on the brink of manhood. Adolf Hitler was a peculiar individual in very many respects. He seems to have been happy in his own company and appears to have been quite content to survive without the need for a wide circle of friends. The sad reality was that he had no friends at all. One of the reasons for this might stem from the constant pattern of movement which affected his early life and may have made it difficult to form long term relationships. He had enjoyed a wide circle of friends in Leonding but this appears to have come to an abrupt halt in Linz. His rapidly declining school record was not helping and there appear to have been difficulties over Hitler's attitude in general. Despite all of his best efforts Hitler was continuing to fare badly in Linz *Realschule*. Hitler's attitude towards women has also proved something of a mystery, he certainly didn't indulge in the headlong pursuit of the opposite sex which characterises so many youths of equivalent age and circumstances.

The death of Alois freed Hitler from the pressures of a fraught parental relationship. Hitler was now the only man in the house and his doting mother smothered and pampered him, acceding to every whim. Hitler now regarded himself as an artist in waiting. He soon set about absorbing diverse cultural influences, the opera, theatre, reading and drawing.

Without the restraining influence of his father's harsh brand of discipline Adolf Hitler seems to have swung to the opposite extreme and become a dilettante. He was determined to become an artist and immersed himself in the arts. He spent more and more time at the opera where he absorbed more and more of the work of Wagner. Hitler worshipped the imagery and lore of the Nibelung ring saga which were then also fashionable in *völkisch* circles. Hitler was inspired by his love of Wagner to take up music himself and, as always, he was indulged by his doting mother who bought him a grand piano and paid for lessons which she could ill afford.

At school Hitler was clearly a trying student. As we have seen Professor Heumar, his form tutor from 1900-1914, stated clearly to the Munich court that he was argumentative, stubborn and difficult. His surviving school reports confirm that Hitler was a below average student. He was something of a trouble maker intent on pushing the pan-German nationalist agenda at every opportunity. He is said to have enjoyed baiting those teachers who did not share his nationalist sentiments by such tiresome expedients as arranging his pencils in uniform blocks of red, black and gold, the colours of the 1848, pan-German movement. His taciturn attitude did not help matters and the Linz *Realschule* soon tired of Adolf Hitler and he was refused permission to complete his studies there. Given Professor Heumar's low opinion of him, that conclusion is understandable. Somehow Hitler managed to scrape enough remedial passes to be allowed entry to another *Realschule* in Steyr twenty-five miles distant, but even this involved re-sitting key examinations and the school at Linz stipulated that he was only allowed to sit his re-examinations on the express condition that he did not return to Linz next term. Hitler was fortunate in finding a place at *Realschule* in Steyr.

In order to complete his schooling Hitler was once more forced into living away from home. Steyr was twenty-five miles distant from Linz and Hitler lived in the home of the Cichini family. The impression of the poverty of his surroundings was emphasised by Hitler who later described his pastime as 'shooting rats from his window'. Academically his results were no better and Hitler's last term of school appears to have been compounded by ill health. Following a hemorrhage of the lungs, Hitler discontinued his studies without completing his Abitur, the exam which would have given him the diploma necessary for entrance to the *Oberrrealschule*, or Technical Institute, the next destination for many students graduating from *Realschule*.

By July 1905, Hitler was back in Linz. His schooling was behind him, and with no real prospect of anything substantial on the horizon, Hitler began to drift through life as he would do for the next seventeen years. One contributing factor was the fact that Klara had moved from Leonding to the small rented flat at Humboldstrasse 31 in the centre of Linz. Living in a household composed entirely of women suited Hitler who seems to have played the part of the indolent young master to the limit. Hitler had plans to study art at the Academy of Fine Arts in Vienna, but there was plenty of time and life continued to pass pleasantly for the idle and indulged young man. For the time being, Hitler was now free to drift through life attending the opera and filling in his extensive free time drawing and reading. Summers were spent in the pleasant country surroundings of Spital with Klara's mother and life was generally good for the young man.

The only respect in which Hitler's life was incomplete was in the social sphere. By the age of sixteen, Hitler had formed no real friendships. Possibly this was as a result of the constant chopping and changing of schools, or more possibly from his awkward and difficult character, but the fact remained that Hitler had made no real friends at *Realschule*.

He was by nature a loner and by 1905, he had become something of a young dandy and had taken to carrying an ivory handled cane on his frequent visits to the opera. This was one of the things which the young August Kubizek, an aspiring music student, noticed about this pale and gaunt youth whom he first encountered at the opera house in Linz as the two were frequent competitors for the best of the standing places. Gradually an acquaintance was formed and for once Hitler was prepared to let down his guard. The two young men formed a friendship which was to endure for the next five years. Hitler and 'Gustl' as he affectionately called his new friend, soon became inseparable companions and took to attending the opera together. It is the written record of this friendship as published by Kubizek which provides just about all we know of Hitler as a teenager. In later years two carefully censored pamphlets by Kubizek were published during the Third Reich era and after the war Kubizek recorded his experiences with the young Adolf in his book entitled 'The

Young Hitler I Knew'. Once again these sources need to be handled with great care especially those published under the eagle eye of Hitler's Third Reich, but they represent some of the few surviving primary sources which throw some light on the life of the young Adolf Hitler. We certainly have no reason to doubt that Kubizek's initial description of Adolf Hitler is totally accurate:

'Adolf was of middle height and slender, at that time already taller than his mother. His physique was far from sturdy, rather too thin for his height, and he was not at all strong. His health, in fact, was rather poor, which he was the first to regret. He had to take special care of himself during the foggy and damp winters which prevailed in Linz. He was ill from time to time during that period and coughed a lot. In short, he had weak lungs.'[17]

Kubizek found that Hitler was furtive concerning his personal life and could erect barriers when it came to providing information. Hitler's famously hot temper was already in evidence and it seemed always lurking just under the surface. Hitler could be sparked into fury by the most banal of enquiries and Kubizek was soon on the receiving end of one such tantrum when he made the mistake of overstepping the mark in an effort to obtain some background information concerning his mysterious new friend and his schooling. It certainly left its mark on 'Gustl' who recalled Hitler's reaction in the pages of 'The Young Hitler I Knew':

"School?" This was the first outburst of temper that I had experienced with him. He didn't wish to hear anything about school. School was no longer his concern, he said. He hated the teachers and did not even greet them any more, and he also hated his schoolmates whom, he said, the school was turning into idlers.'[18]

We know from the reports of his schoolmaster and from Kubizek that Adolf, even as a youngster, had an exceedingly violent temper and was highly strung. He would become upset over the most trivial things, a few

---

17. August Kubizek: 'The Young Hitler I Knew'.
18. Ibid.

thoughtless words, could produce in Hitler extreme outbursts of temper which Kubizek felt were quite out of proportion to the significance of the matter in hand. School clearly carried unhappy memories for Hitler leaving him resentful and alienated. It would appear that he had been bullied and this left him bitter and ill at ease with his former schoolmates. Kubizek recalled the rude reception which Hitler gave to a former school colleague who made the mistake of offering an amiable greeting:

'We were strolling along the Landstrasse when it happened. A young man, about our age, came around the corner, a plump, rather dandified young gentleman. He recognised Adolf as a former classmate, stopped, and grinning all over his face, called out, "Hello, Hitler!" He took him familiarly by the arm and asked him quite sincerely how he was getting on. I expected Adolf to respond in the same friendly manner, as he always set great store by correct and courteous behaviour. But my friend went red with rage. I knew from former experience that this change of expression boded ill. "What the devil is that to do with you?" he threw at him excitedly, and pushed him sharply away. Then he took my arm and went with me on his way without bothering about the young man who's flushed and baffled face I can still see before me. "All future civil servants," said Adolf, still furious, "and with this lot I had to sit in the same class." It was a long time before he calmed down.'[19]

Despite these initial obstacles the familiarity continued and as their friendship deepened Kubizek often found himself as the sole member of an audience listening to Hitler's oratory.

Kubizek soon came to the realisation that their friendship endured mainly for the reason that he was a patient listener. This was fortunate as Kubizek enjoyed his friendship with Hitler and declared that he was satisfied to assume a passive role, even though Hitler would launch into long lectures about things that did not particularly interest Kubizek. Gustl would therefore sit and listen while Hitler held forth on topics as

19. Ibid.

diverse as the excise duty levied at the Danube bridge, or a collection in the streets for a charity lottery. Kubizek soon formed the opinion that Hitler just had to talk and needed somebody who would listen to him as he spoke at length. As an orator in waiting Hitler was undeterred by his audience of one and would make a full speech to Gustl as if he was in a crowded debating chamber. According to Kubizek, Hitler's speeches were already accompanied by vivid hand gestures in the manner which would one day win over the crowds flocking to hear the prophet of National Socialism. During their days in Linz Kubizek noted that Hitler never once was concerned by the fact that his friend was invariably the only person to hear his outpourings. It seems as if Hitler was content to hone his craft and made no attempt to seek out an audience. Kubizek also noted that Hitler was passionately interested in everything he saw and experienced and simply had to find an outlet for his tempestuous feelings, the expression of which Kubizek compared to a volcano erupting. Hitler's new friend recalled how he was soon filled with astonishment at how fluently Hitler expressed himself, how vividly he managed to convey his feelings and how easily the words flowed when Hitler was carried away by his own emotions. Gustl enjoyed the novelty of his new friend's verbal powers but there was an ominous undertone in his observation of the fact that, from an early age, Hitler would tolerate no opposition to his views. This dogged belief in his own opinion and his absolute refusal to yield a position, however untenable, was to prove a fatal flaw in the later career of Adolf Hitler. It was Gustl who first recorded the evidence of this particular trait in the sixteen-year-old Hitler:

'This to me was something new, magnificent. I had never imagined that a man could produce such an effect with mere words. All he wanted from me, however, was one thing – agreement. I soon came to realise this. Nor was it hard for me to agree with him, because I had never given any thought to the many problems which he raised.' [20]

As their friendship deepened and Hitler began to trust his new friend

---

20. Ibid.

Kubizek was eventually afforded some insights into Hitler's private life. Gustl began to pay visits to Humboldstrasse 31. The record of these visits now constitute the only primary source view of life inside the Hitler household in Linz. It also provides a privileged glimpse into how dutifully Klara continued to press her husband's dying wish, by any means available, that her headstrong son could be prevailed upon to bow to Alois' long held belief that Adolf should join the civil service. Kubizek later recalled her desperate efforts in this direction:

'When I first met her, Klara Hitler was already forty-five years old and a widow of two years' standing… She was glad that Adolf had found a friend whom he liked and trusted, and for this reason Frau Hitler liked me, too. How often did she unburden to me the worries which Adolf caused her. And how fervently did she hope to enlist my help in persuading her son to follow his father's wishes in the choice of a career! I had to disappoint her, yet she did not blame me, for she must have felt that the reasons for Adolf's behaviour were much too deep, far beyond the reach of my influence.'[21]

As regards the small family home, Kubizek painted a simple and melancholy word picture of a rather forlorn existence led by the small family who seemed rather friendless, enjoying little contact with the wider world:

'Just as Adolf often enjoyed the hospitality of my parents' home, I went often to see his mother and on taking leave was unfailingly asked by Frau Hitler to come again. I considered myself as part of the family – there was hardly anybody else who visited them.'[22]

Gustl went on to describe the living conditions of the small dwelling. It is interesting to note that as Kubizek's relationship with Hitler grew ever more familiar Hitler was increasingly prepared to expand upon his family circumstances. He allowed Kubizek the opportunity to learn more and more of Adolf's family background. Fortunately for posterity Kubizek faithfully recorded some of the small details of life

---

21. Ibid.
22. Ibid.

in Humboldstrasse 31 which now provides us with a glimpse into the domestic life of Adolf Hitler:

'No. 31 Humboldstrasse is a three-storied, not unpleasant tenement building. The Hitlers lived on the third floor. I can still visualise the humble apartment. The small kitchen, with green painted furniture, had only one window, which looked out on to the courtyard. The living room, with the two beds of his mother and little Paula, overlooked the street. On the side wall hung a portrait of his father, with a typical civil servant's face, impressive and dignified, whose rather grim expression was mitigated by the carefully groomed whiskers à la Emperor Franz Joseph. Adolf lived and studied in the closet, off the bedroom. Paula, Adolf's little sister, was nine when I first met the family. She was a rather pretty girl, quiet and reserved. I never saw her gay. We got on rather well with each other but Adolf was not particularly close to her. This was due perhaps to the difference in age – he always referred to her as "the kid".' [23]

Haninaunt seems to have been absent from Linz at this time, possibly she had gone back to Spital although she would later return to Linz to look after Paula in the aftermath of Klara's death. Kubizek was intrigued by the tangle of family relationships behind the visitors to Humboldstrasse 31. It is a measure of just how much the reclusive Hitler now trusted Gustl that he was prepared to open up with more and more detail concerning his step family and the comings and goings of the various offspring of Alois Hitler. Adolf seems to have been fairly close to his step sister Angela who frequently came to visit Klara, but he had no time whatsoever for Angela's husband – Leo Raubal. Raubal appears to have attempted to assist Klara in her relentless campaign to convince Hitler to follow in his father's footsteps and become a civil servant. This was probably the final nail in the coffin as regards the relationship between the two men. Adolf was far too headstrong to be swayed and we know from Kubizek that anyone disagreeing with Hitler was likely to be on the receiving end of one of his volcanic outbursts.

---

23. Ibid.

Angela was reputed to be highly attractive and this was something which Paula Hitler commented upon to her US interrogators. August Kubizek was also impressed by Angela and recorded his own impressions of this 'striking' young woman who seems to have been the only other regular visitor other than himself.

Hitler's friendship with Gustl continued to develop and it is through Kubizek's writings that we gain an insight into Hitler and the influences which shaped his adolescent life in Linz and Vienna. After the First World War, Hans Mend,[24] a former comrade, sought to suggest that Hitler was a homosexual and went as far as to name a comrade, Ernst Schmidt, as his 'male whore'.[25] Kubizek however makes it clear that Hitler had a normal interest in women, but as always with Hitler there was a peculiar aspect to his behaviour. He appeared to suffer from such a chronic shyness that it made it almost impossible for him to make a direct approach. In his book 'The Young Hitler I Knew', Kubizek tells the awkward tale of how Hitler fell in love with a strikingly beautiful young blonde lady called Stefanie described by Hitler as a *Walküre*. For four years Hitler made Stefanie the object of all his desires and wove a series of fantasies around his future plans for the life that he and Stefanie would lead together. Yet Hitler's fear of rejection was so great that he never once plucked up the courage to approach her directly or even speak to her. Not surprisingly his passions were unrequited and Kubizek paints the rather pathetic picture of Hitler drawing up plans for the house which he and Stefanie would one day share together yet never having the courage to come near to the woman he adored. Hitler became unhealthily obsessed by Stefanie and constantly employed Kubizek on a series of missions to gain as much information as he could about the object of his unrequited love. This sad infatuation endured for four years and yet Hitler never once spoke to the woman he desired so much.

Outside of their love of opera and walking out in Linz the two friends enjoyed the countryside and would take long walks in the picturesque

---

24. Hans Mend: *'Adolf Hitler im Felde 1914-1918'*.
25. Lotmar Machtan: 'The Hidden Hitler' 2001.

peaks surrounding Linz. These idyllic days in the fresh air and hiking through the Austrian countryside were later to serve as the model for the Hitler Youth movement which was closely inspired by Hitler's love of clean air and open spaces which had developed during his days in Linz.

Hitler was passionately interested in military history but Kubizek was not much interested in the subject; he therefore left Hitler to his own devices when he spent two days attempting to ascertain whether the locals had a folk memory of a medieval battle of St Georg. The interests of the two companions did, however, coincide on a visit to Bruckner's tomb which held a mystical and spiritual attraction for the young men. Kubizek recalls Hitler standing for a full hour in meditation and reflection on the spot where Bruckner is buried.

As they walked and talked their way around Linz and its environs, Hitler expanded more and more of his political views. It was around this time that Kubizek began to notice a peculiar verbal tic of Hitler's which took the form of an over reliance on one word in particular; the word was 'Reich'. This word was widely used in Austria to delineate the territory of German influence of which the inhabitants were described as Reichs Germans. Kubizek noted that Hitler's use of the term, for Hitler, signified more than just the German Empire. Though Hitler studiously avoided any more precise definition there was clearly a *völkisch* overtone to the word. This one word was regularly used as a kind of verbal full stop to wind up Hitler's long speeches. Kubizek commented on the fact that whenever Hitler talked himself into a blind alley and was unable to proceed to a logical conclusion, Hitler would employ the catch all solution: 'This problem will be solved by the Reich.' By way of example, when asked by Kubizek where the finance for all his grandiose building projects would come from, Hitler's succinct answer was, 'the Reich.' Kubizek came to the conclusion that for Hitler the word Reich was simply a portmanteau expression, which would provide a magic solution for all the myriad political issues which were troubling him.

- CHAPTER 4 -
HARDSHIP IN VIENNA

LINZ WAS THE provincial capital of Upper Austria, but Adolf Hitler had long harboured a dream of visiting Vienna, the true capital of German Austria. In 1906, despite the family's fragile finances, the self-centred and pampered young man managed to persuade Klara to fund a month long stay in the city which Hitler longed to visit as an unrivalled centre for excellence in architecture, art, music and culture. A hotel would have been beyond his means and it is often conjectured that the young Hitler stayed with his god parents (Johann and Johanna Prinz) but no firm evidence has been unearthed. We do know from his surviving correspondence with Kubizek that he seems to have found no problems in paying for a series of opera tickets for performances of Wagner. Hitler did not warm to Italian masters such as Puccini and Verdi and always preferred to attend even second rate Wagner in minor theatres rather than attend first class performances by any other composer, this prejudice extended even to the German masters including Beethoven and Mozart.

Hitler's 1906 visit proved to be a dress rehearsal for a complete relocation to the city, but his move to Vienna took place in stages as, around this time, Hitler's mother was incurably ill and suffering from cancer. She was desperately ill and was undergoing the most extreme attempts to cure her. Klara was very close to her only surviving son and would no doubt have welcomed his presence as her health declined. The family had now moved to Urfahr and were resident at Blütenstrasse 9. Haninaunt had returned and it seemed that the end was in sight. Despite these depressing circumstances, in the summer of 1907, Hitler followed in his father's footsteps and struck out for Vienna in an attempt to gain access to the School of Fine Art. Like Alois before him the young Adolf was determined to make a name for himself in the sprawling Austrian capital. He was recorded by Kubizek as living in the 6th District, at Stumpergasse No. 29, Staircase II, second floor, door No. 17, in the flat of an elderly woman with the curious name of Frau Zakreys.

Hitler describes himself as being armed with a bulky packet of sketches, absolutely convinced that he should pass the entrance examination quite easily. Hitler based this confident belief on the fact that, at the Linz *Realschule*, he was considered to be by far the best student in the drawing class, and on this slender evidence rashly considered himself an assured success in the world of fine art. Hitler duly sat the examination and despite the fact that his mother lay dying Hitler did not rush back to Linz but continued his Vienna sojourn as he impatiently awaited the results of the examination.

Hitler was eager to have confirmation of the result of the entrance examination but still remained profoundly confident of success. In the pages of *'Mein Kampf'* Hitler recalls how he was so convinced of his impending success, that when the news that he had actually failed the exam finally reached him, it struck Hitler like a bolt from the blue. Hitler was perplexed by his failure and in an effort to understand the reasons for his rejection he arranged to visit the Rector in order to obtain a first hand explanation for the reasons behind this devastating turn of events. The Rector granted his wish and patiently explained to Hitler that the sketches which he had brought unquestionably demonstrated that Hitler would not develop into an artist – but on the positive side, the sketches nonetheless gave very clear indications of a strong aptitude for architectural design. The Rector suggested therefore that Hitler apply for the School of Architecture, which also formed part of the Academy.

On leaving his interview on Hansen Palace, on the Schiller Platz, Hitler was stunned and for the first time had reason to face up to reality. No longer would he be supremely confident in his god given talent as an artist. He was now forced bitterly to rue his former conduct in neglecting and despising certain subjects at the *Realschule*. The simple fact was that Hitler could not gain access to study Architecture in the Academy without the necessary Leaving Certificate from the Middle School.

The fact that his work was considered inferior came as a crushing blow to the formerly confident young man. In October 1907, with his tail firmly between his legs he returned to Linz where his mother was now on her deathbed. Klara was diagnosed with terminal breast cancer and despite all of the best efforts of the Jewish physician, Dr Eduard Bloch, there was no prospect of a cure. In an effort to save money, the family had moved across the Danube to the suburb of Urfahr where rents were cheaper and taxes were lower. The new address was Hauptstrasse 46, but the move was only temporary and the small family finally settled at Blütenstrasse 9. On 21 December 1907, Klara Hitler died. Hitler was distraught over her death. Dr Bloch was genuinely taken aback and recalled that he had never seen anyone so prostrate with grief as Adolf Hitler. August Kubizek gave a moving and melancholy description of her funeral procession which took place on Christmas Eve 1907. The black clad Hitler, pale and gaunt, carrying a top hat under his arm stalked solemnly through the streets of Linz leading a small band of mourners. As if to add an almost unbearable poignancy to the scene the tiny cortege passed the house of Stefanie and Kubizek describes how the angelic figure of Stefanie herself appeared at her window to observe the funeral procession. Hitler naturally imagined this was her means of paying respect to her silent admirer, but Kubizek concluded she had merely been drawn by curiosity on hearing the sound of the church bells. The passing of Klara brought Hitler to a breach with his old life in Linz. He now had no ties to the city and saw his future life in Vienna.

Following the funeral, Hitler claims to have quickly recovered some of his old calm and resoluteness and decided to return to Vienna and work hard to gain admittance to the Academy. The former self-assurance quickly came back, and he had his eyes resolutely fixed on the goal of becoming an architect. In 1908, he returned to the city for the third time. This visit was destined to last several years.

This third time round Hitler did not make the move alone to Vienna. Hitler begged and cajoled Kubizek's parents to allow their son to join him. The plan was for the two friends to provide mutual support and companionship to enable Gustl to attend the music Conservatory while

Hitler studied hard to gain entrance to the Vienna Academy of Art where he would qualify as an architect. Hitler had often invited Kubizek to join him when stating his intention of going to live in Vienna. Kubizek was no fool and was aware that Hitler thought primarily of himself. It was apparent that Hitler harboured a real fear of going alone to Vienna. With his vivid imagination however, Hitler produced convincing and highly alluring pictures for Kubizek of the exciting and varied student life they would lead in Vienna. The attempt to lure Kubizek to Vienna wasn't an entirely selfish mission for Hitler, the long hours spent in the dusty upholsterer's workshop had genuinely impaired the health of Kubizek and his doctor (whom Kubizek claims was 'a secret ally') advised emphatically against his continuing to work as an upholsterer. This cleared the way for the talented Kubizek to make music his profession which fortuitously for Hitler entailed Gustl going to live and study in Vienna.

Hitler's third journey to Vienna was a quite different proposition from his earlier visits. Until now, Hitler had his mother to fall back on, and even though he was living away from Linz, his home still existed as a safe haven to which he could return at any time. Now Hitler had lost even that slender emotional safety net and had gained the additional concern over what would happen to 'the kid'. Fortunately Angela immediately let Hitler know that Paula could now live with the Raubals, but Angela's husband had point blank refused to receive Adolf into his home on the understandable grounds that Adolf had behaved so disrespectfully towards Leo. Leo's snub meant nothing to Hitler, as he never intended to take up residence with the Raubals in any event. The Raubals' kindness towards Paula however relieved Hitler of his greatest remaining burden. Paula continued to live with Haninaunt at Blütenstrasse but at least had a secure protector and safety net. Hitler was now free to follow his own star. Going to Vienna was therefore a final decision from which there was no turning back.

Kubizek was aware that despite the months Hitler had spent in Vienna during the preceding autumn, Hitler had not succeeded in making any friends. Gustl surmised that perhaps this was because he had no desire to do so. Hitler seemed to have no desire for any company other than Kubizek's, although some form of social interaction was available to Hitler in Vienna. The Prinz family who were his Godparents and close relatives of his mother were still living there and Hitler may possibly have lodged with them during his first visit to Vienna in 1906. However on his second visit it seems certain he never went to visit them, this was certainly odd for a young man who set a great deal of store in doing what he considered to be correct. According to Kubizek he did not even mention the Prinz household again. Possibly the wide berth given to his Godparents was an effort to avoid the inevitable questions concerning his work and livelihood. Kubizek was of the opinion that his friend would have willingly suffered starvation and misery rather than have appeared to be in need of help.

In the circumstances nothing was more natural to Hitler than that he should take his friend with him to Vienna, as not only did their joint destinies point in that direction, but Kubizek was the only person with whom he shared the secret of his great love for Stefanie. In the run up to their departure for Vienna, Hitler had begun to talk of Stefanie in a new and more forceful manner. He confided to Kubizek that he was now determined to bring the present fraught state of affairs to an end. At the next opportunity, he would end all of the suspense and finally introduce himself to Stefanie and her mother.

According to Kubizek, Hitler reckoned that he probably needed to linger on in Linz throughout the month of January 1908, until his mother's home was finally disposed of and the estate settled. He confided to Kubizek that he foresaw some heated arguments concerning his future with his guardian – Josef Mayrhofer, a stout citizen of Leonding in whom the late Alois reposed a great deal of trust. Josef wanted to do his best for Adolf, but his vision for Hitler's future involved setting him up with an apprenticeship as a master baker in Leonding.

Old Josef Mayrhofer lived on in Leonding to a ripe old age and often recalled the story of how Hitler came to see him to discuss the question of his inheritance. Hitler began the meeting by firmly refusing to countenance the baker's apprenticeship and declared with the utmost resolution, 'I am going to Vienna again.' Mayrhofer declared that Hitler was a stubborn fellow, like his father and reluctantly agreed to allow him to follow his chosen path. Mayrhofer went on to duly certify the documents which would secure the Orphan's pension necessary to provide an income for Adolf and Paula. In the 1950s, Mayrhofen showed Kubizek the documents which were drawn up in 1908.

'To the Respected Imperial and Royal Finance Administration. The respectfully undersigned herewith request the kind allocation of the Orphans' Pension due to them. Both of these applicants, after the death of their mother, widow of an Imperial and Royal Customs Official, on 21 December 1907, are now without either of their parents, are minors, and are incapable of earning their own living. The guardian of both applicants – Adolf Hitler, born on the 20 April 1889, in Braunau-on-Inn, and Paula Hitler, born on the 21 January 1898, in Fischlam, near Lambach, Upper Austria – is Mr. Joseph Mayrhofer, of Leonding, near Linz. Both applicants are domiciled in Linz.'

The small pension was soon granted and Hitler unselfishly assigned his portion to Paula and with a modest income to rely upon, her future was secure and the road to Vienna was now clear for Hitler. The one remaining obstacle was to convince Kubizek's parents of the wisdom of Gustl's chosen path. Despite the reservations of Kubizek's parents, Hitler was to prove as persuasive as ever and Kubizek was permitted to join Hitler at Stumpergasse 17 for a trial period. Gustl arrived in Vienna in February 1908, and moved with Hitler and a rented grand piano into the larger room of Frau Zakrey's humble two room apartment.

At first the two friends were as inseparable as ever sharing their cramped room and small store of food and branching out into life in Vienna. They regularly visited the opera together, always to hear Wagner. Kubizek later described the mesmeric effect of Wagner's music on Hitler stating that when Hitler listened to the music of Wagner, it was almost as if he were transformed. Hitler, it appeared, willingly allowed himself to be transported back into a legendary world which was in some respects more real to Hitler than the ordinary grey world he saw around him everyday. Listening to Wagner, Hitler was released from the stale, musty prison of Frau Zakrey's spare room at the back of the courtyard, he was transported into the blessed regions of German antiquity, which for him was the ideal world, the highest goal of all his endeavours. Here the revered Wagnerian themes of chivalry, valour, duty and order were embodied in a sublime cloak of musical wonder. Hitler yearned to see these values re-established at the heart of the consciousness of the German people. Hitler had found a life long passion and as he learned more and more about Wagner, Hitler delighted in their common *weltanschauung*. Kubizek noted that as soon as the music of Wagner started, all signs of Hitler's normal violent temperament left him and he became quiet, submissive and even biddable. Kubizek studied Hitler during his Wagnerian reveries and noted how his stern gaze lost its restlessness and intensity as Hitler palpably lost sight of his daily preoccupations which no longer appeared to weigh upon him. It was as if, in the presence of the works of the maestro of Bayreuth, Hitler no longer felt himself to be lonely, an outlaw, kicked around by society. Kubizek describes him as being in a state of 'intoxicated ecstasy'.

These visits to hear Wagner soon inspired Hitler to compose his own *völkisch* inspired opera and he sat down at the piano and began hammering out the first outlines of his opera which was projected to have a libretto and music by Hitler and to be arranged by Kubizek. The opera was based on a projected work by Wagner which had been sketched out but never completed; it concerned the mythological tale Wieland the Smith. Like all too many of his pet projects Hitler lost interest after a few weeks. Kubizek later mislaid the working manuscripts thus robbing posterity of an unbridled opportunity to catch a glimpse into the mind of Adolf Hitler the working artist.

Besides visiting the opera, the politically inclined Hitler was also a frequent visitor to the Cisleithanian parliament, which from 1907, was elected by the then unusual process of universal suffrage by men aged 24 and over. The House of Representatives, the *Reichsrat*, was welcomed as an exciting experiment in democracy and Hitler occasionally dragged Kubizek along with him. The harsh economic climate of Vienna in 1908 and 1909 produced widespread hunger and homelessness.

Huge public rallies were held by those desperate for some kind of relief. This should have been the basis of the *Reichsrat*, but in reality, the house had descended into a farce as a surreal series of pointless proceedings took place daily in the gilded atmosphere of one of Vienna's most beautiful buildings, while vast swathes of the population starved. There were two public galleries, a lower one reserved for nobility and important personages and an upper gallery for the general public. During 1908 and 1909, Hitler was a frequent visitor to the upper gallery. If ever there was a place to convince Hitler of the correctness of his developing view that Vienna was home to a hellish babel of incompatible ethnic groups, it was the Cisleithanian people's parliament of 1908 and 1909.

Completely devoid of decorum, functionality or even common sense, this fantastically weird institution permitted its members to speak in any one of the ten official languages of the empire – but made no attempt whatsoever to translate the words of the speaker or to impose a universal *lingua franca* on proceedings. The result was often chaos which on occasion descended into the lowest kind of farce imaginable. Proceedings were further disrupted by the frequent use of the device of the filibuster under which a member could drone on interminably in Italian or Russian sometimes for days in order to prevent the reading of a bill supported by the German faction. There is a bizarre example of a Czech speaker named Lisy who actually ate a ham sandwich and sipped cognac to give himself energy during a pointless exposition of interminable length delivered merely to prevent the business of the house from moving on to other matters, while outraged citizens who had fought hard for democracy hurled insults at him from the public gallery. The occasions on which the house descended into uncontrollable anarchy were growing more frequent as the harsh economic climate of 1908 and 1909 forced an unruly public to demand changes from an institution riven by ethnic divisions.[26]

The inevitable result was a rise in frustration fuelled by the rank stupidity of the process which led to fist fights on the floor of the house

---

26. Hamman: 'Hitler's Vienna', p. 121.

and the balconies being cleared. Hitler was witness to such scenes, and not surprisingly they coloured his views of democracy for the rest of his life. His description in *'Mein Kampf'* is one of the less colourful word pictures describing the unedifying spectacle of the *Reichsrat* at work:

'A wild gesticulating mass screaming all at once in every different key, presided over by a good-natured old uncle who was striving in the sweat of his brow to revive the house by violently ringing his bell and alternating gentle reproofs with grave admonitions. I couldn't help laughing.'

By 1908, Hitler was not the only one who was laughing, a visit to the parliament had become a source of fun for many Viennese, who at least gained some enjoyment from the lunacy of the proceedings which always seemed to verge on the possibility of a punch up between the heated occupants of the ridiculous circus playing daily in the majestic setting of the Ring Boulevard. It was also considered a source of mirth internationally and many Austrians resented the shame which this brought upon the reputation of their country.

Sadly, the whole rotten institution had begun in the noble spirit of providing a genuine people's parliament as a democratic counterpoint to the rule of the Emperor Franz Josef. The pain of witnessing the resulting ignominy caused great frustration among ordinary Viennese, many of whom had fought hard to achieve such a positive development. However, their well-meaning attempts to protest against the nonsensical proceedings by public interjections from the balcony only added to the general confusion below and frequently resulted in further disruptions as the balconies were cleared of the rightfully incensed members of the public.

At the time Hitler was in the habit of attending the *Reichsrat*, the Austrian Parliament was composed of 233 Germans, 107 Czechs, 82 Poles, 33 *Ruthenians* (Ukrainians), 24 Slovenians, 19 Italians, 13 Croats and 5 Romanians all of whom were entitled to address the house in their own language. There were of course days on which the house proceeded almost normally and Hitler recorded that, on occasion, he listened to speeches 'in so far as they were intelligible'.

On balance the institution was a dismal failure and it was the site of continued spectacle until 1914, when it was closed by an emergency decree. It is not surprising therefore that the impressionable Adolf Hitler should have formed such a negative view on the workings of democracy. Hitler formed the view that only a despot could make way in such circumstances and that seed must have begun to germinate in the mind of the young man who tells us that he sat in silence and pondered on the strange events unfolding before him.

Kubizek returned to Linz shortly after moving to Vienna but it was a temporary move and the two friends continued to correspond as Kubizek made plans to return. A letter from Hitler dated 19 April 1908, still survives and it provides a rare example of Hitler's sense of humour as he responds to the news that Gustl will be bringing a viola with him.

'Dear Gustl, While thanking you for your kind letter, I must tell you how happy I am that your dear father is coming with you to Vienna. If you and your father don't object, I will be waiting for you at the station at 11 A.M. on Thursday. You write that you are having wonderful weather, and this saddens me, for if it were not raining here, we too, and not just the people of Linz, should be enjoying wonderful weather. I am delighted that you are bringing a viola. On Thursday I shall buy two Kronen's worth of cotton wool and 20 Kreuzer's worth of sticking plaster, for my ears naturally. That, on top of all this, you are growing blind, has plunged me into a profound depression: you will play even more wrong notes than before. Then you will go blind and I will eventually go deaf. Alas! Meanwhile I wish you and your esteemed parents at least a happy Easter, and I send them my hearty greetings, and to you, too. Your Friend.'

Despite Hitler's friendly jibes, Kubizek was a fine musician and on his return to Vienna, easily won his place at the Vienna Conservatory and was soon immersed in the whirl of student life in Vienna making extra money by playing the cello and viola and even taking music pupils. Hitler by contrast was simply hiding from reality. Kubizek eventually discovered that his friend was playing a daily charade in which he merely pretended to study. Forced to come clean Hitler admitted that there was no real prospect of him gaining entrance to the school of Architecture. He was too proud to admit it but Gustl noted that his friend was obviously close to penury. As the summer of 1908 rolled round into view the friends continued to enjoy all that Vienna had to offer. A pleasure trip down the river Danube was to prove one of the highlights of the early summer of 1908. Unfortunately, their Viennese idyl was shattered when Kubizek found himself unexpectedly called up to serve in the Austro-Hungarian army. This drove Hitler to apoplexy and he railed at great length against anyone soldiering on behalf of the Empire which Hitler so detested. Hitler attempted to persuade Kubizek to flee to Germany and evade his call up that way, but eventually Kubizek saw sense and reluctantly returned to Linz to face the music. Fortunately for Gustl he was only called upon to serve eight weeks as a reservist leaving him free to return to Vienna in mid-November 1908.

During his friend's long absence from Vienna, Hitler continued to correspond intermittently with Kubizek during the summer and into the autumn of 1908. In return, Kubizek wrote to his friend informing him that he would be back in Vienna from mid November 1908, as agreed. The faithful Kubizek honoured his agreement but on reaching Vienna station on the designated day, Kubizek was dismayed to find no sign of Hitler ready to welcome his friend back to Vienna. Nor was there any trace of him at Frau Zakreys' humble apartment. The realisation slowly dawned on Kubizek that, without giving his best friend any form of notice Hitler had moved on into the depths of metropolitan Vienna leaving no forwarding address. Kubizek was baffled and naturally expected his friend to resurface at any moment, but for Hitler the world had turned once more. It was almost as if he had simply closed the chapter of Kubizek.

The reason for Hitler's abrupt departure from Frau Zakreys' modest apartment appears to have been acute financial embarrassment. Following his father's death Hitler had agreed that the orphan's monthly pension of fifty kronen would be received by Angela on behalf of Paula.

As Hitler got nothing, his slim stock of money soon gave out and rather than face up to the awkward truth and the possibility of having to accept charity from Kubizek, or even worse the Raubals, Hitler seems to have run away from the situation and attempted to make a completely new start, just as Alois would have done.

From this point onwards, the exact narrative of Hitler's stay in Vienna becomes impossible to piece together. We know from the surviving household account book that Haninaunt Johanna, then living at Blütenstrasse 9 with Paula, loaned Hitler the not inconsiderable sum of 940 Kronen. At a time when a labourer's wage could be as low as 1,200 Kronen this was a healthy sum of cash which if prudently eked out could keep a young student in food and rent for a year. Hitler appears to have been reasonably prudent with his money, but by 1909, it was exhausted, leaving him effectively destitute. Following his second attempt to gain admission to Art school, from mid 1908 onwards Hitler found himself friendless and alone and without any trade or reliable means of means of making money, Hitler claims he struggled to survive in Vienna as an unskilled labourer.

We know that on 16 November 1908, Hitler dutifully paid all of the remaining rent he owed to Frau Zakreys and moved to Felberstrasse 22, Door Number 16, where his police registration records that his new landlady was Helene Reidl. He lived there for some nine months but not necessarily as a lodger with his own room, he may well have been a glorified *Bettgeher*. *Bettgeher* were poor people with no fixed abode, often shift workers from the countryside, they paid a small fee for the use of a bed in a private house for a few hours.

In 1910, it was estimated the *Bettgeher* numbered 80,000 in Vienna, and this form of 'hot bedding' was regarded as a threat to the health and morals of the host family. Hitler then moved on from Felberstrasse in August 1909, but that appeared to exhaust his available budget. Hitler was soon reduced to living in the men's homeless shelters and there remains a strong possibility that he may have slipped even further and joined the ranks of Vienna's *Bettgeher* ('bed-goers'). Hitler certainly claimed to have experienced some dreadful living conditions and as he recalled in *'Mein Kampf'* he had experienced for himself the very worst of what Vienna had to offer.

'Housing conditions were very bad at that time. The Viennese manual labourers lived in surroundings of appalling misery. I shudder even today when I think of the woeful dens in which people dwelt, the night shelters and the slums, and all the tenebrous spectacles of ordure, loathsome filth and wickedness.'

The harsh lot of a man reduced to living in Vienna's shelters for the homeless was described by Reinhold Hanisch, an itinerant labourer, who befriended Hitler in the autumn of 1909. By this time Hitler had been drifting around Vienna for over a year and he was clearly at a very low ebb indeed. Hanisch's account of his life with Hitler was later published in three parts by the American magazine 'New Republic' commencing on 5 April 1939, under the very American title 'I Was Hitler's Buddy':

'In the autumn of 1909, after extensive wanderings through Germany and Austria, I arrived as a travelling artisan in Vienna. On the highway I had already heard about a lodging-house and I decided to go there, for I had very little money. I soon found the Asylum for the Homeless, a large modern building behind the South Railway Station. The town's poor stood there in a long row waiting for admittance. Finally the gates were thrown open and our line livened up. Everyone was given a ticket that entitled him to five nights' lodging, and it was punched by the supervisor. Inside, long rows of benches stood on both sides of the hall to accommodate the people. They went in couples to the shower-bath. Those who were full of vermin had their clothing tied up in bundles and disinfected. This "burning-out" of the clothes often damaged them severely. After that the people returned to the hall, the upper part of which was set with rows of tables. Bread was brought in, soup was served, and afterward everyone retired to the dormitories. Cots with wire springs stood along the walls, each covered with two brownish-coloured sheets.'

During 1908, from his own account, it would appear that Hitler had undertaken a series of hard manual jobs to earn what little money he could. With his thin and frail figure, he was clearly unsuited to the task. The prospect of salvation was at hand however in the form of the hand painted postcards of familiar Viennese landmarks which Hitler slowly learned how to produce and sell. During this period of extreme poverty and toil spurred on by a series of unpleasant confrontations with left leaning union officials, Hitler also began to engage in the first small bursts of political activity. Initially his politics were main stream as he records that he attended mass meetings of the Social Democrats and absorbed political newspapers and literature. It was here that his views on the importance of a centralised and interventionist state began to coalesce. The socialist part of the Hitler political agenda was being forged as a result of his struggles in Vienna:

'During my struggle for existence in Vienna I perceived very clearly that the aim of all social activity must never be merely charitable relief, which is ridiculous and useless, but it must rather be a means to find a way of eliminating the fundamental deficiencies in our economic and cultural life-deficiencies which necessarily bring about the degradation of the individual or at least lead him towards such degradation.'

Hitler argued that the task of 'nationalising' a people was first and foremost one of establishing healthy social conditions. It is social improvement above all, Hitler reasoned, which would furnish the necessary infrastructure for the education of the individual. He argued that only when family upbringing and school education were robust and had inculcated in the individual a knowledge of the cultural and economic greatness and, above all, the political greatness of the German Reich then, and then only, would it be possible for the individual to feel proud of being a citizen of the Reich. Hitler maintained that he could fight only for something that he loved and could love only what he respected, and in order to respect a thing the individual must at least have some clear knowledge of the thing he was supposed to respect.

During 1908, Hitler moved further and further away from the mainstream Social Democrat ideal, his brief flirtation with centrist politics faded as he began to drift further and further to the right as he developed his own peculiar ultra-nationalist political agenda. The process of political discovery is detailed in a long and rambling passage which forms Chapter Two of *'Mein Kampf'*. Hitler sets out in painstaking detail to explain something of the chronology and the process by which his own warped logic led away from the Social Democracy which Hitler had initially admired at the time of his arrival in Vienna. Hitler grudgingly accorded Social Democracy respect for its role in bringing about universal suffrage which produced the *Reichsrat*. According to Hitler however, this triumph for Social Democracy gave him an inner satisfaction as he derived in that chaotic assembly, the loosening of the Habsburg grip on power which he hoped would one day undermine the whole Habsburg regime which he so thoroughly detested. The racist aspect of Hitler's politics were evident from his earliest schooling. In his mind, the Slavs represented a virtual bogeyman which his Vienna sojourn did nothing to dispel. Hitler was convinced that the hated Slavs did not possess the necessary capacity for constructive politics and he welcomed every movement that might lead towards the final disruption of the Habsburg Empire as only then would it become possible for the Germano-Austrian population to be re-united with the greater German Reich.

In *'Mein Kampf'*, Hitler states that he originally had no feelings of antipathy towards the actual policy of the Social Democrats. Hitler claimed that he had hitherto regarded 'Social Democracy' and 'Socialism' as synonymous expressions. He wholeheartedly agreed with its avowed purpose of helping to improve the lot of the working classes, but as always, Hitler's nationalist agenda came to the fore and he soon found himself violently opposed to what he viewed as the Social Democrats' hostile attitude towards pan-Germanism in Austria.

Hitler soon radically reassessed his entire opinion of the Social Democrats. In a classic example of paranoia in action, he later claimed to have discovered an unparalleled system for 'duping' the public at the hands of the Jews. In typical delusional fashion, Hitler described how he had come to the conclusion that, 'under the cloak of social virtue', a veritable pestilence was spreading and that if this pestilence be not stamped out of the world without delay it might eventually succeed in 'exterminating the human race'. At the outer core of this 'pestilence' was trade unionism which even Hitler conceded could be harnessed as a force for good and therefore serve the interests of the Reich. Unfortunately, he also concluded trade unionism was more often simply the battering ram of the Social Democrats to be harnessed in the interests of class war.

As a building site labourer in Vienna sometime in 1908, Hitler claimed that he had point blank refused to join a trade union when ordered to do so. He became ever more defiant in his refusal to join when he heard how the union spokesmen disparaged a number of different aspects of his beloved Reich. Hitler listened with incredulity and deepening anger, he later paraphrased the arguments he had heard on the building site. He claimed that the trade unionists criticised the nation 'because it was held to be an invention of the "capitalist" class'. He was incensed when a union official allegedly criticised the Fatherland 'because it was held to be an instrument in the hands of the bourgeoisie for the exploitation of' the working masses'. Hitler continued to spell out his own view of the opinion of his opponents and the authority of the law, 'because that was a means of holding down the proletariat'; religion was a means of 'duping the people, so as to exploit them afterwards', and morality 'was a badge of stupid and sheepish docility'. To Hitler it seemed that all of the *völkisch* and nationalist values of duty and honour which he held so dear were being dragged in the mud. He began to argue with the trades unionists in his usual fervent style. Eventually he claims he was chased off the site by threats of violence and drew the ominous conclusion that all such threats of this nature should, in future, be met with counter violence. Hitler now formed the view that trade unionism was a movement based upon intimidation which Hitler proclaimed was apparent in workshops and in factories, in assembly halls and at mass demonstrations.

- CHAPTER 5 -
THE JEWISH QUESTION

ITLER'S DISGUST WITH his own wretched state in
Vienna was soon projected on to the city he had once admired.
Hitler despised the racial melting pot which he saw around him and
eventually this loathing coalesced into a venomous hatred for the Jewish
race. Vienna did not mark the onset of Hitler's anti-Semitic politics, as
Kubizek recalled that Hitler held anti-Semitic views during their time
in Linz. These youthful views however, were lukewarm and were widely
held in Linz society and Hitler it seems was merely acting in step with
the grain of society. However, what we do know from the pages of *'Mein
Kampf'* is that it was in Vienna that Hitler began to form his own vicious
brand of ultra anti-Semitism. As he gradually settled down to his new
surroundings, Hitler was immediately aware of the racial and cultural
mix of the city. It was now that he came up against the evidence of
what was called the *Judenfrage*, which can be translated as either 'Jewish
question' or 'Jewish problem'.

The term *Judenfrage* was in use from at least the 1840s and it is
interesting to note that both Marx and Engels had made reference to
the 'Jewish question'. It is typical of Hitler that he viewed Marxism as a
Jewish plot even though its progenitor had written in fiercely anti-Semitic
terms during the previous century. In his own essay, *'Zur Judenfrage'*
(On the Jewish Question) written in 1843, Marx used the same vicious
language which would come to characterise Hitler's outpourings and
described the Jews as 'a nation of hucksters'.

The widespread use of the phrase 'Jewish question' was evidence of
the routine anti-Semitism which was an ingrained aspect of Austrian
and German society in the nineteenth and early twentieth centuries.
If there was a 'question' then it was self-evident there had to exist an
answer to that question. Hitler had to break no new political ground on

the road that was to lead to the *Endlösung* (or final solution). He had to do little more than latch on to an existing tide of anti-Semitism which stridently demanded an answer to the Jewish question. The influence of populist politicians such Georg Schönerer had shaped much of the nationalist agenda in Austria for many years and his influence although declining was still widely felt at the time when Hitler was visiting Vienna. As a young man Schönerer became a political activist and was elected to Austria's *Reichsrat* in 1873. Originally a liberal, Schönerer soon developed a political philosophy that featured elements of violent anti-Semitism, anti-Slavism, anti-Catholicism, authoritarianism and pan-Germanism, themes which appealed to many lower class Viennese. As such, Schönerer rapidly became a popular and powerful political figure. In 1879, he formed the Pan-German Party, which would become a considerable force in Austrian politics.

In 1888, Schönerer was temporarily imprisoned for ransacking a Jewish-owned newspaper office and assaulting its employees. This action increased Schönerer's popularity and helped members of his party get elected to the Austrian Parliament. The prison sentence also resulted in the loss of his status as a noble. Schönerer himself was re-elected to the *Reichsrat* in 1897, and later that year helped orchestrate the expulsion of Prime Minister Kasimir Felix Graf Badeni from office. Badeni had proclaimed that civil servants in Austrian-controlled Bohemia would have to know the Czech language, an ordinance which prevented many ethnic German-speakers (the majority of whom could not speak Czech) in Bohemia from applying for governmental jobs. Schönerer staged mass protests against the ordinance and disrupted parliamentary proceedings, actions which eventually caused Emperor Franz Joseph to dismiss Badeni.

Schönerer became even more powerful in 1901, when 21 members of his party gained seats in the Parliament. His career crumbled rapidly thereafter, however, due to his forceful views and eccentric personality. His party suffered too, and had virtually disintegrated by 1907. Nonetheless Schönerer's views and philosophy greatly influenced the young Adolf Hitler and had a particular influence on his drift towards virulent anti-Semitism. It is widely held that it was Schönerer who coined the pseudo-medieval greeting '*Hail*,' or '*Heil*'. His followers also called him 'the Leader' (*Führer*), another term which his movement is likely to have introduced into the vocabulary of nationalist politics. Karl Hermann Wolf was another nationalist politician who was active at the time and who influenced Hitler on his political journey to the right.

The gallery of nationalist opinion formers who influenced Hitler's thinking in his Vienna period is completed by Franz Stein and Dr Karl Lueger the notoriously anti-Semitic mayor of Vienna who held office from 1897-1910. There were obviously a number of factors at work in shaping the anti-Semitic aspects of Hitler's thinking and he certainly attended speeches by Stein and Lueger.

However, according to Hitler, the whole downward curve of world history in the twentieth century that led towards the ignominy of the final solution appears to have stemmed from a single sudden momentary realisation. Hitler sought to claim that the impetus came entirely from within his own experience and was formed in his own mind. He described the world changing moment when passing through the inner City of Vienna, he encountered a figure in a long caftan wearing black side-locks. Hitler records his first thought was: 'Is this a Jew?' They certainly had not adopted this orthodox appearance in Linz. Hitler watched the man stealthily and cautiously; but the longer he gazed at the strange countenance and examined the strange man-alien feature by alien feature, the more the momentous question shaped itself in Hitler's brain: 'Is this a German?'

According to Hitler, this chance meeting led him on a twisted journey of discovery as he researched deeper and deeper into the Jewish question. This self-study course was conducted in libraries, in cheap cafés and from the pages of penny pamphlets. The warped conclusions drawn by Hitler combined with his experiences in the Great War were to result in worldwide misery and the death of millions. In reality, it is more likely that Hitler's views were shaped by Schönerer and Wolf and that the passage in *'Mein Kampf'* represents the moment when Hitler's thoughts began crystallising.

In 1908, Hitler came to the unshakeable conclusion that Social

Democracy was merely the shield behind which lay the 'grimacing figure of Marxism'. Hitler had formed the strange view that a real knowledge of the Jews was the only key whereby one could understand the inner nature and the real aims of Social Democracy. He began to buy pamphlets and books and to study everything connected with the Jews. The more he read the more it seemed that Hitler's own prejudices were confirmed. In his eyes the charge against Judaism became much more grave as Hitler discovered the extent of Jewish activities in the press, in art, in literature and the theatre. In Vienna at the time it was possible to purchase a wide variety of virulently anti-Semitic pamphlets and even newspapers including the notorious *Ostara*. *Ostara* was described as the newsletter of the blonde and the masculist, published by the *völkisch* mystic Jörg Lanz (also known as Jörg Lanz von Liebenfels) it purported to promote an occult world view based on an outlandish racial struggle begun in a remote past.

Ostara was one of the *völkisch* predecessors to *'Der Stürmer'* the viciously anti-Semitic Third Reich journal published by Julius Streicher in the 1920s, which would in time take anti-Jewish propaganda to new levels. The lives of the Jews living in Germany had been typically harsh; during the eighteenth century they had been tolerated but treated very much as second class citizens. The emancipation of German Jews had begun in Prussia in 1812, and was essentially a consequence of the French Revolution and the rise of liberalism. It was not a smooth journey as leading German literary and political figures had declared themselves against this tendency. In 1823, for example, Goethe, hearing that a law permitting the intermarriage of Christians and Jews had been passed, gave himself up to passionate protest predicting the gravest consequences from this new concession. Bismarck, speaking as a deputy in the Prussian Parliament in 1847, said that he was not an enemy of the Jews and was willing to grant them every privilege – except that of holding office in a Gentile state. In 1848, however, the revolutionary movement brought the Jews an officially recognised measure of emancipation although a complete removal of all restrictions did not become a fact in law until 1869.

Throughout the nineteenth century an anti-Jewish current was latent in educated German circles, growing stronger as the consequences of Jewish emancipation became more apparent. The wide spread anti-Semitic trend found expression in the anti-Jewish stances adopted by notable figures such as Schopenhauer, Wagner and Moltke. With the appointment, however, of the Court-Preacher Adolf Stoecker, called from Metz to Berlin by Emperor Wilhelm I, there began an anti-Marxian movement which soon broadened into an anti-Jewish campaign, making Stoecker the leading apostle of German anti-Semitism in the late nineteenth century.

Prominent among other anti-Jewish agitators were noblemen like Max Lieberman von Sonnenberg and Graf Ludwig zu Reventlow, the brother of Ernst. By 1893, the anti-Semitic Party in Parliament had sixteen deputies, and strong and influential economic groups, such as the *Landbund* and the *Deutschnationale Handlungsgehilfen-Verband* were now active in the *völkisch* movement and in opposition to Jewry.

The word *völk* could mean 'proletariat' amongst those on the left, however for those on the right it signified 'race'. Hitler was all the time moving further and further to the right and the subject of race was at the very heart of his thinking. Although the primary interest of the Germanic mystical movement was the revival of pagan traditions and customs, a marked preoccupation with purity of race soon came to motivate some of its increasingly politically oriented offshoots. One of these was the *Germanenorden*, a secret society founded in Berlin during 1912. It was around this time that Hitler may well have been exposed to *völkisch* concepts such as Aryanism. The *Germanenorden* required its candidates to prove that they had no 'non-Aryan' bloodlines and required from each a promise to maintain purity of his stock in marriage. Pseudo-masonic principles were quickly added to the eclectic mix of the mystical and the romantic to produce a powerful sense of purpose for what were essentially a pretty disparate bunch of nonsensical ideas. Nonetheless the influence of the *völkisch* movements continued to spread and with it the power of the *Germanenorden*. Local groups of the sect began to meet to celebrate the summer solstice with arcane ceremonies, and the solstice soon became the most important neo-pagan festivity in *völkisch* circles and later in Nazi Germany.

Intellectuals began to meet to read the Icelandic Eddas in their native tongue. It was this branch of the *völkisch* movement quickly developed a hyper-nationalist sentiment and allied itself with anti-Semitism, then rising throughout the Western world. It is interesting to note that *völkisch* methods and ideas were also gaining currency outside Germany. In Oxford, the celebrated writer J.R.R. Tolkien regularly met with a group of like-minded colleagues to revel in the power of hearing the Eddas read aloud in old Icelandic. The Gothic/Norse overtones of Tolkien's race-obsessed master work would undoubtedly have struck a very warm chord in *völkisch* circles had it been published at the time.

Lanz claimed that, in 1908, an impoverished Hitler had turned up on his doorstep seeking to buy copies of the magazine in order to complete his collection. Lanz stated that he had given Hitler the magazines plus the fare so he could ride home on the train. Hitler himself makes no mention of any such meeting, or indeed any mention of Lanz. Consciously or otherwise Hitler's political philosophy absorbed and adopted some of the ideas and many of the phrases and terminology of the *völkisch* fringe. The idea that there once had existed a race of Aryans who fought for the Nordic world against the *untermensch* was accepted unquestioningly by Hitler and slipped into his thought processes to emerge years later as part of the National Socialist dogma. It must be concluded that in 1908, at that stage in his development, Hitler was clearly receptive to nationalist and ultra-racialist ideas which were embraced by the *völkisch* movement. The *völkisch* concept of a *volksgemeinschaft* or national community excluded the Jews and anti-Semitic ideas were widely promulgated. *Völkisch* pamphlets were in wide circulation and many outlandish ideas were already beginning to gain traction, among them was the neo-pagan religion of *Wotanism*.

Hitler had hitherto despised the overtly anti-Semitic press as vulgar and uncouth, but he now saw the liberal policy of his favoured broadsheet papers as forming part of a cunning and despicable way of deceiving the readers in all manner of devious and underhand ways, many of which were so subtle as to be invisible to the untrained observer. In Hitler's fevered brain for example the deluded idea soon took root that brilliant praiseworthy theatrical criticisms were always lauded upon the Jewish authors, while adverse criticism was reserved exclusively for the Germans.

Hitler also took it upon himself to research the part which the Jews played in the social phenomenon of prostitution. Inevitably his prejudices were once more confirmed and in the pages of 'Mein Kampf' Hitler described how a cold shiver ran down his spine when he first ascertained that it was the same kind of 'cold-blooded, thick-skinned and shameless' Jew who showed his consummate skill in conducting the flesh trade in the big city.

Hitler claimed that he had now learned to 'track down the Jew' in all the different spheres of cultural and artistic life, and in fact he found various manifestations of this life everywhere. Hitler now came to the 'realisation' that the Jews were the leaders of Social Democracy and that the Social Democratic Press was also predominantly controlled by Jews.

Hitler described himself as making an effort to overcome his natural reluctance by setting out to read the Marxist Press; but in doing so his aversion increased all the more when he discovered that the people who wrote and published this 'mischievous stuff' from the publisher downwards, all of them were Jews too. Hitler's massive burden of outrage and prejudice weighed even heavier with the discovery that the public leaders of Marxism, like Marx himself were mainly Jews as were the Social Democratic representatives in the Imperial Cabinet as well as the secretaries of the Trades Unions and even the street agitators. It seemed to Hitler that everywhere the same sinister picture presented itself. Hitler saw evidence of the conspiracy everywhere he looked. It was on this basis that Hitler declared himself happy to know 'for certain' that the Jew is not a German.

Hitler had now identified Judaism as his arch enemy and he soon began to heap his prejudices on the shoulders of his unfortunate adversaries. Chief among the many faults which Hitler brought to the long suffering door of the Jewish race, was an alleged universal tendency to twist the truth – which Hitler called the 'dialectical perfidy' of that race. Hitler maintained it was futile to try to win over such evil people with argument. He had drawn the conclusion that their very mouths distorted the truth and stated that the Jews consistently disowned the words they had just used only to adopt them again a few moments afterwards if they were needed to serve their own ends in the argument. Hitler summed up the tautological argument which forms Chapter Two of 'Mein Kampf' with the tortured conclusion that the Jewish doctrine of Marxism should be opposed as it repudiates the aristocratic principle of nature and substitutes that wonderful vibrant force and energy with the dead weight of numerical mass.

These were the convoluted assembly of political ideas and prejudices which had formed during the years of suffering in the warped brain of the young Adolf Hitler. By late 1909, however, the worst of the period of suffering in Vienna was behind him. Hitler states that he had so far improved his position that he no longer had to earn his daily bread as a manual labourer. He was now working independently as a postcard painter. He used water colours to make individual postcards of Vienna's landmark buildings. This living was a very poor one indeed, but it provided Hitler with enough to meet the bare exigencies of life. Yet Hitler still comforted himself with the faint hope that this was nonetheless a step in the direction of the architect's profession to which he still aspired. Peddling postcards was not as physically exhausting as mending roads and according to Hitler when he came home in the evenings, he was no longer dead-tired as formerly, when he had been unable to look into a book without falling asleep almost immediately. Hitler now painted in order to earn his daily bread, and studied because he liked to do so.

As Hitler's circumstances slowly improved he was able to leave the world of night shelters behind him and he was ultimately able to transfer to the comparative luxury of the new model men's hostel at Meldemannstrasse 27. The construction of the dormitory in 1905 was financed by a private charitable foundation which aimed at reducing the number of *Bettgeher* in Vienna. It is typical of Hitler's ungrateful and hypocritical nature that his own life was revolutionised by the efforts of a charitable trust, yet years later, he himself in the pages of *'Mein Kampf'* maintained that charitable relief was 'ridiculous and useless'.

The six-story dormitory on Meldemannstrasse was a dream facility for Hitler, it was among the most modern of its kind and was still almost new, having opened in 1905. It was lit by gas lamps and even some electric light bulbs, and in the bitter Viennese winters was heated by a modern steam heater. On the ground floor there was a large mess hall where inexpensive meals could be had, there was also a reading room with a supply of daily newspapers and a library. The underground floor housed cleaning rooms, a luggage room, a bicycle storage room as well as shoemaker's and tailor's workshops. Moreover, the dormitory included a sick room with a resident physician, a disinfection chamber for the de-lousing of new residents, washrooms, a shaving room and a bathroom with sixteen showers and four bathtubs.

The actual dormitory was located on the upper four stories. Each of the 544 residents was allocated a small cabin of his own, measuring 5ft by 7ft. The cabins, which were unlocked each evening at 8 P.M. and had to be vacated by 9 A.M., had a lockable door, a light bulb, a bed, a small table, a clothes-hanger and a mirror. The weekly rent was 2.50 crowns which was roughly equivalent to what a *Bettgeher* would normally have to pay for the use of a bed. This made Meldemannstrasse 27 a very attractive and affordable lodging for unskilled labourers or journeyman artisans with an annual income of about 1,000 crowns. When the dormitory opened, the Viennese press praised it as 'fantastical quarters, a paradise on earth' and as a 'wonder of elegance and inexpensiveness'. It must have felt like a heaven-sent oasis for Adolf Hitler who was slowly beginning to haul himself up from the lowest rungs of society. According to police registration files, Adolf Hitler – at the time unemployed and living off the sale of his paintings – lived in the dormitory for three years, from 9 February 1910 to 24 May 1913, when he finally moved to Munich.

Hitler himself has provided no details about his daily life in Vienna, but several of his Meldemannstrasse co-residents later published their recollections of Hitler's stay in the dormitory. They all report in common, that he read the newspapers each morning in the non-smoking area of the reading room, where he also painted, discussed politics with other residents and on occasion gave some of his trademark rambling speeches.

Some of the co-residents of the dormitory with whom Hitler became involved included a number of his Jewish friends including Eduard Löffner and Josef Neumann. He also met the Viennese druggist Rudolf Häusler, who later moved to Munich with Hitler in 1913, and a rival painter called Karl Leidenroth.

Among the men who seized the opportunity to make a few crowns by writing about Hitler's residence in the dormitory was an anonymous contributor who wrote reports that appeared in Czech newspapers in the 1930s. Although many of the details appear to be accurate, an inability to identify the author or corroborate the evidence means that the same cannot be relied upon. Also writing and easily identifiable as genuine was Karl Honisch who wrote a report for the Nazi party archives in 1938. Next, there was Josef Greiner, an itinerant worker who published two slim volumes of memoirs in 1938 and 1947, and was initially considered to be an accurate source. However as a result of a number of glaring inaccuracies Greiner has now been dismissed as a fraud who never actually met Hitler. For example, Greiner places Hitler in Vienna in 1907-1908, at which time we know for certain that Hitler was still living in Linz. Greiner also claims that at one point Hitler attempted to rape one of his models, despite the fact that Hitler painted exclusively still lives, architecture and spurned the human form. His surviving work displays a distinct inability to render even tiny human forms in proper perspective. He appears never to have painted male or female subjects at any time during his stay in Vienna. Greiner also claims that Hitler contracted syphilis from a Leopoldstadt prostitute and made the fanciful claim that in 1945, Hitler did not commit suicide, but instead fled from Berlin in an airplane.

One source we can trust to a much greater extent, is the memoir written by Reinhold Hanisch, a vagabond and part-time labourer who became an enemy of Hitler's and died in Buchenwald in 1937. His recollections were posthumously published in 'The New Republican' in 1939, and, according to him, the subjects which invited Hitler's interest could be broadly grouped under the wide canopy of the *völkisch* movements that had developed during the late 19th century in the German Empire.

Although he was an enemy of Hitler's from around 1912, Reinhold Hanisch has provided what appears to be the most reliable account of his life with Hitler between 1909 and 1912. In 1910, Hanisch operated as Hitler's agent, selling his paintings and obtaining commissions. Hanisch was a colourful character with a chequered past and a habit of assuming false names. Some of his claims are highly implausible. He claims to have taught Hitler to sing *'Die Wacht am Rhein'*, a song which Hitler would have known very well from his youth. Despite this, much of the remaining memoir can be substantiated. In his memoir, Hanisch produced a vivid picture of Hitler as he knew him, and of the circumstances that had a share in the formation of Hitler's character.

Hanisch himself was a German-Bohemian who, like Hitler, held Austrian citizenship. He was not a Jew, but Hanisch had the ultimate misfortune to cross Hitler sometime in 1912, and ended up on the losing side of a criminal court case which saw him jailed for his part in defrauding Hitler of some small sum of money.

Hanisch first met Hitler in 1909, when both were living in the Asylum for the homeless. He knew just low Hitler had fallen and, in contrast to the principled young man whom Kubizek felt would never be reduced to accepting charity, Hanisch claimed that Hitler had sunk much lower. Hanisch went on to form a working partnership which grew into a friendship with Hitler and in his memoir he described how Hitler had in fact become so desperate he had actually been reduced to begging in the street:

> *'The neighbour on my right looked sad, and so we asked him questions. For several days he had been living on benches in the parks where his sleep was often disturbed by policemen. He had landed here dead tired, hungry, with sore feet. His blue-checked suit had turned lilac, from the rain and the "burning" in the asylum bleached*

it. We gave him our bread because he had nothing to eat. An old beggar standing near by advised him to go to the convent in the Gumpendorferstrasse; there every morning between nine and ten soup was given to the poor. We said this was "calling on Kathie", probably because the name of the Mother Superior was Katherine. My neighbour's name was Adolf Hitler.

He was awkward. The Asylum meant to him an entirely new world where he could not find his way, but we all advised him as best we could, and our good humour raised his spirits a little. I was also "calling on Kathie" daily, and we became close friends. He told us that he was a painter, an artist, and had read quite a lot, that his father was a small customs official in Braunau-on-Inn and that he had attended the Realschule in Linz. Now he had come to Vienna in the hope of earning a living here, since he had already devoted much time to painting in Linz, but had been bitterly disappointed in his hopes. His landlady had dispossessed him and he had found himself on the street without shelter.

After he was forced out of his room he had spent several evenings in a cheap coffeehouse in the Kaiserstrasse, but now he was entirely without money. For days he hadn't eaten anything. One night in his great distress he begged a drunk gentleman for a few pennies, but the drunk man raised his cane and insulted him. Hitler was very bitter about this, but I made fun of him, saying, "Look here, don't you know you should never approach a drunk."

Life on the breadline continued to be very hard indeed and Hanisch described how, when the winter cold set in, conditions for the poor became so much harder. Hitler and Hanisch continued the process of daily 'calling on Kathie' to receive their welcome bowl of soup and afterward strolled to the Western Railway Station. Here Hitler sometimes seized the opportunity to carry a passenger's bag for a few pennies. All too frequently however Hitler found no employment at all, and he was lucky to receive a share of bread from Hanisch. When the night shelters were opened Hanisch recalled how Hitler used to go with others to the one in Erdberg. Ironically this shelter had been endowed by the

Jewish Baron Koenigswarter, and the Asylum where Hitler occasionally lived was also a Jewish foundation. From Erdberg, Hitler and Hanisch often went to Favoriten and then to Meidling, a two-and-a-half-hour walk, for soup and bread. Hanisch recalled how in 1909, Hitler had no winter overcoat and how in his thin jacket he shivered with cold and was blue and frostbitten. He was not earning enough with his package-carrying for food, and in the evening according to Hanisch he was sometimes reduced to living on horse-sausage or the like given to him from the kindness of his fellow down and outs. It was a miserable life, and Hanisch recalled how he once asked him what he was really waiting for. Hitler answered, 'I don't know myself.'

When Hanisch learned of the fifty kronen orphan's pension which Angela was receiving from the Austrian state he suggested to Hitler that the situation was now grown so desperate that Hitler should approach his half-sister, Angela, for a sum of money as emergency relief. Hitler maintained he could not do that, as his sister was just married and needed the money for Paula's upkeep. Hanisch strongly pressed Hitler to request at least some small sum of money, because his health was clearly suffering and he was becoming worse off every day. Hitler had developed a noticeably bad cough, and Hanisch was afraid Hitler was going to become seriously ill. Finally, Hitler relented and agreed to write back to Linz. Accordingly, Hanisch, along with a salesman from Austrian Silesia took Hitler to the Cafe Arthaber, opposite the Meidling Southern Station. Seated in the coffee house Hanisch claims they oversaw Hitler as he wrote a letter to his sister, asking for some money to be sent *Poste Restante*.

A few days before Christmas Eve 1909, the money arrived. That evening as usual Hitler came to the Asylum and, while standing in the line, pulled out a fifty kronen note from his pocket and showed it to Hanisch. Hanisch was panic stricken and told Hitler not to show it again on the sensible grounds that if anyone in this environment saw it Hitler might be robbed or pursued for loans.

The money from Angela produced a transformation in Hitler's fortunes. Hanisch advised him to buy a second-hand winter overcoat in the Jewish quarter, but Hitler was afraid he would be cheated there. The pair went together to the *Dorotheum*, the pawnshop operated by the government, and there, Hitler for twelve kronen purchased a dark winter overcoat. With the balance of the funds Hitler was able to move from the Asylum into the *Maennerheim* (men's home) on the Meldemannstrasse.

The chronology between *'Mein Kampf'* and the Hanisch memoir are at odds on a number of points. Hanisch claims it was he who first suggested that Hitler should take up work painting postcards while Hitler maintains he had already put manual work behind him and was earning a living from painting long before the two met. We shall never know the truth for certain but Hanisch clearly had experience of the frustration which was often felt by those who had direct dealings with Hitler. Hanisch stated that Hitler's characteristic first response to the suggestion that he paint postcards was that Hitler would first rest for a week, then begin work. Hitler all his life had an indolent attitude towards work which would later drive his Third Reich subordinates to distraction. He liked to sleep late and would constantly find excuses to put off pressing work matters. Hanisch was against the idea of Hitler resting up for a week and cautioned Hitler that now he had a little money he should be careful not to spend it at once. The frugal Hitler countered that he couldn't spend it all in a week anyway. Besides, Hitler was afraid that, without a licence, there might be trouble with the police. Eventually it seems that Hitler gave in to Hanisch's commercial overtures and in February 1910, Hanisch too moved into the Men's Home and began to act as Hitler's sales agent peddling Hitler's postcards in the taverns of Vienna.

According to Hanisch, Hitler appears to have been something of a dilettante, he was very slow worker, and easily distracted. There were frequent political debates in the men's home and Hitler was always ready to lay down his brush to take up an argument. Hanisch frequently had to lecture him on the need to speed up his output as the cards had begun to sell moderately well in the Viennese taverns. Hanisch described how he was often driven to despair by bringing in orders that

Hitler simply wouldn't honour. Around Easter 1910, Hanisch recalled how he and Hitler had earned forty kronen on a big order, and divided the spoils equally between them. Next morning, Hanisch claims he came downstairs and asked for Hitler, to be told that he had already left with a Jewish acquaintance called Neumann, who was also an occupant of the *Maennerheim*. Hitler had apparently gone sightseeing around Vienna with Neumann and had spent much of that time in the Museum. When Hanisch confronted the returning Hitler and asked him whether he was going to keep on working, Hitler answered that he must recuperate after each burst of activity, that he must have some leisure and that he was not a 'coolie'. Hanisch recalled that Hitler was able to sell his water-colours almost solely to Jewish dealers. He claims that Hitler sold to Jacob Altenberg of the Wiednar Hauptstrasse, who also had a branch in the Favoritenstrasse. There was another Jewish shop in the Favoritenstrasse, owned by Landsberger, who also bought from Hitler, and there was Morgenstern in the Liechtensteinstrasse, who often bought from him and sometimes recommended Hitler to private customers.

In common with Kubizek, Hanish stressed that in his early Vienna days Hitler was by no means the virulent anti-Semite that he was in the twenties. Hanisch did note however that one of Hitler's sayings was 'the end justifies the means' and was not at all surprised that Hitler later incorporated strident anti-Semitism into his programme for the National Socialists. It would appear to support the supposition that the catalyst which finally triggered Hitler's rabid anti-Semitic behaviour still lay ahead in the events of the Great War culminating in the *Dolchstosslegende* and his post-war meetings with the like-minded zealots such as Julius Streicher.

In the men's home, Hanisch recalled Hitler had helpful advisers who were Jews. A one-eyed locksmith called Robinsohn often assisted Hitler and, since he was a beneficiary of an accident-insurance annuity he was sometimes able to spare a few pennies. In the *Maennerheim*, Hitler often found a Jewish audience who listened to his political debates. According to Hanisch, the Jewish salesman called Neumann became a real friend to Hitler. Neumann worked with another Jew who was buying old clothes and peddling them in the streets and he often gave Hitler the old clothes even he couldn't sell. Neumann was a good-hearted man who liked Hitler very much and who, in return, appears to have been highly esteemed by Hitler. Hitler confided to Hanisch that Neumann was a very decent man, because if there were any small debts Neumann paid them, though he himself was still very much in want.

At that time Hitler lived in the *Maennerheim*, Theodor Herzl and the Zionist question were very much on the agenda. The question of a return to Palestine for the Jews was raised in Herzl's book *'Der Judendtaat'*. Hitler and Neumann had long debates about Zionism. Neumann stated his position was that if the Jews should leave Austria it would be a great misfortune for the country, for they would carry with them all the Austrian capital. In an ominous portent of the 'fines' which Hermann Göering would later levy on Germany's Jews, Hitler countered Neumann with the assertion that the Jews were welcome to leave but the money would obviously be confiscated, as it was not Jewish, but Austrian.

Neumann eventually went to Germany in 1910. According to Hanisch, he tried hard to persuade Hitler to join him and spoke enthusiastically of the things they could achieve together in Germany, but Hitler wasn't able to make up his mind and Neumann stepped out of the pages of history.

Like Kubizek, Hanisch confirmed that Hitler carried a high opinion of love and marriage, but his strong condemnation of men's disloyalty didn't prevent him from having, what Hanisch considered to be, a very small regard for women. Hitler appears to have been something of a misogynist. Hanisch recalled how Hitler, in order to prove his own self-control, had told him of an experience he remembered from when he was young. During one of his vacations from high school, in the country, Hitler met a milkmaid who appealed to him, and who liked him, too. Once, as she was milking the cow and he was alone with her, she behaved in a rather forward manner. Hitler suddenly thought of the eventual consequences and ran away, 'like the chaste Joseph', knocking over a big pot of fresh milk in his hurry. Hitler had no practical experience but this proved to be no obstacle and Hitler used to lecture on the subject of women with his usual abandon. Hanisch recalled Hitler stating that it was the woman's fault if a man went astray. In Hitler's opinion a decent man could never improve a bad woman, but a woman could always improve a man. All during this time, of course, Hitler was living in the deepest misery in Vienna. He was so poor and so ill fed that he was hardly conscious of any needs, and his poverty prevented him from having anything to do with women. Besides all of this Hanisch was convinced that Hitler's strange idealism about love would have kept him from any frivolous adventures and in any event Hitler certainly wasn't the kind of man at that time for any girl to fall in love with. His poor clothes, the tangled hair falling down over his dirty collar, these are the reasons that he probably never knew any more than a yearning for Stefanie or indeed any other girl.

Life in Vienna continued to be hard for Hitler. By 1909, he was no longer able to afford the opera tickets which had once been so important to him. Hanisch recalled that Richard Wagner was still Hitler's great passion. Hitler worshipped Wagner, not just as a musician, but also as a revolutionist, who had taken part in the struggles of 1848. As a result of his current plight, Hitler sympathised with Wagner's ceaseless struggle to find a patron in King Ludwig. His enduring poverty meant that the gilded theatre of Vienna Opera was now closed to him and Hitler was pathetically reduced to visiting the scenic railway in the Prater, where he could hear the organ play 'Tannhaüser'. Hanisch recalled how Hitler listened quietly and then explained the action to him. Once he grabbed my hand excitedly and said, 'That's the passage! Do you hear? That's the passage!'

On the way home to Mendlemenstrasse 27, Hanisch remembered how Hitler tried to explain the opera and sang some passages. According to Hanisch, in his excited way, he could only hum a few tones and fidget with his arms. But he could describe the scenes very well, and what the music meant. Hanisch formed the conclusion that Hitler did not have a real understanding of music, though he had more of a sense for what was presented on the stage and what had to be performed. His enthusiasm was total and undimmed by his present plight. Hitler espoused that opera was actually the best form of divine service, but Hanisch rejected the claim stating dismissively that 'everything about him was somewhat exaggerated.'

Hanisch also recalled that in the scenic railway there was always a great deal of Mozart played, usually from 'The Magic Flute', which Hitler detested. Hanisch once remarked that Mozart was greater than Wagner, which sent Hitler into one of his paroxysms of denial. Hitler vehemently maintained that Mozart fitted the old sentimental times but in the modern world he had been outlasted. Wagner was a fighter, there was more greatness and power in Wagner; besides there were now more people in employment, especially in the orchestra.

Eventually a dispute arose between Hanisch and Hitler, which according to Hanisch was over Hitler's constant failure to deliver his commissions on time. Hanisch's version of events was that Hitler maintained that he needed to be in the mood for artistic work prompting Hanisch to ridicule Hitler as a hunger artist. Hitler retorted that, because he had once worked as a domestic in Berlin, Hanisch was a mere house servant. As a result of this quarrel, Hanisch, who had some artistic skill of his own, moved out of the Asylum and looked for a private lodging and decided to work independently.

Within a few days Hanisch had obtained a large order and was happily making his way home when he met a postcard salesman named Loeffler, who also stayed in the Asylum and was one of Hitler's circle of acquaintances. Loeffler reproached Hanisch for having misappropriated a picture by Hitler which led to a violent argument. In the middle of it a policeman walked up and took the pair to the Commissariat of Police. Since he had no identification papers Hanisch was held for living under an assumed name, which was a criminal offence. Hanisch claimed to have done this purely in order to avoid Hitler tracking him down and demanding a list of customers – nonetheless Hanisch hoped that Hitler would remember their former friendship and clear up this error so that then the whole affair would turn out satisfactorily. Hanisch described how he was then taken to the Brigittenau Police Commissariat and confronted with Hitler. To the great disappointment of Hanisch, Hitler declared that Hanisch had indeed misappropriated a water-colour of his, worth fifty kronen. Hanisch objected and maintained that he had sold the painting with Hitler's consent and that Hitler had received his share of the twelve kronen paid. Hitler denied this and furthermore denied that he had authorised Hanisch to sell the picture. At the trial two days later appearances were against Hanisch who was sentenced to a short term. After the sentence had been passed the prisoner angrily called out to Hitler, 'When and where will we see each other again to make a settlement?' The pair did meet again but there was to be no settlement. The last time Hanisch met Hitler was in August 1913, on the Wiedner Hauptstrasse. Hitler had just sold some things to the art shop of Jacob Altenberg, the meeting seems to have been strained but cordial; after that the pair never met again.

The matter would probably have rested there, but Hanisch was arrested in Vienna in 1936, after it had become known that he had written his memoir of the events between 1910 and 1913, and that he was now attempting to find a publisher. The additional charge, from Berlin, was that Hanisch had tampered with and falsified some water-colours done by Hitler at the time described in Hanisch's memoirs. They had been sold at a high price to a Berlin dealer and the surrounding publicity had drawn Hanisch back into the spotlight.

In 1937, Hanisch was arrested and sent to Buchenwald. Some time later the public was informed that Hanisch had died in Buchenwald concentration camp after a sudden illness. According to the official report he had died of pleurisy which had developed in just three days. It is no surprise that Hanisch should disappear so conveniently as the Nazi authorities were understandably apprehensive concerning the possibility of publication of the Hanisch memoirs.

- CHAPTER 6 -
THE DRIFTER IN VIENNA AND MUNICH

IN MAY 1913, Adolf Hitler was a twenty-three-year-old living rough in Vienna; he had come to the city from his home town of Linz in order to further his aspiration to study either as an artist or an architect. Not surprisingly for a young man with limited talent and no suitable educational qualifications, a doorway into either of his chosen careers had not materialised. After five fruitless years in the city engaged in the unsuccessful pursuit of a new life, he was embittered, destitute and homeless. The optimistic young man who aspired to a professional respectability had, by 1913, been reduced to living the life of a down and out in Vienna, eking out an existence by painting and selling tourist postcards. He lived in the dismal surroundings of a men's hostel at Mendlemennstrasse 27 with other itinerant men who had fallen on hard times during the great depression which then gripped the whole of Austria.

Not surprisingly Hitler was shamed and degraded by the unhappy outcome of his Viennese sojourn and it is understandable that Hitler eventually came to despise the city which was the location for the worst and most humiliating experiences of his life. Moreover, under the influence of his nascent racial agenda, he came to view the bustling Austro-Hungarian capital as being entirely dominated by Slavs and Jews. For Hitler the city represented a melting pot of races, a process which Hitler later described as inexorably diluting the racial purity of his precious German *völk*. According to his own account in *'Mein Kampf'* Hitler moved from Austria to Germany for what he later described as 'political' reasons. However, on all of the available evidence, it appears he may actually have moved for a combination of economic and personal reasons connected with his desire to avoid further misery; and more importantly, the looming prospect of compulsory service in the Austro-Hungarian army.

For companionship during the move to Germany Hitler took with him an acquaintance named Rudolf Hausler who had also lived in the Vienna men's hostel. The pair decided against the obvious move, to the Prussian capital at Berlin, and settled instead on a move to Munich – the elegant capital of the state of Bavaria. The move to Munich got off to a good start and they soon found lodgings in the city with the family of Herr Josef Popp, a Munich master tailor. Herr Popp lived in modest circumstances, but he boasted of having travelled as far as Paris and therefore considered himself a man of the world. The Popp family lived at Schleissheimerstrasse 34 and Frau Anna Popp in particular seems to have quickly developed something of a soft spot for Hitler, the man she dubbed the 'Austrian charmer'.

Although Hitler soon developed a cordial relationship with the Popps, the business of sharing a room with Rudolf Hausler progressed somewhat less smoothly. Hausler justifiably objected to Hitler's habit of reading late into the night by the light of a smoky petrol lamp, and eventually Hausler was driven to find his own room elsewhere. Relations between the two however continued to be cordial and the pair remained close until, on the outbreak of the Great War in 1914, Hausler moved back to Vienna to enlist in the Austro-Hungarian army. Even after the war the relationship endured and Hausler later became a senior Nazi functionary in Vienna.

Despite the small hiccup with Hausler, Hitler was at last living in the embrace of what he described as a 'true city of the Reich'. The Hitler family had briefly lived in Passau in Bavaria and Hitler was happy that he was now once more living in his beloved Bavaria for the first time since his infancy. His love affair with the city of Munich was to last all of his life and he later recorded his impressions with great affection in the pages of *'Mein Kampf'*:

At last I came to Munich, in the spring of 1912. The city itself was as familiar to me as if I had lived for years within its walls. This was because my studies in architecture had been constantly turning my attention to the metropolis of German art. One must know Munich if one would know Germany, and it is impossible to acquire knowledge of German art without seeing Munich.

All things considered, this pre-war sojourn was by far the happiest and most contented time of my life. My earnings were very slender; but after all I did not live for the sake of painting. I painted in order to get the bare necessities of existence while I continued my studies. I was firmly convinced that I should finally succeed in reaching the goal I had marked out for myself. And this conviction alone was strong enough to enable me to bear the petty hardships of everyday life without worrying very much about them.'

It is important to note that Hitler claims to have moved to Munich in 1912, while all the other sources, including the Police records in Vienna, still point to him being a resident of Vienna and living in Mendlemennstrasse 27 until at least 24 May 1913. His former business associate Reinhold Hanisch gives an even later date for the move and states that Hitler was still in Vienna as late as August 1913. In any event, we can be certain that it was not until 1913 that Hitler finally made the decision to leave Austria and strike out for a new life Germany.

Whatever the true date, the move to Munich was an auspicious one for Hitler who developed a renewed sense of purpose after his fruitless struggles in Vienna. That new energy was inspired by the charms of the sophisticated capital of Bavaria which Hitler later recalled in the pages of 'Mein Kampf':

'Moreover, almost from the very first moment of my sojourn there I came to love that city more than any other place known to me. A German city! I said to myself. How different to Vienna. It was with a feeling of disgust that my imagination reverted to that Babylon of races. Another pleasant feature here was the way the people spoke German, which was much nearer my own way of speaking than the Viennese idiom. The Munich idiom recalled the days of my youth, especially when I spoke with those who had come to Munich from Lower Bavaria. There were a thousand or more things which I inwardly loved or which I came to love during the course of my stay.

But what attracted me most was the marvelous wedlock of native folk-energy with the fine artistic spirit of the city, that unique harmony from the Hofbräuhaus to the Odeon, from the October Festival to the Pinakothek, etc. The reason why my heart's strings are entwined around this city as around no other spot in this world is probably because Munich is and will remain inseparably connected with the development of my own career; and the fact that from the beginning of my visit I felt inwardly happy and contented is to be attributed to the charm of the marvelous Wittelsbach Capital, which has attracted probably everybody who is blessed with a feeling for beauty instead of commercial instincts.'

In 1913, there is no question that Hitler could certainly have used a few more finely honed commercial instincts of his own. Hitler's move to Munich had been made possible, in part at least, due to his inheritance of a small legacy from his father's estate; and it would appear he also relied upon the continued support of his long suffering Aunt Johanna. Nonetheless, his small store of money was quickly exhausted and he was soon living hand to mouth once more. We know that Hitler had been a sickly youth with chest problems and it is not surprising that five years of strain and poor diet in Vienna combined with his continuing struggles in Munich left their mark on his already poor health.

Writing in the pages of *'Mein Kampf'* in 1924, Hitler markedly described his reasons for moving to Munich from Vienna as 'political', but there is a strong suspicion that the move may actually have been in search of a better life. There is certainly strong circumstantial evidence that the move was connected with Hitler's desire to avoid compulsory service in the Austro-Hungarian Habsburg Army. Hitler was a subject of the Austro-Hungarian Empire and his age group was due for compulsory military service in 1913. The suspicion that he was a draft dodger grows even stronger when one considers the passage in the book, 'The Young Hitler I Knew', by Hitler's friend August Kubizek. Kubizek recalled the time in 1911, when he himself had been called up for service and Hitler had strongly urged that his friend should flee to Germany as the best means to avoid military service in the Austro-Hungarian army.

If it was indeed his intention to avoid military service by a move to Munich then Hitler had clearly not bargained on the co-operative and efficient relations between the authorities on either side of the Austro-German border. It did not take long before Hitler was tracked down by the Austrian Government. His problems were compounded when a policeman arrived at Schleissheimerstrasse 34 to inform Hitler that he was now faced with the immediate prospect of having to report for military service for the despised Habsburg Empire. If we are to accept his own account Hitler received the news of his call up very late and too late to actually report for duty in Linz as required. He urgently enlisted the help of a Munich lawyer Ernst Hepp and with the help of the Austrian embassy in Munich he was narrowly able to avoid being branded as a deserter. Hitler and Hepp quickly set to work and were successful in their aim of obtaining dispensation for Hitler to report late and to attend for his medical in nearby Salzburg rather than distant Linz. Having obtained that official sanction, Hitler seems to have finally resigned himself to his fate, and in February 1914, he dutifully rushed back to Salzburg ready to do his military service.

Fortunately from Hitler's point of view the debilitating effects of his years of struggle in Vienna, combined with his poor health record, were readily apparent. He failed his medical examination and, by this stroke of fortune, was lucky enough to be spared Austrian military service.

It is important to note that Hitler escaped on entirely legitimate grounds by virtue of the fact that he was deemed physically unfit for the peace-time army. In later years the circumstances surrounding Hitler's call up for service in the Austro-Hungarian army would take on enormous significance for him and would lead to a series of scornful gibes being leveled at Hitler by his political opponents who claimed, with some justification, that he was a 'draft dodger' on the run from the Austro-Hungarian Army. What was less convincing was his opponents' claim that he had been somehow unwillingly enlisted into the ranks of the Bavarian army.

Due to the overwhelming strength of the circumstantial evidence Hitler could not risk a fight with those newspapers which habitually referred to him as an Austrian draft dodger. Finally however, in 1932, the SDP supporting newspaper *'Echo Der Woche'* stepped over the mark by mistakenly labelling him a 'deserter' from the Austrian army. Hitler knew this was untrue and in order to protect his precarious reputation, he was able to take court action against the newspaper safe in the knowledge that he could not lose on this narrow definition of the literal truth. With the help of the testimony of his former colleagues Hitler easily won his court case. The evidence however had to stand up to the full scrutiny of the law and Hitler was able to produce incontestable evidence in the form of an official statement from the Austrian authorities:

> *'Office of the State Government, State Registry Office, Nr. 786*
> *Official Statement*
> *Adolf Hitler, born on 20 April 1889 in Braunau am Inn and resident of Linz, Upper Austria, son of Alois and Klara (maiden name, Pötzl), was found by examination of the 3rd age group in Salzburg on 5 February 1914 to be "too weak for military or support service", and was declared "unfit for military service".*
>
> > Linz, 23 February 1932,
> > signed Ovitz '

There are many grey areas concerning the facts behind the life of Adolf Hitler, but in this one instance at least, we can be certain of what happened. Adolf Hitler dutifully reported himself to the military authorities at Salzburg, on 5 February 1914, but was found to be unfit (*'zu schwach'*) for military service. We can be confident therefore that it was a relieved, and no doubt surprised, Adolf Hitler who returned to Munich in February 1914. His lodgings at Schleissheimerstrasse 34 were still available to him and his unremarkable life continued much as before; until in August 1914, world events conspired to change the course of his life forever.

- CHAPTER 7 -
HITLER AND THE LIST REGIMENT

W E KNOW FROM his own account that Adolf Hitler
delighted in the prospect of war in his lifetime. In the pages of
'Mein Kampf' he declared himself thoroughly disappointed by the fact
that he had been born into a period of lasting peace. Somewhat bizarrely
he confesses that he yearned for war and actually rued the fact that,
during his own boyhood, the world was relatively peaceful and there was
no current major armed conflict taking place. However that situation
was soon to change, to Hitler's lasting delight the spectre of war loomed
eventually in South Africa and he avidly followed events from afar:

'Then the Boer War came, like a glow of lightning on the far
horizon. Day after day I used to gaze intently at the newspapers
and I almost 'devoured' the telegrams and communiques, overjoyed to
think that I could witness that heroic struggle, even though from so
great a distance. When the Russo-Japanese War came I was older and
better able to judge for myself. For national reasons I then took the
side of the Japanese in our discussions. I looked upon the defeat of the
Russians as a blow to Austrian Slavism.'

By 1913, like so many others, Hitler sensed that a European war was
almost inevitable and he later confessed that, as an Austrian subject,
what he had feared most was that Germany would become involved in
a conflict which did not affect Austria. In such an event it was Hitler's
great fear that the Austrian State, for domestic political reasons, would
not come to the aid of her ally:

'Many years had passed between that time and my arrival in
Munich. I now realized that what I formerly believed to be a morbid
decadence was only the lull before the storm.'

In 1934, after Hitler had become Chancellor of Germany, the

writer and party member Heinz A. Heinz was authorised by the Nazi party to interview those who had known Hitler during his wilderness years in the lead up to the Great War. The results of these interviews were published for foreign consumption in book form under the title 'Germany's Hitler' which first appeared in 1934. Building on those interviews Heinz was able to describe the scenes around Munich in 1914. By then the population of Europe were already aware that they were sitting on a powder keg. The complex series of European alliances between the great powers, all pointed in one dismal direction – war. Heinz, writing with many dramatic flourishes, including the verbatim quotes and copious exclamation marks which mark German writing of the period, described the circumstances in which Hitler found himself in the run up to the outbreak of the long anticipated European war:

'It was in his lodgings at Frau Popp's that the young student painter first heard of the shot at Sarajevo. There was a tremendous babble going on suddenly outside; in the street below people came running together; a word floated up to his ears, and on his going down presently to find out what the commotion was all about… Thus Frau Popp, breathless with excitement, "Der osterreichische Thronfolger Erzherzog Franz Ferdinand ist ermordet worden!" (The Austrian heir, Archduke Franz Ferdinand, has been assassinated!)

Hitler pushed past her into the street. Thrusting his way into a press of people, staring open-mouthed at a placard, he read the announcement of the crime for himself. The perpetrators, it seemed, had already been arrested.'

Heinz goes on to state that 'the whole world gasped at the news'. No one in Munich required to be particularly well posted as to the political situation just then to realise that this must mean an explosion in the Balkans. The Wittelsbachs, the Bavarian royal family, had received the unfortunate Archduke and his wife as recently as March 1913, and they certainly foresaw great political consequences of a war between Austria and Russia, which would presage the World War.

Heinz also recalled how the city of Munich seethed with indignation and in Vienna, too, the mood was angry and there were flashpoints all over the city as mobs threatened the Serbian Legation. This murder was understood to have been the overt act of a conspiracy which Austria-Hungary suspected to have its origin in Serbia. The bomb throwers at Sarajevo, and Princip, the man who shot the Archduke, were viewed as emissaries of Serb secret societies whose aim was dissolution of the Dual Austro-Hungarian Monarchy and the establishment of a pan-Serb State. The popular conjecture was that all of this was to be achieved with the assistance of France and England who were bent on hampering Germany's economic expansion.

Hitler was a man who devoured newspapers and he could therefore grasp the impending consequences better than Frau Popp. There followed a few days of high tension, then, on Saturday 1 August 1914, in response to the news of Russian mobilisation, came what Heinz described as the 'reluctant' Imperial order for the mobilisation of Germany's great war machine. For Adolf Hitler, what he described as 'the most memorable period' of his life had now begun. Faced with the prospect of that mighty conflict, it seemed to him that all of his past fell away into oblivion. With a wistful pride, Hitler, in the pages of 'Mein Kampf', looked back on the days of war with a warm enthusiasm and a delight that fortune had permitted him the honour of taking his place in that 'heroic struggle.'

Ironically, the Sarajevo flashpoint and the outbreak of war with Serbia made it certain that the Austria-Hungarian Empire would indeed be involved in fighting side by side with Germany. For Hitler, the outbreak of war which married Germany and Austria-Hungary as allies in which he could take part as a soldier fighting for the Kaiser, was a deliverance from the distress that had weighed upon him during his long sojourn in Vienna:

> 'I am not ashamed to acknowledge today that I was carried away by the enthusiasm of the moment and that I sank down upon my knees and thanked Heaven out of the fullness of my heart for the favour of having been permitted to live in such a time.'

Hitler appears to have been correct in forming his view that the Great War was certainly not forced on the masses; the outbreak of war seems to have been conjured into existence almost as if it were the subject of a popular demand. For Hitler it appeared as if there was a common desire to bring what he called 'the general feeling of uncertainty' to an end once and for all. He was intensely proud of how more than two million German males voluntarily joined the colours, ready to shed the last drop of their blood for the cause. Although even Hitler had to concede, in keeping with the western allies, the German people did not have the slightest conception of how long the war might last. People dreamed of the soldiers being home by Christmas and that then they would resume their daily work in peace. Had they known the awful truth, the universal mood of optimism would have been far less bullish.

In 1914, the state of Bavaria still maintained its own standing army, however, in the event of war, the Bavarian army formed a component part of the Imperial German Army. As such the Bavarian army took its marching orders from Prussia and, although it still maintained its own recruiting and logistical systems based in Munich, it came firmly under the direct control of Berlin. On the outbreak of war the ageing Prince-Regent Ludwig III, remained at the Residenz in Munich. His son, Crown Prince Rupprecht, however, departed for the Front where he was to serve with distinction as a senior Imperial German Army commander. Rupprecht's brother Prince Ludwig Ferdinand, at once presented himself for a military surgeon, while his sister, Princess Pilar, became a nurse.

The streets of Munich were now filled with field-grey uniforms and there was a corresponding surge of military activity. According to Heinz the enthusiastic spirit of war filled the state of Bavaria:

> 'Youth everywhere was sanguine and high-spirited. The sense of war flew to everybody's head like wine. There were processions and great cheering. If peasants called to the colours from the Bayerischer Wald, the mountains and the Franconian plains scarcely knew what it was all about, they only needed to learn that the Fatherland was threatened, to become as conspicuous for their enthusiasm at this moment as later they were to become conspicuous for bravery.'

Every day it seemed troops were moving off for the front. There were enormous parades as the companies massed in great open spaces and swore their oath of allegiance anew; the priests and bishops of the Protestant and Catholic churches blessed their departure; the trumpeters sounded the *Zum Gebet*; and to the accompaniment of blood-stirring martial music, and the tumultuous leave-taking of the townsfolk, masses of men entrained for the Front. Day after day crowds assembled in dense thousands before the Feldherrnhalle on the Odeonsplatz and burst into *'Die Wacht am Rhein'*. The normally reserved student painter from Vienna joined the crowds and sang along with them as lustily as the rest.

It is no surprise therefore that Hitler was part of the cheering crowd on Munich's Odeonsplatz photographed by Heinrich Hoffmann on Sunday 2 August 1914. In the famous photograph Hitler can be clearly seen waving his hat enthusiastically and welcoming the news that war had been declared on Russia the day before. Even more momentous news was to follow as France and Britain both entered the fray over the next few days. At the outbreak of the First World War, unlike his friend Hausler, Hitler did not return to Austria. He had successfully, and entirely legitimately, evaded military service for the Habsburgs and he intended to keep it that way. Hitler later recalled how he had often longed for the occasion to prove that his enthusiasm for pan-German national ideal was not 'mere vapouring'. He now felt a proud almost religious sense of joy at the prospect of being able to take the ultimate test of loyalty on the field of combat in the service of the German Reich.

No sooner had the Munich crowd begun to disperse than Hitler, the recent Austro-Hungarian reject, volunteered for service in the Bavarian army. According to the account published by Heinz, Adolf Hitler rushed upstairs to his 'studio' in the Popp apartment and dashed off an application to the Kabinettskanzlei of the Prince Regent for permission to enlist in a Bavarian Regiment which, in time of war, fought within the framework of the Imperial German Army. Hitler's own version of events appears in *'Mein Kampf'*, and he tells us that, immensely to his astonishment and jubilation, the very next day brought the answer. The Herr Kabinettschef of the Prince-Regent Ludwig III accepted the young Austrian's proffer of service, and directed him to report himself immediately at the nearest barracks. Hitler records that he fell on his knees and thanked God. His reaction seems to have been typical of the passionate enthusiasm of those first few weeks of the War with high-spirited, patriotic, untried youth debouching on every Front. Captain Otto Schwink was, later in the war, charged with the task of writing an official account of the Germans at Ypres. His official version appeared in 1917, and he too looked back with misty eyes to the heady days of 1914, which so enthused the young Adolf Hitler. Captain Schwink recalled how this enthusiasm produced the men who would fill the ranks of the 6th Bavarian Reserve Division which would include Adolf Hitler in its ranks.

'Whoever has lived through those great days of August 1914, and witnessed the wonderful enthusiasm of the German nation, will never forget that within a few days more than a million volunteers entered German barracks to prepare to fight the enemies who were hemming in Germany. Workmen, students, peasants, townspeople, teachers, traders, officials, high and low, all hastened to join the colours. There was such a constant stream of men that finally they had to be sent away, and put off till a later date, for there was neither equipment nor clothing left for them. By 16 August, before the advance in the west had begun, the Prussian War Minister in Berlin had ordered the formation of five new Reserve Corps to be numbered from XXII to XXVI, whilst Bavaria formed the 6th Bavarian Reserve Division, and Saxony and Würtemburg together brought the XXVII Reserve Corps into being. Old and young had taken up arms in August 1914, in their enthusiasm to defend their country, and 75 per cent of the new Corps consisted of these volunteers, the remainder being trained men of both categories of the *Landwehr* and the *Landsturm*, as well as some reservists from the *depôts*, who joined up in September. All these men, ranging from sixteen to fifty years of age, realised the seriousness of the moment, and the need of their country: they were anxious to become useful soldiers as quickly as possible to help in overthrowing our malicious enemies. Some regiments consisted entirely of students; whole classes of the higher educational schools came with their teachers and joined the same company or battery. Countless retired officers placed themselves at the disposal of the Government, and the country will never forget these patriots who took over commands in the new units, the formation of which was mainly due to their willing and unselfish work.'

Despite having been declared unfit for Austro-Hungarian service only the year before, Hitler, although he was not even a German national, had somehow succeeded in obtaining permission to join the List Regiment (later known as 16th Bavarian Reserve Infantry Regiment, or the 16th RIR for short). Hitler later explained his reasons for making his direct appeal to the Price Regent:

'I had left Austria principally for political reasons. What therefore could be more rational than that I should put into practice the logical consequences of my political opinions, now that the war had begun. I had no desire to fight for the Habsburg cause, but I was prepared to die at any time for my own kinsfolk and the Empire to which they really belonged. On 3 August 1914, I presented an urgent petition to His Majesty, King Ludwig III, requesting to be allowed to serve in a Bavarian regiment. In those days the Chancellery had its hands quite full and therefore I was all the more pleased when I received the answer a day later, that my request had been granted. I opened the document with trembling hands; and no words of mine could now describe the satisfaction I felt on reading that I was instructed to report to a Bavarian regiment. Within a few days I was wearing that uniform which I was not to put away again for nearly six years.'

Initially the uniform which was issued to Hitler did not represent the characteristic German uniform of 1914. There were insufficient *pickelhaube* helmets to equip the new battalion, and the recruits of the List Regiment had to be issued with the old style peaked oilcloth caps (*Landsturmmuetzen*) of the very same design as those worn during the 1812, War of Liberation and very similar to those worn by the British Expeditionary Force in 1914. This unfortunate item was to cause the List Regiment great difficulty and a number of casualties during the early battles of 1914. Despite the problems with supply of standard head-gear however, there were at least sufficient uniforms to go round and Hitler received his *feldgrau* tunic. The greenish-grey issue jacket was universal in the Imperial German Army and distinguished from the other regiments by having the regimental number 'RIR 16' sown in red onto the epaulettes. Another item of uniform equipment which was issued was a thick leather belt worn around the waist of the uniform jacket; the uniform was completed by a *feldgrau* trouser on which a red stripe was sown down the outside of the leg. The trousers were then tucked into the famous leather 'jack' boots to complete the look of a 1914 soldier in the service of the Kaiser.

On the surface Hitler's decision to enlist as a soldier in the ranks of the Bavarian army was a typically perverse action. After all, he had apparently gone to great lengths only six months previously to avoid military service. Hitler had now joined up on the instant as '*Kriegsfreiwilliger*' (war-time volunteer), and to his obvious delight found himself properly enrolled as Infanterist Number 148 in the 1st Company of the List Regiment.

The explanation to this apparent conundrum however lies in Hitler's life long political support for the pan-German nationalist *Grossdeutschsland lossung* (greater German solution). Hitler's own attitude towards the conflict was simple and clear. He believed that it was no longer a case of Austria fighting to get satisfaction from Serbia, but rather a case of the wider German peoples fighting for their own future existence. His fevered imagination pictured the Germanic lands hemmed in by enemies on all sides and furthermore entirely without the opportunity to expand horizons by overseas colonization. It was on this flimsy basis that Hitler, and so many others in 1914, surmised that it was necessary for the survival of the German Empire that Germany must assert herself in Europe by force of arms. Hitler was certainly anxious to play his part in a struggle with which he could empathise, but he wanted to play the precise part that suited him; and that meant service in the Imperial German Army not the hated Austro-Hungarian Army with its Slav influences.

For better or worse the pan-German nationalist Adolf Hitler was now firmly enrolled as a war-time volunteer number 148 in the 1st Company of the List Regiment. This formation was one of nearly 800 or so regiments to serve in the Imperial German Army on the Western Front in the Great War. In common with the other recruits, Hitler had only one worry during those optimistic early war days. He harboured a fear that his regiment might arrive too late for the fighting at the front. Every announcement of a victorious engagement produced an increasing concern, which further increased as the news of further victories arrived. Hitler wanted to see action, he was soon to get his wish – and he would not be found lacking.

In the meantime Hitler's regiment then began a short but intensive basic training programme, which was held in the premises of a large public school on the Elizabethplatz in Munich.

A fellow recruit was Hans Mend, who was to play a major role in the story of Private Hitler's War. Mend was an extremely colourful character who had convictions for fraud. In 1930, when Hitler was on the brink of power, Mend published his account of his service alongside Hitler entitled Adolf Hitler Im Felde 1914-1918, (Adolf Hitler At War 1914-1918) it was essentially a hagiography, but there were elements of the book which were critical of the character of Adolf Hitler. Initially it seems the book found a measure of favour with the Nazi party, but once Hitler had attained power it was disowned and supressed, all unsold copies were ordered to be withdrawn and pulped and all library shelves were cleared of the book. Like Reinhold Hanisch, Mend had come to an irrevocable breach with Hitler and despite a belated attempt to join the Nazi party, Mend was consigned to a concentration camp before dying of natural causes in the early 1940s. Mend's account is exaggerated and self-serving, it must therefore be treated with extreme caution. However, it is nonetheless written by someone who did actually serve with Hitler, and there is no reason to doubt every single word. Mend claims that he first noticed Hitler during the time the regiment was in training in Munich and tells us he first took Hitler to be an 'academic', of whom there were many in the List Regiment. Mend was struck by the manner in which Hitler lavished attention of his newly issued rifle:

'I saw him for the second time on another day, as he pottered about with his rifle. He regarded it with the delight of a woman with her jewelry, while I secretly laughed to myself.'

On the Exerzierplatz of Munich, Hitler and the List regiment embarked on a period of intensive training, with the focus on the usual exercises consisting of army drills, learning how to march in step, form fours, file evolutions, route marching and bayonet practice. What was missing was the time to develop the rank and file into proficient marksmen, and this deficiency was to come home to haunt the List Regiment when it came face to face with the highly trained British regulars who were trained in the art of marksmanship and could deliver a much higher rate of accurate and sustained rifle fire.

On 8 September 1914, the men were gathered together to hear the 49-year-old commander of the List Regiment, Colonel Julius von List, address his recruits. Their commander was well aware that training time was ridiculously short, his words were preserved for posterity in the Official Regimental history by Franz Rubenbauer:

'Comrades! I welcome with all my heart and full confidence all officers, doctors, and officials, all Offiziersstellvertreter, NCOs, and troops. Our Regiment, whose men for the most part are untrained, is expected to be ready for mobile deployment within a few weeks. This is a difficult task, but with the admirable spirit which animates all members of this regiment, not an impossible one... With God's blessing, let's begin our work for Kaiser, King, and Fatherland!'

Hitler and the Listers were not destined to remain in Munich barracks for long and on 7 October 1914, he found the time to bid a fond farewell to the family of the tailor, Josef Popp. Frau Popp later recalled how he requested that, in the event of his death, the Popp family should write to his sister on his behalf and suggest that she might perhaps like to receive his few possessions. According to Frau Popp he then informed the Popps that, in the event that Paula did not wish to have his property, then the Popps were free to dispose of them as they wished. Frau Popp wept, and after shaking hands with Josef, Hitler took his leave and embarked on his 'great adventure'.

On 8 October 1914, the recruits took their oaths and swore allegiance to Kaiser Wilhelm II but also to King Ludwig III of Bavaria, and to Hitler's own monarch, Kaiser Franz Josef. Standing next to Hitler was Ernst Schmidt, who would become Hitler's closest wartime companion. Schmidt was another List veteran who would later write his own hagiography which was more acceptable to Hitler. Schmidt noticed Hitler's extraordinary appetite; he would not be the last to comment on the voracious appetite of the slender Austrian:

'On the day of the swearing-in, there was a double-ration of roast pork and potato salad. Hitler told me several times that the festive day remained particularly pleasant in his memory, as he was always hungry. During the war he was known for being always hungry, and could become ill when the food supply was delayed.'

With the men sworn in, the List Regiment was ordered to prepare to march off for a few weeks further training at Lechfeld, a pleasant town at the confluence of the Lech and the Danube about seventy miles west of Munich. Here the wide river meadows provided ideal terrain for the divisional training exercises which were to follow as the List Regiment combined with three other Regiments to form the 6th Bavarian Reserve Division (6th BRD). The men were all glad of the change, and left the city, after a tremendous send-off from the populace, still anxious that they might not be afforded the opportunity to come to grips with the enemy before the War was over. Adolf Hitler recalled his memories of these halcyon days in the pages of 'Mein Kampf':

'As the scene unfolds itself before my mind, it seems only like yesterday. I see myself among my young comrades on our first parade drill, and so on until at last the day came on which we were to leave for the front. In common with the others, I had one worry during those days. This was a fear that we might arrive too late for the fighting at the front. Time and again that thought disturbed me; and every announcement of a victorious engagement left a bitter taste, which increased as the news of further victories arrived.'

On Saturday 9 October, the 1st Company of the 16th Bavarian Reserve Infantry including Adolf Hitler in its ranks set off on foot for

Lechfeld, and began the long march which would take them seventy miles west of Munich to the confluence of the rivers Lech and the Danube. Burdened by the weight of the full packs on their backs, they marched off in pouring rain which continued for the next eleven hours. Not surprisingly, Hitler found the march hard going and he voiced his frustrations in the letter he wrote to Frau Popp on 20 October 1914:

> 'We were on our feet from 6.30 A.M. to 5 P.M. and during the march we took part in a major exercise, all of this in constant rain. I was put up in a stable, soaked through and through. There was no possibility of sleep.'

The next day the company continued their march to Lechfeld on what was described as a bitterly cold Sunday, they marched for thirteen hours before bivouacking in the open for the night. Finally, on 11 October 1914, Hitler and the rest of the 1st Company reached Lechfeld in mid afternoon. The regiment was to receive no respite after its gruelling march and immediately embarked upon a programme of further training.

Franz Rubenhauer, an officer of the List regiment who was later to produce the bulk of the material for the regimental history, recalled the detail of their activities:

> 'We still gratefully remember the warm welcome we received from the local population, in the places where we had our living quarters, after the exhausting daily exercises on the vast Lechfeld, or from the practice firing range in the meadows of the Lech, singing marching songs with high and clear voices; old and young were out and about and marched with us. After we were dismissed for the day, they took us back into their homes, where the food waited ready for us on their stoves.'

While they honed their skills at Lechfeld, the List Regiment did not have too long to worry about missing out on the war. Their rapid, and wholly inadequate, bout of basic training in Munich and Lechfeld was now drawing to a close and the day duly arrived when the List Regiment departed on active war service.

On 20 October, Hitler wrote to Frau Popp, bringing her up to date on all that had happened to him since he departed Munich and informing her that he would soon be moving out for the front:

'We are going on a four-day journey, probably to Belgium. I am tremendously excited... After arrival at our destination I will write immediately and give you my address. I hope we get to England.'

The fresh warriors of the List Regiment now boarded a troop train which headed north and west and, just as Hitler had hoped, they soon deduced that their fate was indeed to fight on the Western Front. During the Great War, the Russian Front was regarded as the softer option and Hitler would no doubt have been very happy in the realization that the List Regiment was destined to see action where the fighting was hardest. As the train continued its journey north and westwards, Hitler, for the first time in his life, saw the Rhine river. The magical music and narrative of the mighty Ring of the Nibelung cycle of operas by Richard Wagner had long been an inspiration to Hitler. As the regiment journeyed westwards, Hitler recalled a dramatic episode when the first soft rays of the morning sun broke through the light mist and revealed the gigantic Niederwald Statue. Hitler described the powerful moment when with one accord the whole troop train broke into the strains of *'Die Wacht am Rhein'* at which point Hitler emotionally declared that his heart was 'fit to burst'.

In later years former Private Ignatz Westenkirchner, another of Hitler's List comrades, was also interviewed by Heinz A. Heinz, the Nazi propagandist who was commissioned to write a biography of Hitler entitled 'Germany's Hitler' which appeared in the Thirties. Heinz described his first impressions of Herr Ignaz Westenkirchner, who at that stage was an ex-service man, and former war-time comrade of the Führer. He was, in 1934, thanks to the influence of Adolf Hitler, employed on the *'Völkischer Beobachter'*, the official Nazi newspaper based in Munich:

'A somewhat small-built man, this Ignaz Westenkirchner, thin, with a clean-shaven face much lined and worn, and, of course, somewhere about the Fuhrer's own age. He wore a simple blue suit and had a regular galaxy of various-coloured pencils sticking out of

the pocket in his jacket. He had a job in the dispatching department of the paper, hence the multi-coloured pencils. He received the writer in the waiting-room of the offices of the Völkischer Beobachter in Munich. But we repaired immediately to a quieter room where we could talk in comfort. "Dear me, yes," said he, "the Führer remains ever the good comrade that he was! you shall have the whole account of our doings on the Western Front...."

The *Führer* himself also touched upon of his War experiences in 'Mein Kampf', but it is a brief version which concentrates heavily on the events of October 1914, so we are lucky to have Herr Westenkirchner's verbatim story as told to Heinz. No doubt refreshed by the very similar passage in 'Mein Kampf', as Westenkirchner began to unfold his story to Heinz A. Heinz he described the excitement of the journey to Flanders in almost identical terms to Hitler's description:

'We were all in topping spirits that day, our heads stuffed with no end of war nonsense, sure as eggs is eggs the glorious fighting would be all over by Christmas or the New Year at latest. We reached the Rhine that night. Lots of us south Bavarian chaps had never seen the Rhine before, and then in the dawn, I remember as if it were yesterday, how it just struck us all to see the sun drawing up the mist from the river and unveiling before our dazzled eyes that splendid statue of Germania which looks down from the Niederwald. How we yelled the "Wacht am Rhein", the whole lot of us for the first time going out to war.'

The journey to the front for Hitler may have been something of a mythical pageant with Wagnerian overtones, but as they neared the front the grim realities of the first of the modern wars gradually enveloped the enthusiastic volunteers. The infantry tactics of August 1914 had not kept pace with the advances in artillery and machine guns. The result was to be the 'slaughter of the innocents' which produced a huge German casualty toll as flesh met steel in Flanders.

- CHAPTER 8 -

THE BATTLE FOR GHELUVELT

THE LIST REGIMENT were at last on their way to war, but even with modern transportation systems the problem of moving such an enormous mass of men and material placed a terrific strain on the rail system and Ignatz Westenkirchner recalled the frustrations of the latter stages of the slow and tortuous journey to the front:

'It took us two days to reach Lille as our train only crawled from that point onward. Across war-ravaged Belgium we provided reinforcements for the 6th Bavarian Division of the Army of the Crown Prince Rupprecht. The great battles of the Marne and the Aisne were over by this time; Antwerp had fallen; the first phase of the Battle of Ypres in which the Allied enemy had made every effort to effect a great turning movement round our right flank, clearing the Belgian coast line, and forcing us out of Bruges and Ghent, had failed.'

Writing in the regimental history of the List Regiment Franz Rubenhauer recalled the arrival of the regiment in Lille:

'On the morning of 23 October 1914 between 7 and 9 o'clock, our troops arrived in Lille. There had been lengthy delays. For long hours the trains stood immobile at open stretches, then crawled forward from station to station at a snail's pace of 8 kilometers per hour. After a few hours, as Lille approached, unbroken cannon fire was heard in the Westerly direction of Armentièeres, fliers were seen circling in the brightly illuminated sky – one already felt the vicinity of the Front.'

Hitler's regiment de-trained and marched into Lille. This was the first time Hitler had ever travelled beyond the borders of German-speaking territories. Stopping at the courtyard of the Old Stock Exchange, the men were ordered to sleep on the hard flagstones for the night after which they halted in Lille for four days and the scene was recorded in the diary of the List Regiment's chaplain, Father Norbert, a somewhat eccentric figure who habitually dressed in a monk's habit:

'Lille, and in particular the central station, was a terrible sight. The entire train station was a shambles. The wounded lay everywhere. 1,200 houses were said to have been destroyed in the bombardment, most of them grandiose buildings. There were burntout gables and smoking piles of rubble everywhere, along with crying and begging women and children, and withdrawn, sullen men. In the military hospitals, of which there are fifteen in the city, lie about 4,000 soldiers, most of them seriously wounded, but no clergymen; the French priests are not allowed to visit the injured due to fear of espionage. Because the enemy received intelligence from the church tower, through signs and the chiming of the hour and the direction of the hand, the clergymen were arrested and were not allowed to enter the rectory again.... My accoutrements – or monk's habit – excited everywhere a great commotion amongst friends and foe alike. I was even to be arrested as a spy, as a result of my dress. For five hours I was closely watched by a constable and 15 men, until the mistake was cleared up.'

In addition to the Popp family Hitler was also in correspondence with Herr Ernst Hepp, the Munich lawyer who had previously represented Hitler in his troubles with the Austrian government over his failure to report for military service. It provides a revealing insight into the affairs of the List Regiment from Hitler's contemporary viewpoint. In a letter written in February 1915, Hitler recalled for Herr Hepp in some detail the circumstances in the lead up to the early engagements:

'After a really lovely journey down the Rhine, we reached Lille on 23 October. We could already see the effects of the war as we travelled through Belgium. We saw the conflagrations of war and heard its ferocious winds. As far as Douai, our journey was reasonably safe and quiet. Then came shock after shock. In some places, the base artillery had been destroyed in spite of the strongest defense. We were now frequently coming upon blown up bridges and wrecked locomotives. Although the train kept going at a snail's pace, we encountered more

and more horrors: graves. Then in the distance we heard our heavy guns.

'*Toward evening we arrived in Lille, which was knocked about rather a lot in the suburbs. We got off the train and hung about around our stacked rifles, and shortly before midnight we were on the march; and at last we entered the town. It was an endless monotonous road left and right with miserable workmen's dwellings, and the countryside blackened with smoke. The pavements were poor and bad and dirty. There were no signs of any inhabitants, and there was no one on the street after 9 P.M. except the military. We were almost in danger of our lives — because the place was so full of guns and ammunition carts — and through them, we eventually reached the Citadel. We spent the night in the courtyard of the stock exchange building. This pretentious building was not yet completed. We had to lie down with full packs, and were kept at the ready. It was very cold on the stone pavement and we could not sleep. The next day we changed our quarters, and this time we were in a very large glass building. There was no lack of fresh air, the iron framework was still standing, and the panes of glass had been smashed into millions of fragments in the German bombardment. During the day, something more was attempted. We inspected the town and, most of all, we admired the tremendous military equipment; and all of Lille lay open, the gigantic shapes of the town rolling before our astonished eyes. At night there was singing, and for me it was the last time.*'

The time for the List Regiment to engage in action was fast approaching and on 27 October at 1:00 am, shortly before they were due to march off to the front, Hitler's regiment was mustered in the Place de Concert, to hear an 'Order of the Day' by the Bavarian Crown Prince Rupprecht who railed against the Englishmen opposing them.

'*We have now the fortune to have the Englishmen on our front, the troops of that people whose antagonism has been at work for so many years in order to surround us with a ring of enemies and strangle us. We have to thank them above all for this bloody, terrible war.... when you meet up with this enemy, demonstrate to them that the German cannot be swept so lightly from world history, show them through German blows of a quite special kind. Here is the enemy who stands most in the way of the restoration of peace. Onwards!'*

Hitler was full of patriotic fervour and he was eager for the fight and every detail of his new world was to be savoured. The Hepp letter continued the narrative of the lead up to the fight at Gheluvelt:

'On the third night, about 2 A.M., there was a sudden alarm and, about 3 A.M., we marched away in full marching order from the assembly point. No one knew for certain why we were marching, but in any case we regarded it as an exercise. It was rather a dark night, and we had hardly been marching for twenty minutes when we turned left and met two columns of cavalry and other troops, and the road was so blocked there was no room for us.'

Ignatz Westenkirchner also recalled the build-up to the first engagement which formed part of a larger offensive which was known to the British as the First Battle Of Ypres and to the Germans as Langemark:

'We had established a line to the sea (Nieuport), and we Bavarians amongst the rest coming up in time for the great offensive of 31 October and 1 November, when for forty-eight hours two and a half German Army Corps stormed the Wytschaete Messines Ridge, saw the beginning of the second phase of that enormous struggle. From Lille where we put in perhaps half a day we proceeded by train again to a place called Ledeghem, but after that it was all marching. Now we were within earshot of the guns: the thunder on the Front became even nearer. The country seemed awfully flat and monotonous; the only villages we passed were nothing but heaps of gaping ruins. Dead horses blown up like balloons lay in the ditches. We got the stench of them. We went through places called Dadizeele and Terhan, and approached Becelaere, a half-demolished village, the centre of the enemy's First Division.'

On 29 October 1914, the List Regiment was temporarily attached to the 54th Reserve Division, and it was with this division that the untried men of the regiment experienced their first action. They were sent forward to relieve a hard-pressed Württemburg unit and took some casualties as a result of their non-standard *Landsturmmuetzen* head gear which so closely resembled the British 1914 pattern caps. Hans Mend was engaged as a runner in the thick of the action and he recalled the devastating effect of the rounds fired by the men on his own side who were under the mistaken impression that the Listers were British troops.

> *'We reached Becalaere and were immediately in action and already this first day endured enormous losses. Since the troops of the List Regiment had received as headgear with their equipment militia caps the Würtemmburgers, in the belief that they were English, had fired violently on them, through this error many had to lose their lives.'*

With English and Belgian shells falling all around, the battle continued for three days, with fierce causalities on both sides. Hitler and the 1st Company advanced and retreated into a storm of fire four times until eventually the village of Gheluvelt finally fell into German hands. Ignatz Westenkirchner was also present at the action and his account closely matches the description which appears in *'Mein Kampf'*:

> *'Here the fire was intensely hot. We advanced in the face of a bombardment. It was already night, cold and wet. We came well within range, scrambling over the muddy broken ground, taking whatever shelter we could behind hedges, in ditches and in shell-holes, our way lit by the glare of houses burning like torches in the lurid blackness, and fell at last upon the enemy, in a hand-to-hand fight, man to man, fiercely thrusting with our bayonets.'*

The task for the 1st Company of the List Regiment was to take up positions just to the north of the main road to Ypres and to co-operate with the Württembergers and other elements of the 54th Reserve Division in order to capture the village and open the road to Ypres. The chateau of Gheluveldt village was captured by the Listers but fell back into the hands of the British after a ferocious counter attack by the men of the Worcester Regiment. We are fortunate that we also have Adolf Hitler's letter to Ernst Hepp which provides us with a surprisingly detailed account of the reality of service in a front-line unit during the early months of the Great War.

'Then morning came. We were now a long way from Lille. The thunder of gunfire had grown somewhat stronger. Our column moved forward like a giant snake. At 9 A.M., we halted in the park of a country house. We had two hours' rest and then moved on again, marching until 8 P.M. We no longer moved as a regiment, but split up into companies, each man taking cover against enemy airplanes. At 9 P.M., we pitched camp. I couldn't sleep. Four paces from my bundle of straw lay a dead horse. The animal was already half decayed. Finally, a German howitzer battery immediately behind us kept sending two shells flying over our heads into the darkness of the night every quarter of an hour. They came whistling and hissing through the air, and then, far in the distance, there came two dull thuds. We all listened. None of us had ever heard that sound before. While we were huddled close together, whispering softly and looking up at the stars in the heavens, a terrible racket broke out in the distance. At first it was a long way off, and then the crackling came closer and closer, and the sound of single shells grew to a multitude, finally becoming a continuous roar. All of us felt the blood quickening in our veins. The English were making one of their night attacks. We waited a long time, uncertain what was happening. Then it grew quieter and at last the sound ceased altogether – except for our own batteries – which sent out their iron greetings to the night every quarter of an hour. In the morning we found a big shell hole. We had to brush ourselves up a bit, and about 10 A.M. there was another alarm and, a quarter of an hour later, we were on the march. After a long period of wandering about we reached a farm that had been shot to pieces and we camped here. I was on watch duty that night and, about one o'clock, we suddenly had another alarm; and we marched off at three o'clock in the morning. We had just taken a bit of food, and we were waiting for our marching orders, when Major Count Zech rode up: "Tomorrow we are attacking the English!" he said. So it had come at last! We were all overjoyed; and after *making this announcement, the Major went on foot to the head of the column.'*

The 'English' which Major Count Zech was referring to consisted of elements of the Worcester Regiment in position between the village of Gheluvelt and the town of Ypres. Also in the vicinity were some companies of the Scottish regular regiment, the renowned Black Watch. Although this was not a full scale battle it was to prove a bitterly fought encounter. Hitler only ever fought in two engagements and, not surprisingly, the events of October and early 1914 were destined to feature heavily in the pages of *'Mein Kampf'*.

The List Regiment had well and truly received its baptism of fire on 29 October 1914, and the casualties suffered by the List regiment in October 1914, were severe. Hitler's description of the regiment's first taste of combat reads like political hyperbole – until we compare it to the other accounts of the fighting, all of which confirm the ferocity of the engagement:

'And then followed a damp, cold night in Flanders. We marched in silence throughout the night and as the morning sun came through the mist an iron greeting suddenly burst above our heads. Shrapnel exploded in our midst and spluttered in the damp ground. But before the smoke of the explosion disappeared a wild 'Hurrah' was shouted from two hundred throats, in response to this first greeting of Death. Then began the whistling of bullets and the booming of cannons, the shouting and singing of the combatants. With eyes straining feverishly, we pressed forward, quicker and quicker, until we finally came to close-quarter fighting, there beyond the beet-fields and the meadows. Soon the strains of a song reached us from afar. Nearer and nearer, from company to company, it came. And while Death began to make havoc in our ranks we passed the song on to those beside us: Deutschland, Deutschland Über Alles, Über Alles In Der Welt.'

Hitler and the List Regiment acquitted themselves well during the fight around Gheluvelt, but casualties, amounting to two thirds of the strength of the regiment, were very high – even by Great War standards.

Hans Mend, who had since become Colonel List's personal messenger, described the battle on the morning of the first day as 'a last awakening for many of my comrades'. Mend reported that the skies were flaming red from the burning villages as they marched towards their first battle and claimed that he clearly recalled the figure of Adolf Hitler near the head of the regiment bent forward and with a smile on his lips. Mend tells us that he wondered to himself how this slightly built man would manage if he had to carry a full field pack. However Mend would later revise his estimate of Hitler who seems to have overcome his early health problems and proved himself to be made of the right stuff for the life of a soldier:

There were few in the regiment as healthy or as full of stamina as Hitler. With unbelievable toughness, he endured the greatest strains and never showed any weakness. The battle-ordinance, to which Hitler also belonged, was far more exposed to enemy fire than the companies themselves, for while the latter could always find cover in the terrain, the ordinance staff were constantly on the move with messages; and I am amazed even today, how Adolf Hitler came through the war so fortunately.'

Hitler was to become very familiar with the distant aspect of the town of Ypres. His war would start near the town and four years later it would also end there. Twenty-four years later during one of his rambling monologues which were later collected together and published as 'Hitler's Table Talk', the *Führer* recalled the first tantalising glimpse of the town which would remain within the grasp of the German armies but which would never fall to them.

'My first impression of Ypres was – towers, so near that I could all but touch them. But the little infantryman in his hole in the ground has a very small field of vision.'

Hitler's description of the battle for Gheluvelt is detailed at great length in his letter to Ernst Hepp. The fight clearly made a huge impression on him and he went to some trouble to ensure that Herr Hepp had all of the details. The situation was fluid and confused, and although trenches were beginning to appear on the battlefield, this was one of the last occasions on the Western Front on which armies would manouver in the open:

'Early, around 6 A.M., we came to an inn. We were with another company and it was not till 7 A.M. that we went out to join the dance. We followed the road into a wood, and then we came out in correct marching order on a large meadow. In front of us were guns in partially dug trenches and, behind these, we took up our positions in big hollows scooped out of the earth; and waited. Soon, the first lots of shrapnel came over, bursting in the woods, and smashing up the trees as though they were brushwood. We looked on interestedly, without any real idea of danger. No one was afraid. Every man waited impatiently for the command: "Forward!" The whole thing was getting hotter and hotter. We heard that some of us had been wounded. Five or six men brown as clay were being led along from the left, and we all broke into a cheer: six Englishmen with a machine gun! We shouted to our men marching proudly behind their prisoners. The rest of us just waited. We could scarcely see into the steaming, seething witches' caldron which lay in front of us. At last there came the ringing command: "Forward!"

We swarmed out of our positions and raced across the fields to a small farm. Shrapnel was bursting left and right of us, and the English bullets came whistling through the shrapnel; but we paid no attention to them. For ten minutes, we lay there; and then, once again, we were ordered to advance. I was right out in front, ahead of everyone in my platoon. Platoon-leader Stoever was hit. Good God! I had barely any time to think; the fighting was beginning in earnest! Because we were out in the open, we had to advance quickly. The captain was at the head. The first of our men had begun to fall. The English had set up machine guns. We threw ourselves down and crawled slowly along a ditch. From time to time someone was hit, we could not go on, and the whole company was stuck there. We had to lift the man out of the ditch. We kept on crawling until the ditch came to an end, and then we were out in the open field again. We ran fifteen or twenty yards, and then we found a big pool of water.

One after another, we splashed through it, took cover, and caught our breath. But it was no place for lying low. We dashed out again at full speed into a forest that lay about a hundred yards ahead of us. There, after a while, we all found each other. But the forest was beginning to look terribly thin.

At this time there was only a second sergeant in command, a big tall splendid fellow called Schmidt. We crawled on our bellies to the edge of the forest, while the shells came whistling and whining above us; tearing tree trunks and branches to shreds. Then the shells came down again on the edge of the forest, flinging up clouds of earth, stones, and roots; and enveloping everything in a disgusting, sickening, yellowy-green vapor. We can't possibly lie here forever, we thought and, if we are going to be killed, it is better to die in the open. Then the Major came up. Once more we advanced. I jumped up and ran as fast as I could across meadows and beet fields, jumping over trenches, hedgerows, and barbed-wire entanglements; and then I heard someone shouting ahead of me: "In here! Everyone in here!" There was a long trench in front of me and, in an instant, I had jumped into it; and there were others in front of me, behind me, and left and right of me. Next to me were Württembergers, and under me were dead and wounded Englishmen.

The Württembergers had stormed the trench before us. Now I knew why I had landed so softly when I jumped in. About 250 yards to the left there were more English trenches; to the right the road to Leceloire was still in our possession. An unending storm of iron came screaming over our trench. At last, at ten o'clock, our artillery opened up in this sector. One – two – three – five – and so it went on. Time and again a shell burst in the English trenches in front of us. The poor devils came swarming out like ants from an ant heap, and we hurled ourselves at them. In a flash we had crossed the fields in front of us, and after bloody hand-to-hand fighting in some places, we threw (the enemy) out of one trench after another. Most of them raised their hands above their heads. Anyone who refused to surrender was mown down. In this way we cleared trench after trench.

At last we reached the main highway. To the right and left of us there was a small forest, and we drove right into it. We threw them all out of this forest, and then we reached the place where the forest came to an end and the open road continued. On the left lay several farms – all occupied – and there was withering fire. Right in front of us, men were falling. Our Major came up; quite fearless, and smoking calmly; with his adjutant, Lieutenant Piloty. The Major saw the situation at a glance, and ordered us to assemble, on both sides of the highway for an assault. We had lost our officers, and there were hardly any non-commissioned officers. So all of us, every one of us who was still walking, went running back to get reinforcements. When I returned the second time with a handful of stray Württembergers, the Major was lying on the ground with his chest torn open, and there was a heap of corpses all around him.

By this time, the only remaining officer was his adjutant. We were absolutely furious. "Herr Leutnant, lead us against them!" we all shouted. So we advanced straight into the forest, fanning out to the left, because there was no way of advancing along the road. Four times we went forward, and each time we were forced to retreat. From my company, only one other man was left besides myself, and then he, too, fell. A shot tore off the entire left sleeve of my tunic but, by a miracle, I remained unharmed. Finally, at 2 A.M. we advanced for the fifth time; and this time, we were able to occupy the farm and the edge of the forest. At 5 P.M., we assembled and dug in, a hundred yards from the road. So we went on fighting for three days in the same way, and on the third day the British were finally defeated. On the fourth evening we marched back to Werwick. Only then did we know how many men we had lost. In four days our regiment consisting of thirty-five hundred men was reduced to six hundred. In the entire regiment there remained only thirty officers. Four companies had to be disbanded. But we were all so proud of having defeated the British!'

Despite all the inherent evils of the job, Hitler had a love of soldiering which never left him, but even wearing his most rose-tinted glasses, he must have known that his audience was unlikely to be taken in by a description of eager units advancing towards each other singing patriotic songs. It is certainly true that in the intensive battles of the early war units would sing a snatch of 'Der Wacht am Rhein' which was the proscribed means of verbal recognition in the early stages of the war, but this activity had a distinct purpose. Hitler's less dramatic description of the withdrawal of the List Regiment from the line is much more convincing:

'After four days in the trenches we came back. Even our step was no longer what it had been. Boys of seventeen looked now like grown men. The rank and file of the List Regiment had not been properly trained in the art of warfare, but they knew how to die like old soldiers.'

The official regimental history of the 16th RIR also described the fight around Gheluvelt in detail. It was a highly significant event in the history of the regiment and the fight for Gheluvelt on 31 October 1914 was described in suitably dramatic terms:

'The losses grow under the violent fire that the enemy hurls steel toward the attackers from cannons and machine-guns. They lean, and fall down on their knees among the hedges, mown down by a burst of fire; but the yawning gaps are always filled again by fresh fighters. Our artillery's lack of ammunition is clearly noticeable; it can offer the attack no effective support. Morning passes in tough, bloody stand-up fights. A horrifying battle fills the battlefield. The howls, hisses, crashes of the heavy shells of English naval cannons constantly bursting between the lines; the rolls of machine-gun salvos, and the clatter of infantry weapons; the fire rises from violent storms to raging assault, to eerie hurricane. Whole rows drop while pushing forward, crash back again, break in on themselves. Is it not mad to advance in this fire? And new waves push in, repeated hour after hour. The excitement is unproductive; all reserves are already used up. At last at 3 o'clock in the afternoon the enemy's key-point, the windmill – on the south-slope of the area from where so much (havoc) has been created – is brought under heavy fire by our artillery, is caught cleanly, and is shattered with a few direct hits. For a moment, enemy fire falls*

silent. It is like a deep, eerie breathing-space. Then it breaks out with
strengthening force: a single fire-spitting mouth of hell: but on – must
go on – forwards! Then, at the critical moment, the assault signal
of the buglers is heard over the whole fighting front! Knapsacks are
discarded; everyone pulls himself up: Bavarians, Saxons, Swabians,
all closed together; there are no more stops; only forwards! A thousand-
voiced "Hurrah" roars across the battlefield – a single violent victory
cry – and, like a wild surf, the storm waves throw themselves at the
village! – Gheluvelt is ours!'

Adolf Meyer of the List Regiment writing in his diary recalled one of the defining moments of the battle. This was the instant when Colonel List was killed by a British shell. It is not surprising that in all the confusion of battle there are differing accounts of the death of the Colonel. According to Meyer, List was killed fighting in the very front ranks. His diary entry records the effects of the fighting:

'Only a few regiments have had to give such a heavy toll in blood
in their first fight, the proud List Regiment had melted down to the
strength of a battalion, the brave regimental leader, Colonel List,
felled by a direct hit in the furthest forward line.'

Hans Mend writing in his book, gives a completely different account of the circumstances of the Colonel's death. Mend was an eye witness and recalled how he was on his way to see Colonel List, who was then engaged in setting up headquarters in the recently captured Gheluvelt chateaux. As he approached the building Mend witnessed what he described as 'three heavy English shells' crashing into the building.' According to Mend this was the real cause of the death of Colonel List:

'I could see nothing any more, and could no longer breathe for
dust. Hearing cries of help coming from the chateaux, Mend rushed
forward and was able to describe the scene as an eyewitness in which
he attempted to assist in the rescue effort which was being performed
by a group of Saxons, a few telegraph operators sprang immediately to
the aid of the wounded. At once, one cried out: "The Bavarian colonel
is also dead!" In my horror, I left my horse unattended, and sprang to
the side of Colonel List, now covered by a tent flap. I lifted this away

and saw that blood welled from his mouth. Our brave commander, who was a true leader of his troops, was no more.'

With the death of its commander the regiment lost its immediate association with the name of its first commander and was officially known from henceforth as the 16th Bavarian Reserve Infantry Regiment (16th RIR), but the veterans such as Hitler continued to refer to the regiment by its old title which is used interchangeably throughout the various personal accounts.

A fuller description of the fight for Gheluvelt was given by Captain Otto Scwink in his book 'The Germans at Ypres 1914':

'After sufficient artillery preparation the British stronghold of Gheluvelt was to be attacked from south and east simultaneously. Colonel von Aldershausen, commanding the 105th Infantry Regiment, was to direct the attack from the east. Besides two battalions of his own regiment, there were placed under his command the 1st Battalion of the143rd Infantry Regiment and a strong mixed detachment from the 54th Reserve Division, mainly belonging to the 245th Reserve Regiment and the 26th Reserve Jäger Battalion. The 99th Infantry Regiment was to make the attack from the south.

During the morning, in spite of the heaviest fighting, no success was achieved, and isolated attacks were repulsed by British counter-movements. At about 11 A.M. our converging attack was begun. The commanders of the 54th Reserve and 30th Infantry Divisions with their artillery leaders, as well as the general commanding the XV Corps, were again in the foremost lines, though the last, General von Deimling, was wounded almost at once by a shell-splinter. Towards midday the attack began to gain ground. His Majesty the Kaiser, who had arrived at the battle headquarters of the Sixth Army, watched the infantry working its way through the maze of the enemy's obstacles and entrenchments. It was well supported by artillery, some of the guns being moved forward with the front line. The British and French artillery fired as rapidly as they knew how, and over every bush, hedge and fragment of wall floated a thin film of smoke, betraying a machine-gun rattling out bullets. But it was all of no avail: the attackers kept on advancing. More hostile strongholds were constantly being discovered; even all the points known to be of importance could not be given sufficient bombardments by our artillery, so that many attacks had to be delivered against fresh troops in good sheltered entrenchments untouched by our guns. Many of our gallant men were killed, and the officers, who were the first to rise in the assault, were the special target of the enemy's sharpshooters, well trained in long colonial wars. Once our troops entered an enemy's position, the resistance was only slight, and the German showed his superiority in single combat. It was only the enemy's counter-attacks, delivered with remarkable accuracy and rapidity, that regained some of his lost ground, but they did not, however, compromise the general success of the day. The XXVII Reserve Corps pressed forward into the dense woods near Reutel, which were defended by a strong system of obstacles and by a quantity of machine-guns, hidden in some cases up in trees.

While this was in progress the last assault on Gheluvelt was taking place. The attacks from east and south both broke into the village, and by 3 P.M.. the whole place with its château and park was in German possession. Colonel von Hügel took his storming parties of the 54th Reserve Division northwards through and beyond the village, while Captain Reiner galloped his batteries close up to it. It was then, however, that fresh hostile reserves were launched against Gheluvelt.

The 16th Reserve Regiment of the 6th Bavarian Reserve Division was hurried up to meet them, its gallant commander, Colonel List, dying a hero's death during the movement. For a short time our own artillery fired into the backs of the Bavarian ranks: for the men were wearing caps and were thus mistaken for British troops. Nevertheless the enemy's counter-attack failed and Gheluvelt became and remained ours, and we captured besides 17 officers and 1,000 men, and 3 guns.

The enemy prevented our further advance beyond Gheluvelt by a heavy fire from a new and strong position along the edge of the woods west of Gheluvelt.'

After four days of fierce fighting, the battle for Gheluvelt petered out with the Germans in control of the village. The prize had been won at great cost as Ignatz Westenkirchner recalled twenty years later when interviewed by Heinz A. Heinz:

'It was our baptism of fire. Four days we had of this at Becelaere and Polygon Wood and Gheluvelt, four days and nights – sheer hell! Of the three thousand men of the Regiment List, only five hundred came safely out of it. The rest were killed, or wounded, or had vanished. We had gone into battle as youngsters, we came out of it worn, scarred, exhausted men. No longer recruits, we were soldiers of the fighting line.'

This was the beginning of Hitler's war, and even he was soon forced to admit that a feeling of horror soon replaced the romantic fighting spirit. His description of the aftermath of the fighting is close to the reality of what had occured. The List Regiment had lost over two thirds of its strength in killed and wounded in those two brutal engagements.

'We went into rest billets for a couple of days at a place called Werwick; then found ourselves in the thick of it again at Wytschaete. We broke through the enemy line north of Messines and turned the left flank of the trenches held by the London Scottish. But what ground or advantage we gained at one moment was lost the next. The enemy was forced to retire; but he came on again a few hours later.'

The List Regiment had paid a very heavy price in its first battle which can be attributed variously to a lack of training, inappropriate equipment and, most of all, a tendency on the part of the German Officer Corps to underestimate and depreciate the fighting qualities of the British regulars who formed the opposition. This produced in the German rank and file a dangerous over-confidence which led to unnecessary risk taking and consequently to high casualties. As a result of the propaganda which they were fed, the men of the List Regiment were certain that they would prevail against an enemy which would simply melt away under their onslaught. The reality was completely different, their opposition were the regular units who were to become known to posterity as the famous Old Contemptables. These regular full time soldiers possessed a fierce determination to succeed, an aggressive attitude and had the training to make their presence felt in the field. The men of the Worcester Regiment and the Black Watch left an indelible impression on the mind of Adolf Hitler who later recalled his growing disillusionment in the pages of 'Mein Kampf':

'Faced with the Tommies in person in Flanders, after the very first days of battle the conviction dawned on each and every one of them that these Scotsmen did not exactly fit with the image they (the High Command) had fed us. The results were devastating for now the German soldier felt himself swindled by this propaganda.'

The victorious List Regiment withdrew, decimated and exhausted, to Commines to lick its wounds. As the men began to recover, the rumour mill was soon in action and the story began to circulate that the survivors were to be transferred to the Eastern Front. At the time of the Great War the Russian Front did not sound the note of dread which it would come to embody in the Second World War, and there was real appetite, even a wish, for the mooted transfer. The episode was reported in the official regimental history:

'In those days, although the regiment had no way of knowing, this wish was almost fulfilled. On 19 November an advance notice was sent to Crown Prince Rupprecht from the high command that six divisions, among them our 6th BRD, were to be placed under the command of Hindenburg, who had already won a decision in the East. But the List Regiment's luck would not be sweet. This did not happen.

Without rest, the difficult activity of fortification work began. New trenches were built, and connected by communications trenches… a front was built with toughness and speed, by the sweat and blood of the best. This collaborative work was for Life; Death was the employer. The sooner it was complete, the less time for the enemy to fire, the deeper the trenches, the more secure the shelter, the safer the cover against shrapnel, the better to withstand shells. After establishing regimental headquarters in the Grand Palace at Messines, the List Regiment was to endure many harrowing weeks of constant pressure from British troops and artillery.'

- CHAPTER 9 -
GEFREITER HITLER

FROM ALL OF the evidence available to us it would appear that the fighting for the farm at Becelare and the village of Gheluvelt was the only occasion on which Hitler fought with rifle in hand. By early November, the time of a brief action against the London Scottish near Wijtschaete, we know he was already serving as a regimental messenger. However the brief combat at Gheluvelt seems to have been enough for Hitler to distinguish himself in the field. It is conceivable that, even during his first taste of fighting near Gheluvelt, Hitler was already being entrusted to carry messages in the field. If that was the case it is not beyond the bounds of possibility that he may never have fired a shot in anger as a rifleman. Hans Mend certainly gives the impression that Hitler was already employed as a despatch runner at some time during the first engagement and describes Hitler in action: 'He lined up fearlessly for the most difficult messages, he was one of the best and most reliable battle ordinance men.' Mend also quoted the opinion of one of the officers of the List Regiment: 'I still can't understand how he puts his life at such risk when he owns not a single stone in Germany, he is certainly a strange one and lives in his own world, otherwise he is a capable individual.' Westenkirchner however gives a different account and clearly recalled Hitler fighting as an infantryman. We will never know the truth for certain but, in any event, Hitler certainly carried out the duties assigned to him to the satisfaction of his commander and in recognition for his service as a runner, by 9 November he was selected to serve permanently at Regimental headquarters. He was to acheive the remarkable distinction of serving in that capacity and in that regiment for the next four years.

With the excitement of the opening engagements behind them, for the men of the List Regiment the misery of fighting in the Ypres salient soon took hold. Hans Mend wrote an evocative passage in his memoirs which summed up the drudgery of those days as the reality of the true nature of this war to end all wars began to make itself known.

'Days and weeks passed, for all of us in a state of the greatest stress, which cost many good comrades their lives.... Even if filthy, sulfur-yellow like a canary, with bullet holes in the great coat or dispatch case, the lucky ones among us were glad to be able to march safely back into our quarters. With steaming coffee or a "Blue Henry" (a Schnapps) the adventures of the preceding day were made light of, through wit and humor. In all of this, Adolf Hitler was no spoilsport, on the contrary, he livened things up with his ideas and interruptions: but he never spoke about his work.'

Hitler may not have spoken about his work to Mend, but he did send a very lengthy letter in February 1915, to Ernst Hepp which contains a great deal of detail concerning Hitler's early service in the war and touches upon the award of the Iron Cross Second Class:

'Since that time we have been continually in the front lines. I was proposed for the Iron Cross, the first time in Messines, then again at Wytschaete by Lieutenant Colonel Engelhardt, who was our regimental commander. Four other soldiers were proposed for the Iron Cross at the same time. Finally, on 2 December, I received the medal.

My job now is to carry dispatches for the staff. As for the mud, things are a bit better here, but also more dangerous. In Wytschaete during the first day of the attack three of us eight dispatch riders were killed, and one was badly wounded. The four survivors and the man who was wounded were cited for their distinguished conduct. While they were deciding which of us should be awarded the Iron Cross, four company commanders came to the dugout. That meant that the four of us had to step out. We were standing some distance away about five minutes later when a shell slammed into the dugout, wounding Lieutenant Colonel Engelhardt and killing or wounding the rest of his staff. This was the most terrible moment of my life. We worshipped Lieutenant Colonel Engelhardt.

I am sorry, I will have to close now. The really important thing for *me is to keep thinking about Germany. From eight in the morning to five in the afternoon, day after day, we are under heavy artillery fire. In time even the strongest nerves are shattered by it. I keep thinking about Munich, and there is not one man here who isn't hoping that we shall soon finish off this rabble once and for all, make mincemeat of them, at whatever the cost. The hope is that those of us who have the good fortune to see our homeland again will find it purer and less corrupted by foreign influence. The sacrifices and misery exacted daily from hundreds of thousands of people, the rivers of blood flowing every day against an international world of enemies will, we hope, result in smashing Germany's external enemies and bring about the destruction of our internal internationalism. That would be better than any territorial gains. As for Austria, it will come about as I have already told you.*

Once more I express my heartiest gratitude and remain your devoted and grateful ADOLF HITLER.'

The same Lieutenant Colonel Engelhardt whom Hitler mentions in his letter obviously harboured a measure of mutual respect for Hitler. In a 1932, pamphlet, 'Facts and Lies', he is quoted describing Hitler's act of bravery which it is thought led to the award of the Iron Cross 2nd Class.

'Once as I emerged from the wood at Wytschaete during a fierce attack, in order to make some observations, Hitler and an orderly from the Regimental Staff planted themselves bang in front of me to shield me with their own bodies from machine-gun fire.'

The fact that Hitler had distinguished himself in the fighting was also recognised by him being awarded *gefreiter* status. In the English speaking world the term *gefreiter* is problematic and has caused some difficulties in interpreting the Hitler story. The Imperial German Army used a large number of terms to indicate the status of a soldier which had no direct counterpart in the English or American forces. Hitler for example could be referred to by the title *kreigsfreiwilliger*, or wartime volunteer, which was used to differentiate professional career soldiers from those who had joined for the duration. Over the centuries the German military tradition has also harnessed a variety of unique incentives to encourage good conduct in the ranks. One of these was to recognise reliable private soldiers (who were known by the title *infanterist* in the Bavarian army) and rewarding them with an easier life. The word *gefrieter* evolved from older German and Dutch – meaning 'freed' or 'liberated' person. The award of the title *gefreiter* brought with it a series of negative rights which meant the *gefreiter* did not have to perform many of the most menial duties which the private soldiers loathed so much. The holder of the title *gefreiter* was literally freed from sentry duty. It is important to realise that *gefreiter* was not a rank which brought with it the right to issue orders to other men; as such it was little more than a signifier which indicated that this man was considered to be a trustworthy private soldier. A better term might be Private First Class, but the revised status also brought with it a tiny rise in pay: an *infanterist* received 70 pfennigs per day while a *gefreiter* received 75 pfennigs.

Hitler was elevated to *gefreiter* status in November 1914, but in contrast to the popular conception in the UK and the USA, he was certainly not promoted to the equivalent rank of a corporal. In the Bavarian army of 1914, the rank of corporal had its own directly equivalent rank which was called *korporal*. In the Prussian army the equivalent term was *unteroffizier*. It is clearly a substantial error therefore to translate *gefreiter* to corporal, but regrettably this is what so often happens. In the Bavarian army of 1914, *korporal* was the lowest rank from which orders could be given to subordinates. The '*gefreitene*' on the other hand, although they were recognised as reliable private soldiers, had no power of command over other men. The term helped to differentiate between proven and unproven *infanterists*, it aided Officers and NCOs to identify those who had distinguished themselves and who could be counted upon. To assist that process such men were addressed as 'liberated' or '*gefreitene*'. The holder of the title remained an ordinary private soldier nonetheless and was not authorised to give any form of command. It certainly is confusing but the reality is that Hitler had merely been recognised as a reliable and trustworthy soldier and was rewarded by being exempted from sentry duties.

Hitler's contemporaries such as Westenkirchner understood the subtext of the situation and in the inter-war translations of Nazi books such as Heinz's 'Germany's Hitler', Hitler is referred to as a private and later as a lance corporal. Alexander Moritz Frey however consistently refers to Hitler as a 'private' and indeed this appears in the title of the unpublished article, which came to light after the war, 'The Unknown Private – Personal Memories of Hitler'.

In order to get round this difficulty the term *gefreiter* is frequently equated with the British rank of lance-corporal, but even this is not altogether helpful as there was no direct equivalent in the Bavarian army. The mistaken assumption that a 1914 Bavarian *gefrieter* was equivalent to an non-commissioned officer took root during World War II. To add to the confusion, by 1940 the role of the *gefreiter* in the *Wehrmacht* had changed to a role which was indeed equivalent to a junior non-commissioned officer such as a lance corporal. The upshot of this difficulty in translation has led to the creation of the popular myth that Hitler was promoted with the equivalent rank of *unteroffizier* or *korporal*, this is simply untrue. Of one thing we can be certain; Hitler never was a corporal.

After the brief flurry of excitement which surrounded their arrival in Flanders, the men of the List Regiment soon had to settle down to the routine of life in the waterlogged and muddy trenches which were to become infamous during the Battle of Paschendale. Hans Mend summed up the miserable experience of the first year in the trenches.

> *'It was of small satisfaction to us that the positions of our opponents were just as bad as our own, for the English had also suffered heavily from the mass of water forcing its way into the trenches. Once they tried, by opening the sluice valves, to flood our position but our pioneers had prevented this plan in time.... To put it bluntly, the way our troops existed was not to be envied.'*

Despite all of the privations, Hitler certainly demonstrated a keen appetite for soldiering, but Hans Mend noted the gloomy mien which *Gefreiter* Hitler had begun to exhibit. Mend writing about this period recalled how one day he observed an infantryman standing with his rifle at his feet lost in contemplation:

'From his stance, I immediately recognized Adolf Hitler. Two dead men, in whom he seemed very interested, lay in front of him. He looked around and stretched his head, as though sensing danger. But in spite of the greatest danger to life and limb, he remained next to the dead men. Once he turned in my direction, probably since he recognized me and wanted to see how I would get through this crater field. Next day I asked what he found so interesting and Hitler answered, "I took a look at two dead men on whom grass was already growing." I replied that it was absolutely unnecessary to remain at that place, unless you want to catch moles. Hitler tugged at his mustache, as if to say, "Dispatch rider Mend, you look after yourself, I'll look after myself." Before we parted, I remarked: "Your bones could be lying in that corner of the battlefield at Messines."'

Ignatz Westenkirchner also recalled this settling down period in the wretched landscape around Ypres. In his 1934 interview with Heinz A. Heinz he described the course of the first winter:

'The weather got ever colder and colder. As the winter set in, the line hereabouts established itself and the fighting was no longer so fierce until the turn of the year. When I say this I mean it wasn't so fierce in comparison with what was to come later! Looking back now, all that business at Becelaere and Wytschaete was child's play to the fighting still ahead. For the most part all that first winter we occupied trenches between Messines and Wulverghem. Our line was consolidated by then and it held like steel for four years. By now Hitler was a trench runner, whose duty was to keep up communication between Company and Regimental Headquarters. There were eight or ten of us altogether. We were very pally and made a mob by ourselves. There were even times when things couldn't be said to be too bad – when we got parcels from home and letters. We shared out, of course. Sometimes, even, we had a game with 'Tommy.' We stuck a helmet on the point of a bayonet and shoved it above the parapet, when it would be sure to draw immediate fire. Even Hitler, who was usually so serious, saw the fun of this. He used to double himself up with laughter.'

Hitler later maintained that his enthusiasm for the war cooled down gradually, but the realisation for most of his comrades was harsh and sudden. Any remaining and exuberant spirits were soon quelled by the fear of ever-present death. Self preservation inevitably took over from military ardour and even a gung-ho character like Hitler recognised this moment when duty was eclipsed by survival:

> 'A time came when there arose within each one of us a conflict between the urge to self-preservation and the call of duty. And I had to go through that conflict too. As Death sought its prey everywhere and unrelentingly a nameless Something rebelled within the weak body and tried to introduce itself under the name of Common Sense; but in reality it was Fear, which had taken on this cloak in order to impose itself on the individual.'

The cooling of martial ardour wasn't just limited to the German side of the line. On 25 December 1914, the famous Christmas truce took place and was most marked just to the south of Messines, almost exactly where Hitler's regiment was stationed. Heinz A. Heinz writing in 'Germany's Hitler' gives us the view from the English side of the trenches and quotes Field-Marshal French:

> 'It was that first winter of the War, the Germans took a very bold initiative at several points along our Front in trying to establish some form of fraternisation. It began by individual unarmed men running from the German trenches across to ours holding Xmas trees above their heads. These overtures were in some places favourably received and fraternisation of a limited kind took place during the day. It appeared that a little feasting went on, and junior officers, non-coms, and men on either side conversed together in No Man's Land. When this was reported to me I issued immediate orders to prevent any recurrence of such conduct....'

According to Heinz, popular opinion in England was against the belligerent attitude of the Generals. Heinz fondly imagined, and not without some good reason, that the sentimental English public liked the idea of a Christmas truce, and credited the Christian gesture to the 'gentler Bavarians' in the Imperial German Army. In any event the truce was short lived and was never to be repeated.

The List Regiment was soon plunged back into the unremitting grind of daily life at the front. The course of the Great War was inexorably turning against Germany and allied superiority in men and material was already beginning to make itself felt. In March 1915, there was an unexpected new posting for the regiment. The British had regained the initiative and were ready to unleash a major offensive which would become known to posterity as the Battle of Neuve Chapelle. Balthaser Brandmayer was another of Hitler's comrades who wrote a memoir of his war-time service alongside Hitler. He had not seen action in the opening battles of 1914, but he was with the List Regiment as it was rushed in to position to defend Neuve Chapelle:

> 'Alarms were sounded at noon from all directions.... An hour later we found ourselves sitting in a military train, where this would take us no one knows. Some suspect that we will be going to Russia, others to Lorraine. The overloaded train rolls slowly and carefully into the deepening night. We freeze: scarcely a word is spoken.'

The sudden train journey was far shorter than expected and those who had hopes of a transfer to Russia were again disappointed. The men de-trained and once more found themselves in Lille, and learned of the disconcerting news that British regiments had broken through the German front line, as each of the companies of the List Regiment arrived they were formed into ranks and marched off as quickly as possible to a new destination; the town of Neuve Chapelle. The British had succeeded in making a small incursion into the German lines and the fighting was tough and bloody. In order to recapture the lost territory the 6th BRD, Hitler's parent division, was thrown into battle in piecemeal fashion. Regiments, battalions, detachments, companies, and batteries were rushed onto the battlefield as soon as they arrived at the railway station, and as a result were divided up among the Prussian formations holding the line. According to the Bavarian official History the result was a motley crew which was only just able to stitch together a defence. Hans Mend was an eye witness to the events and he recalled the confusion bordering on panic as the Germans scrambled to react to the British offensive:

'*The confusion came into being because the different formations from our regiment, as they disembarked from their trains, were immediately marched to the Front and had gone into action, on their own account, between Prussian troops. The battle orderlies, Hitler, Lippert, Schmidt, and Weiss had the task, in so far as possible, to re-establish the connection, which was made all the more difficult by the frightful fire and the soggy ground underfoot. Hitler said later in Fournes that he had to deliver reports by creeping forward from one shell-hole to another, and that sometimes the sulfur fumes only allowed him to see 10 metres to the Front. During the lulls in the fighting he paced around like a restless tiger in the farm at Halpegarde.... Even the Colonel said: "I can scarcely believe that my orderlies can come through this fire..." The most dangerous time for a dispatch runner is delivering a message for the first time from a new position. I said to Hitler "You're a mole. You'll come through all right, just don't let them shoot you in the guts." "That's my business, my dear Mend," Hitler replied that the communications trenches leading to the positions further forward provided little protection, they were not deep enough and already, on the first crossings, caused many casualties. Adolf Hitler had to take these dangerous paths several times daily and, if he wanted to come through safe and sound, was obliged to crawl rather than march. Not even the slightest movement escaped English snipers, exposed to the heavy barrage on the way from Fromelles to the fighting zone.... Hitler reported "Every shell-hole is being bitterly contested. Because of our barrage, the English have been cut off from all possible help. Many are hanging on the electric barbed-wire, and screaming horribly." As we knew him to be a man who never exaggerated and, who expressed himself carefully in such situations, we knew now that a bloody fight was being waged. His expression also attracted attention. He must have seen much horror and have joined in the fighting himself; the expression of the eyes in his thin yellow face told us much.*'

For most men in the trenches the lure of self preservation outweighed the desire to serve one's country; Hitler was different, for him the call of duty took precedence over self preservation. At Neuve Chapelle, the amazing reservoir of will power which Hitler was able to summon up on occasion asserted its incontestable mastery. His sense of duty, obedience to the national cause and an obsessive devotion to the German Reich had won out and Hitler remained steadfastly obedient to his adopted country's call even in this most unforgiving of environments. At a more mundane level Hitler was also noticeably different from the other men in his unit, as he had no contact with his family in the shape of his sister Paula, or his half sister Angela, and he received no parcels from home. This was noted by his colleagues such as Ignatz Westenkirchner:

'He owned up to me sometimes how stoney broke he was. Poor chap, he never had a cent! I blurted it right out once – "Haven't you got anyone back home? Isn't there anyone to send you things?" "No," he answered, "at least, no one but a sister, and goodness only knows where she is by this time." There were letters and parcels awaiting us there – all except for Hitler. He just looked the other way and busied himself knocking the mud off his boots and doing what he could to clean his shirt.'

Hans Mend was another of the men of the List Regiment who also noted the sad situation of *Gefreiter* Hitler who received little in the way of mail and no parcels whatsoever:

'When he was not fired at, he would often say on his return: "Today an old woman would have had no trouble in getting through"…. Hitler often looked completely exhausted; the best nerves can fail. However, he always pulled himself together…. I never saw him receive a field packet. Nor would he accept presents from us, though we often made the offer. Occasionally he refused with a brief thank you. He was uninterested in home leave. The trenches and Fromelles were his world and what lay beyond did not exist for him.'

As Mend observed, by early 1915 Hitler had thrown himself fully into the world of soldiering. The List Regiment was his new family and he proved himself a dedicated and genuinely courageous soldier. All of the main witnesses to Hitler's deeds in the trenches are united in testifying to the fact that he was absolutely dedicated to his duty and did not shirk from even the toughest and most dangerous assignments.

However, that is not to say that Hitler was popular. He certainly was not an easy companion. Some of his colleagues recall that he was a tiresome individual who marched to the beat of a different drummer. His main critic in this respect is Alexander Moritz Frey.

Moritz Frey was serving in the ranks of the List regiment alongside Hitler, he was a writer turned medic. After the war Frey became a very popular German science fiction writer who reached his peak of popularity in the thirties, he also contributed to the long running Bavarian based humour magazine *Simplissimus*. Long after his death in 1954, an obscure unpublished essay by Frey entitled 'The Unknown Private – Personal Memories of Hitler', was discovered in an archive in the German town of Marbach. Frey was no friend of Hitler's and unwaveringly refused to join the Nazi party. He remained critical of Hitler even into the thirties and he eventually had to flee the country when the attentions of the SA grew too strong. It was during the war that Moritz Frey first became sceptical of Hitler. He mistrusted him and soon formed the view that the thin Austrian was a schemer and conniver who used his talents with words to his own ends, but even Frey had to testify to the fact that Hitler was not a coward and, although he was no hero, he did not lack the courage to be able to withstand the rigours of the front:

'When people claim that he had been a coward, that's not true. But he also wasn't brave, he lacked the composure for that. He was always alert, ready to act, back-stabbing, very concerned about himself. All his comradeship was an act – an act cleverly chosen for the simple and naïve – to make himself popular and to create a striking impression. He knew the tricks that one could use to throw nuggets to the youngsters that they would happily swallow.'

Not everyone who fought alongside Hitler was in accord with Moritz Frey's harsh views. A young Lieutenant called Fritz Wiedemann respected Hitler's qualities as a soldier despite his decidedly 'unmilitary' bearing. Wiedemann would later be promoted to Captain and was destined to become Hitler's adjutant from 1935 until 1939, when he was dismissed following a disagreement over Hitler's foreign policy. Despite his differences with Hitler, Wiedemann was firmly of the opinion that Hitler was a fine soldier and that Hitler's account of his war experiences in 'Mein Kampf' was essentially true. Wiedmann eventually fled to America, but he too was adamant that Hitler fundamentally told the truth concerning his war record. 'I never caught him lying or exaggerating when he told of his recollections.'

Balthasar Brandmayer was another comrade from the Great War who produced a written account of his service alongside Hitler. He was not present during the opening battles and first met Adolf Hitler on 30 May 1915, after recovering from injuries during the 9 May attack on Neuve Chapelle. Brandmayer returned to the ranks of the 16th RIR and was given the position of *meldegänger* and joined Hitler's tight knit little group. Writing in his memoirs Brandmayer later recounted his first encounter with Hitler in a bunker occupied by the Regimental runners:

'He had only come back fatigued after a delivery. I looked at him for the first time in my life. We stood eye to eye facing one another.... He was like a skeleton, his face pale and colorless. Two piercingly dark eyes, which struck me especially, stared out of deep sockets. His prominent mustache was unkempt. Forehead and facial expression suggested high intelligence. I can still see him today as he stood before me then, loosening his belt buckle. Along with Max Mund, Adolf Hitler became my inseparable comrade.'

Unlike the rest of the grumblers and moaners who make up armies everywhere, Hitler, it seems, was obsessive in his dedication to duty. We are told he was a ready volunteer for difficult missions and always seemed to find a way to get the message through the most threatening shell fire even if he was sometimes reduced to crawling on his belly like a snake. Private Westenkirchner was another of the List regiment who felt that Hitler was unfairly maligned after the Great War. He gave vent to his frustrations when interviewed by Heinz A. Heinz in 1934, and, as a Nazi supporter, Heinz was naturally quick to take up the argument on his *Führer's* part.

'Among the innumerable libels with which the Führer has no time to concern himself, if he is to get on with the job of governing Germany at all, is that which accuses him of skulking during the War.

He is supposed to have managed somehow or other to have kept well out of the firing line.'

By 1932, the 'innumerable libels' which Heinz referred to were increasingly appearing in print and Germany's left leaning newspapers were quick to seize upon any opportunity to criticise Hitler. In order to refute the allegations a number of pamphlets concerning Hitler and his service in the Great War were prepared and issued to the public. The first was written by Dagobert Dürr and was entitled Adolf Hitler, *'der deutsche Arbeiter und Frontsoldat'* (Adolf Hitler the German worker and front-line soldier). It was published during the first round of the 1932 presidential election. Heinz A. Heinz was able to draw upon this and the later 1932 pamphlet entitled *'Tatsachen und Lügen um Hitler'* (Facts and Lies About Adolf Hitler) to support his case that Hitler was a trusted and doughty fighter. The Nazi pamphlets were both published in the wake of the 1932 court case which Hitler successfully pursued against *'Echo Der Woche'* which had published an article which was critical of Hitler's Great War service. That court case was part of the fall out which marked the bitterly fought 1932 presidential campaign, the second round of which was held on 10 April 1932. According to the 'Facts and Lies' pamphlet Hitler also took action against a member of the S.P.D. who had falsely claimed that Hitler had received a prison sentence for deserting the German army, and for which he had been granted amnesty by Kurt Eisner. The allegation was adjudged to be slanderous and in this instance the defendant had to pay a 50 Mark fine. The S.P.D party was also the principal publisher of the story that Hitler had shirked his Great War duties. At Fournes in particular, it was alleged that Hitler had always been 'far from the action'. The court was unimpressed from the outset and a temporary ban was imposed on an S.P.D pamphlet. In the subsequent court proceedings, the judge heard all of the evidence including the testimony of many of Hitler's former comrades. On the basis of the evidence before him he ruled that the claim was patently untrue. We should not overlook the fact that his judgement was based on an impressive number of sworn statements by witnesses, either on paper or directly before the court.

The 'Facts and Lies' pamphlet published on behalf of the Nazi party in 1932, is particularly interesting as it reproduces the testimony of a substantial array of accurate official testimony which was used in the trial. The pamphlet has been dismissed by some authorities. Thomas Weber in particular disregards the court testimony as being the inevitable product of the bond between former comrades, but there is no evidence to support the suggestion that Hitler's former comrades went out of their way to lie on his behalf. The pamphlet should therefore be taken at face value and it goes a long way towards producing the hard evidence which contradicts the idea that Hitler was a coward who skulked in the rear areas. No less than three of *Gefreiter* Hitler's commanding officers gave evidence in the trial with the highest appreciation of his soldierly qualities. These men adhered to a strict code of honour and held the utmost respect for the organs of the state. Their evidence certainly stood up well in a court of law in what we must remember was still the pre-Nazi era. There is therefore no justifiable reason why these statements should not carry proper weight in the historical record. The 'Facts and Lies' pamphlet was quick to capitalise on the court victory over the S.P.D and its newspaper, and in order to make further capital the Nazis reproduced a number of excerpts from the sworn statements:

> *'I want to stress that, when during the attack on the axe-shaped piece of forest (later called the Bavarian Forest), I left the cover of the forest near Wytschaete to better observe the attack, Hitler and another courier from the regimental staff, the volunteer Bachmann, placed themselves in front of me to protect me from machine gun fire with their own bodies.'*
> *Signed: Engelhardt, Major General (retired),*
> *former commander of the Bavarian R.-R.-F.-R. 16 (List).*

> *'I can only give former Corporal Hitler the greatest praise for his extraordinary accomplishments. Fournes was a village behind the regiment's battle line. It served as a recovery area for battalion relieved from the front, and also served as the seat of the regimental staff during calmer periods. The village was within the danger zone, and*

was frequently under rather heavy fire. During battle, the regimental headquarters was moved about 3/4 of an hour forward to Fournelles, and orders had to be carried to the front line. The path was often under enemy machine gun and artillery fire. I can never remember a single time when Hitler was absent from his post. Hitler may wear the medals he earned with pride...'

Signed: Satny, Colonel (retired),
former commander of the Bavarian R.-F.-R. 16 (List).

'Mr. Hitler, as corporal, was a courier for the regimental staff, and was not only always willing to carry out hard tasks, but did so with distinction. I stress that the List Regiment, as might be expected from its history, was at the toughest parts of the front, fighting in frequent major battles...'

Signed: Baligand, Colonel (retired),
last commander of the Bavarian R.-F.-R. 16 (List).

'At particularly dangerous points I often was asked for volunteers, and at such times Hitler regularly volunteered, and without hesitation...'

Signed: Bruno Horn,
Lieutenant with the Bavarian R.-F.-R. 16 (List).

'Hitler never hesitated in the least in carrying out even the most difficult order, and very often took on the most dangerous duties for his comrades.

Couriers for the regimental staff had to be among the most reliable people, because serving as a regimental courier during battles and skirmishes required iron nerves and a cool head. Hitler always did his duty, and even after his severe thigh wound, volunteered to be sent back to his regiment from the reserve battalion immediately after his release from the hospital...'

Signed: Max Amann,
former sergeant with the Bavarian R.-F.-R. 16 (List).

'I often met Corporal Adolf Hitler as he served as courier to and from the front. Anyone who understands the duties of a courier – and any soldier who has served at the front does – knows what it means, day after day and night after night to move through artillery fire and machine gun fire from the rear...'

Signed: Joseph Lohr,
officer candidate with the Bavarian R.-F.-R. 16 (List).

'It is true that Hitler was nearly blinded by a courier mission during a heavy gas attack, even though he was wearing a gas mask...'
Signed: Jakob Weiß,
NCO with the Bavarian R.-F.-R. 16 (List).

'Hitler received the Iron Cross, First Class, during the spring or summer of 1918 for his outstanding service as a courier during the great offensive of 1918, and in particular for his personal capture of a French officer and about 15 men, whom he suddenly encountered during a mission, and as a result of his quick thinking and decisive action, captured.

Hitler was seen by his fellow couriers, and many others in the regiment, as one of the best and bravest soldiers.'

Signed: Ernst Schmidt,
with the Bavarian R.-F.-R. 16 (List) from November 1914 until
October 1918.

According to the pamphlet, the most sensational moment of the trial came during the testimony of Hitler's regimental comrade Michel Schlehuber. Schlehuber was a Social Democrat and had been a trade union member for 35 years. He was certainly not a Nazi and was actually called as a witness by the opposing side; it was to prove a disastrous decision for Hitler's opponents:

'I have known Hitler since the departure for the front of the Bavarian R.-I-R. 16. I came to know Hitler as a good soldier and

faultless comrade. I never saw Hitler attempt to avoid any duty or danger. I was part of the division from first to last, and never heard anything then or afterwards bad about Hitler. I was astonished when I later read unfavorable things about Hitler's service as a soldier in the newspapers. I disagree entirely with Hitler on political matters, and give this testimony only because I highly respect Hitler as a war comrade.'

Signed: Michael Schlehuber

The overwhelming testimonies given by Hitler's former colleagues appear to be genuine. They were certainly strong enough to convince the court and stood up to the rigours of the German legal system at a time before Hitler had tasted political power. There is no question of any legal fix and we must surely therefore accept the verdict of the court.

It is clear from the weight of support that Hitler was certainly not, as he is all too frequently depicted, the lonely outcast devoid of friends and lacking in respect from his comrades. That is not to say that Hitler behaved in a regular manner. He was not typical of the average soldier and Hans Mend again noticed his changes of mood, which he felt may have been connected to Hitler's increasingly poor health:

'In twenty-three months had not once spent half a day in Lille, had never taken home leave and never once reported sick was suddenly very sick and coughed heavily, but none of us could convince him to report to the doctor.'

Mend blamed the unhealthy conditions at the front for Hitler's declining health and noted that although there was little snow or frost, the area was subject to persistent falls of freezing rain. It heralded a miserable Christmas and Mend noted that during the second Christmas of the war the sickly Hitler was apparently even more miserable than his long suffering comrades.

'Many lay in wet clothes, with a high fever, on wet bunks in the barracks. Only a few were able to dry their uniforms in the ovens installed there; most, therefore, returned on the march to the Front

with the same wet covering they'd arrived in. Clinging to the body and soaked through with mud and dirt, these bits of uniform offered no protection at all against the cold. Mass illness was the inevitable consequence, and whole companies had to be placed on sick leave by the doctor. The only advantage our troops had during the wet season was that they had no fear of attack by the enemy, for they were just as badly off. When Hitler came back from the trenches at night, he often lay on his wooden bunk in wet clothes. During the three days of Christmas, he spoke not a word to anyone, and we were unable to explain why he was so surly. At that time, he was perhaps taking it to heart that everyone at home had forgotten him, and that nobody had sent either a Christmas greeting or present.… When he returned from a mission on Christmas Day, he sat deep in thought, sunk in a corner with his helmet still on his head, and no one was capable of stirring him out of his apathy.'

In marked contrast to Hans Mend, who was sympathetic to Hitler's plight, Alexander Moritz Frey maintained a very circumspect view of Hitler. He suspected him of playing to the gallery and attempting to create a false picture of dedication and suffering. In contrast to Mend's claim that Hitler never reported sick, Moritz Frey recalled how Hitler had refused some routine medication which Moritz Frey had prescribed for a throat infection. Moritz Frey formed the opinion that Hitler did this in order that he could play the martyr's role and gain additional recognition for his selflessness:

'I gave him some sort of tablet to swallow. He had a mild temperature and a raw red throat. Although it was as good as nothing and it would normally have been ignored at the front, I advised him nonetheless to register for a doctor's appointment the next day. He thought for a moment, hesitated – and then shook his head… clenched determination in his eyes. No, he didn't want that, he said opaquely. In the later course of his illness, he made sure that it was talked about among his fellow soldiers and that it also came to the ears of the officers that Hitler has a 'terrific throat infection' but is doing his duty nonetheless.'

Given the ineffectual qualities of many medicines dispensed at the time, this may appear to be a rather harsh judgement but Moritz Frey was a man of conviction and he remained a genuine opponent of Hitler. Almost alone among the old soldiers of the 16th RIR Regiment, Moritz Frey refused to surrender to the allure of the Nazi party even though Hitler later extended a personal invitation for him to join.

- CHAPTER 10 -

FOXL

ALTHOUGH MANY OF his comrades appear to have held a high regard for Adolf Hitler, in typical Hitler fashion, the bulk of his own warmth appears to have been reserved, not for his comrades, but for his beloved dog. There was no doubt that Hitler absolutely doted upon Foxl (Foxy) a little white terrier who deserted from the British lines and attached himself to Hitler and whose devotion seems to have been totally reciprocated. Long after the Great War, on the night of 22-23 January 1942, Hitler told the story of his favourite companion during one of his late night rambling monologues which was recorded by Bormann and later collected together and published as 'Hitler's Table Talk' by Sir Hugh Trevor Roper:

'It was in January 1915 that I got hold of Foxl. He was engaged in pursuing a rat that had jumped into our trench. He fought against me, and tried to bite me, but I didn't let go. I led him back with me to the rear. He constantly tried to escape. With exemplary patience (he didn't understand a word of German), I gradually got him used to me. At first I gave him only biscuits and chocolate (he'd acquired his habits with the English, who were better fed than we were). Then I began to train him. He never went an inch from my side. At that time, my comrades had no use at all for him. Not only was I fond of the beast, but it interested me to study his reactions. I finally taught him everything: how to jump over obstacles, how to climb up a ladder and down again. The essential thing is that a dog should always sleep beside its master. When I had to go up into the line, and there was a lot of shelling, I used to tie him up in the trench. My comrades told me that he took no interest in anyone during my absence. He would recognise me even from a distance. What an outburst of enthusiasm he would let loose in my honour! We called him Foxl.'

Hitler clearly had a great attachment to his little companion and from his misty eyed recollection some 25 years later it seems to have been one of the most important and memorable relationships which he formed during the Great War.

Meanwhile the unremitting grind of trench warfare continued and a key witness to the next phase of the war was Private Westenkirchner who recalled the next episode in Hitler's war. The List Regiment, in the wake of the battle of Neuve Chapelle, took up new positions in a fairly quiet sector of the Front which was to become a second home to Hitler and his comrades:

'After a time, the regiment found itself in Tourcoing, and then, in the spring of 1915 when the British offensive hurled itself against Neuve Chapelle, we moved up in that direction, and occupied trenches in the neighbourhood of Fromelles. Here we remained, more or less, until the following autumn. As I said, Hitler and I were Meldegänger. For the sake of mobility we carried no arms except a small revolver. Our despatch wallets were attached to our belts. Generally two of us were sent out together, each bearing the same despatches, in case anything happened to the one or the other. The despatches were always sealed and marked with one, two or three crosses, according as they required time, haste, or express speed. It was no joke this despatch bearing, especially as Fromelles stood on a bit of a height, and to reach it from the troops in the plains and valleys below we had to toil up slopes raked by the enemy's machine-gun fire every inch of the way. I can see Hitler before my eyes now, as he used to tumble down back into the dug-out after just such a race with death. He'd squat down in a corner just as if nothing'd happened, but he looked a sketch – thin as a rake, hollow-eyed and waxy white.'

Somehow Hitler survived the gruelling ordeal described by Westenkirchner and the arrival of the fine summer weather at last provided some respite from the misery produced by the mud of winter and spring 1915, but the ever present danger from shelling meant that Hitler and his colleagues had to spend a great deal of their time in one of the concrete bunkers which still dot the landscape around the small town of Fromelles. The fighting around Ypres was also characterised by mining and countermining which could result in a sudden and deadly explosion at any moment. Ignatz Westenkirchner again takes up the saga of the many forms of death which might await the participants in Hitler's war:

'It was pretty beastly in those dug-outs all that summer. I shall never forget it. Nothing got on a man's nerves more than to have the ground blow up right under his feet. You never knew whether or not you were sitting bang on top of a powder magazine. Suddenly there'd come the most sickening sensation as a mine was sprung, and the next thing you'd know was that ten or twenty of your pals and comrades, chaps who'd been at your elbow only a minute before, were flying around in ten thousand bloody bits. That wanted some sticking, I can tell you! By September the English were pressing the attack all along our Front harder and harder. On the night of the 25 September 1915 our position was pretty precarious; it seemed as if something decisive one way or the other must at last come off. The air was full of the screaming of shells and of the hideous hissing and crashing of the whizz-bangs. Suddenly our Company Officer discovered that telephonic communication with the next section had broken down, and Hitler and another man got the order to go and find out what was wrong. They made it somehow, but only got back by the skin of their teeth utterly done in. The wire had been cut: an attack in force was imminent. Warnings must be sent further afield. Hitler received the order a second time. It was nothing less than a miracle how he escaped with his life as he came out on the road between Fromelles and Aubers. It was literally raining shells. The attack, however, failed. How we withstood it I can't tell. I only thought to myself at the time how lucky our English and Indian prisoners ought to think themselves to be out of such a hell.'

The British attack which took place on 25 September 1915, in the Fromelles sector burned itself into the memory of the men of the List Regiment who were by now officially dubbed the 16th RIR. From their positions at Fromelles, Hitler and Schmidt, who were sent out to reconnoitre, brought back the disconcerting news that the British had secretly brought a number of large cylinders to the Front. With the wind blowing towards the 16th RIR positions, there was the imminent danger of a British gas-attack. At this difficult juncture Hitler was again sent out to reconnoitre, this time he took with him Balthasar Brandmayer. The two made their reconnaissance and were heading back to make their report at Regimental H.Q., when the messengers were caught in the middle of a heavy British barrage. The terrifying incident was later described in detail by Balthasar Brandmayer:

> 'Stones and iron fragments whizzed above our heads. We bent low, racing across open country. I could scarcely lift myself from the ground any more (and) still Hitler urged me onwards, onwards! I cannot understand how Hitler could look around, with no cover... while calling to me: "Brandmoari, get up!" He seemed without nerves.... Sweat dug deep rivulets into our faces. More falling than running, we reached the command dugout. Paralyzing tiredness weighed like lead on my burning limbs. I threw off my helmet and webbing and sank, dead-tired, into my bunk. I expected Adolf to do the same, but how wrong I was! As I turned around, I saw him sitting near the exit, helmet on head, buckled up, and waiting for the next order. "You're crazy!" I cried out angrily. "How would you know?" was his prompt reply. There was no man under his uniform, only a skeleton.... He had an iron nature.'

- CHAPTER 11 -

HITLER RUNS OUT OF LUCK

ON 4 AUGUST 1942, around midday, Hitler was holding forth in one of his rambling monologues known to posterity as Hitler's tabletalk and he recalled the scene as the 16ᵗʰ RIR arrived for the first time on the battlefields of the Somme. The regiment was to go into action near the town of Bapaume which was a hotspot in this most ferocious of battles:

> *'When we went into the line in 1916, to the south of Bapaume, the heat was intolerable. As we marched through the streets, there was not a house, not a tree to be seen; everything had been destroyed, and even the grass had been burnt. It was a veritable wilderness. Marching along the roads was a misery for us poor old infantrymen; again and again we were driven off the road by the bloody gunners, and again and again we had to dive into the swamps to save our skins! All the thanks we got was a torrent of curses "Bloody So-and-Sos" was the mildest expression hurled at us.'*

At the time when Hitler and the 16ᵗʰ RIR were transferring to the Somme, Alexander Moritz Frey undertook the rail journey in the company of Private Hitler and the man who was then known as Sergeant Amann:

> *'I sat together with Max Amann and Hitler in the same train compartment… Hitler sat opposite us, sleeping with his mouth open. He slept with his chin hanging down and had stretched out his feet in such a way that Amann, with his short fat legs (he always had plenty to eat due to his connections) was wedged in. Amann gave the sleeping man a kick against the shinbone. Hitler gave a start. "Kindly keep your joints to yourself!" said the sergeant in a commanding tone. Hitler understood, then he went red. For a moment he looked liked he wanted to lunge at the other man, but immediately managed to*

keep his temper under control and he said nothing. Amann said, in a sarcastically pacifying tone, "Yes, I mean you, Private Hitler."'

They could not have known it at the time but Hitler and the men of the 16th RIR were marching into the gates of Hell. They were about to face an ordeal which made all of their previous trials seem mild by comparison. The Battle of the Somme, was a long-drawn-out affair. It lasted, in fact, some three and a half months, from 1 July 1916, well on into the autumn. The battle is often considered solely from the British perspective but it was in fact an allied offensive and was planned on a single front of about twenty-five miles and was preceded by immense preparations and reinforcements in men and material. The French were initially successful but despite some small gains amounting to around eight miles the British failed to break the German line. The reason was, of course, that the German lines consisted of an entire belt of territory scored with lines behind lines, every one of which had to be taken and cleared and held before the British could be said to have broken through.

The British failed to do so and at frightful cost and over two months were spent in trying to secure objectives marked down for the first day or two of the battle: it took weeks upon weeks to decide the possession of a single patch of woodland; prolonged struggles waged backwards and forwards over a few metres of contested ground. The futility of the German attack on Verdun was balanced by the desperate defence of Bapaume. The Somme, even more than Verdun, was to prove the crucible which ultimately ground down the German army. The flow of losses which began on 1 July 1916, were irreplaceable. During their short ten day spell in the lines near Bapaume, the 16th RIR suffered 120 casualties for every day. Ignatz Westenkirchner naturally recalled the awful reality of the fighting as experienced by both he and Adolf Hitler:

'That Somme Battle, a witches' cauldron of horror and fire and death, went on for weeks. Some time before we'd all been issued with fresh equipment. Now, on the 25 September, we were marched off to Haubourdin, there to entrain next day for Longwy. From there we marched endlessly it seemed to us through Cambrai to Fremicourt, where we set to work at top speed to dig ourselves in, constructing

On 29 May 1913 a police report form for Adolf Hitler was created by the Munich police. Although Hitler had already arrived in Munich on 25 May 1913, an arrival date of 26 May 1913 was stated. From the document it is clear that he intended to stay for two years.

The police report form for Rudolf Häusler proves that he and Hitler came to Munich on 25 May 1913, and that the two lived together in a small room at the tailor Joseph Popp's house from 25 May 1913 to 16 February 1914.

A certificate of residence from 10 September 1929, and a notification card to prove that Hitler came to Munich in May 1913 and not 1912, as Hitler stated time and again.

Although Hitler stated that he neither received nor requested money from relatives, the district court noted that on 4 May 1911 Adolf Hitler received large amounts from his aunt Johanna Polzl, to cover his studies as a painter.

A watercolour painted by Adolf Hitler, from the collection of Heinrich Hoffmann. In the years of 1913 and 1914, Hitler often painted this view of the oldest house in Munich. The building would survive the war and this very scene may be viewed today.

During the years of the Third Reich, the Popps' house at No. 34 Schleißheimerstraße, carried a plaque indicating that Hitler had lived there until August 1914. Hitler had indeed lived here with Rudolf Häusler from 25 May 1913 to 16 February 1914. Hitler remained here as a sole lodger until 16 August 1914 when he left for active service with the Imperial German Army.

A Bavarian officer reading out the German declaration of war in August 1914.

On Sunday, 2 August 1914, a twenty-five year old Adolf Hitler was amongst thousands of people gathered at the Odeonsplatz in Munich. The crowd joined in exuberant enthusiasm for the war and Heinrich Hoffmann was on hand to record the scene. He later identified Hitler as a figure in the crowd.

The earliest known photograph of Regimentsordonnanzen (Regimental Orderlies) and messengers Ernst Schmidt, Anton Bachmann and Adolf Hitler. Seated at Hitler's feet is the English Terrier named Foxl, who came to be Hitler's most treasured companion. The photograph was taken in April 1915 in Fournes.

Hitler with his comrades in September 1915, at the Regimental Command Post in Fromelles. Photograph by Hans Bauer: (Front row, left to right) Adolf Hitler, Josef Wurm, Karl Lippert, Josef Kreidmayer. (Middle row, left to right) Karl Lanzhammer, Ernst Schmidt, Jacob Höfele, Jacob Weiss. (Back row) Karl Tiefenböck.

In this photograph taken at the beginning of September 1916, Hitler is seen alongside his colleagues and his faithful dog Foxl in the rear area at Fournes. (Front row, left to right) Adolf Hitler, Balthasar Brandmayer, Anton Bachmann, Max Mund. (Back row, left to right) Ernst Schmidt, Johann Sperl, Jacob Weiss and Karl Tiefenböck.

The badly damaged town of Fromelles, where the Regimental Headquarters of the 16th RIR was situated from 17 March 1915 to 27 September 1916. Even in the rear areas, such as this, long-range shelling was a constant menace.

Orderly Sergeant Max Amann (left) pictured at La Bassée station in March 1917.

A German position at Fromelles, pre-1915. Trenches such as these were frequently knee-deep in water.

The conditions in the water-logged frontline trenches near Fromelles were appalling, as this photograph from May 1915 graphically demonstrates. The men of the 16th RIR lived and fought in these conditions.

German trenches on the Aisne during the Great War. The photograph is undated, but the men are not wearing helmets so this is early in the war, possibly 1914 or early 1915.

Adolf Hitler in 1916 in the rear area at Fournes.

Adolf Hitler and Karl Lippert in mid-1915 in Fournes.

Adolf Hitler, then a battalion-messenger, seen in May 1915 with his rifle slung over his shoulder. Hitler was in the process of delivering a message. This photograph first appeared in the Official Regimental History of the 16th RIR.

Hitler, accompanied by Max Amann and Ernst Schmidt and aides, after the victory over France on 26 May 1940. The group were photographed on their tour to visit the positions they had occupied during Great War in Flanders.

Hitler with his comrades in May 1916 in Fournes: Balthasar Brandmayer (front), (left to right seated) Johann Wimmer, Josef Inkofer, Karl Lanzhammer, Adolf Hitler, (left to right standing) Johann Sperl, Max Mund.

Hitler with (right to left) Max Amann, Wehrmacht adjutant Gerhard Engel, Ernst Schmidt and adjutant Julius Schaub on 26 April 1940 at the same location in Fournes, some 24 years later.

Hitler (left with helmet), and next to him Balthasar Brandmayer, pose for the camera in a bunker near the frontline section of Reincourt-Villers in September 1916.

Hitler on 26 October 1916, in the Prussian Association of the Red Cross hospital in Beelitz near Berlin, where he was brought after being wounded on 5 October 1916.

From soldier to Führer.
These four portraits illustrate the change in Hitler's face and moustache between the years of 1915 to 1921.
(Clockwise from top left) Hitler pictured in 1915, 1916, 1919 and 1921.

A photograph of members of the POW camp guard contingent at Traunstein taken in early January 1919. Hitler (left circle) and Ernst Schmidt (right circle) served here guarding Russian POWs until 11 February 1919.

From 20 February to 8 March 1919, Hitler (seen standing in the centre at the rear of the photograph) helped to guard the Munich Central Train Station, he is pictured here with his fellow guards.

The remains of the German trenches at Wytschaete near Ypres. Hitler served on this sector of the front and was awarded the Iron Cross 2nd Class for his actions at almost this exact spot.

The remains of a German block house at the Bayernwald near Ypres. Hitler spent the war carrying messages to and from locations such as this.

trenches, traverses and dug-outs day and night. We took part in the battle on the 2 October and found ourselves in the sector between Bapaume and La Barque. It was all new ground to us, and we messengers were lost half the time. We relieved the 21st Regiment. The men came straggling back scarcely recognisable in their mud, blood and rags. Once a shell dropped plump into the middle of our dugout. For the moment the lot of us were too stunned to know what had happened. Then we saw four of us lay dead, and seven others lay hideously wounded spouting blood on the ground. That was the first time Hitler caught one. A splinter had gashed him in the face.'

Balthasar Brandmayer was another of Hitler's colleagues who recorded his impressions of the horrendous ordeal which the Imperial German Army was forced to endure on the Somme battlefield:

'There were dead and buried everywhere. We fell from shell hole to shell hole. Multicolored flares arched heavenwards, and burst into countless streams. This was always the moment after which we leapt for another freshly turned-up crater in which to disappear. Shrapnel, filth and iron rained mercilessly down on us. The blood almost stagnated in my arteries, it could only be a few seconds longer – then, yes – then an armored-steel force ripped at bodies already scratched and torn. My nerve failed. I just wanted to lie where I was, I sank hopelessly into insupportable apathy.... Then Hitler spoke kindly to me, gave me words of encouragement, said that someday all our heroism would be rewarded a thousand fold in the Fatherland.... We returned... uninjured. Our faces were no longer recognizable.'

Not surprisingly with the constant presence of death just around the corner, even Hitler would eventually use up his store of good fortune. However even in the face of such overpowering danger Hitler continued to do his duty. Ignatz Westenkirchner was another Lister who vividly recalled the terrible events which were played out on the battlefield of the Somme:

'On the night of the 5 and 6 October 1916 Hitler was on the go with messages between our lot and the 17th the whole time. For the most part he and his comrade were dodging high explosive in the

open, just waiting between earthquakes and volcanoes to make the
next bit there and back. The enemy was doing his utmost to smash the
German line, but in spite of unprecedented ferocity, the attack was
completely foiled. We didn't give way an inch. By day we lay as close
underground as we could. Otherwise, the slightest sign of life on our
part brought the enemy aeroplanes into play and bombs were dropped
right from overhead. Of an evening, as a rule, Hitler was despatched
to Brigade Headquarters at Bapaume. To get there he ran such a
gauntlet between exploding mines and burning houses, that for the
most part his own clothes singed on his back. Over and over again the
company was only saved by our artillery from the English onslaughts.'

On 12 October 1916, Lucky Linzer finally ran out of the commodity
that had sustained him for over two years of war. While on duty near the
town of Bapaume during the Battle Of The Somme he was wounded in
either the groin area or the left thigh. The aftermath of the incident was
witnessed by Ignaz Westenkirchner:

'From 7 October for five days and nights it isn't too much to say
that we trench runners got no sleep and nothing but snatch grub to
eat. Our numbers grew ever fewer and fewer. The stunning din in the
air never let up for one moment. All was the wildest uproar of death
by shot and shell and cannonade. The thing grew unendurable, not
to be believed. It took six runners now to get a message through, three
pairs of them set out on the off chance that one man, perhaps, might
succeed. Our Lieutenant called for volunteers – only Hitler responded,
and a chap named Ernst Schmidt. The thing was rank suicide. This
time only Schmidt got back. Hitler had been hit in the left leg. Later
on the regimental stretcher-bears brought him in. They took us out of
the line on the 13 October. Only a handful of us, apathetic with shock
and exhaustion, stumbled off, making our way as best we could over
the corpses of our comrades.'

According to Private Westenkirchner, the battle of attrition which
the British generals had planned for was beginning to take its toll:

'The companies got smaller and smaller; hardly thirty men went to
a company now. And in this shape we awaited new onslaughts. The

bombardment was incessant. At length, however, we went into rest billets at Sancourt.'

As the days passed it became evident that although Hitler's wound was serious enough to merit a spell in hospital, it was not so severe as to incapacitate him permanently, but it was certainly enough to disable him for some months and would require a period of convalescence. Accordingly he was sent to the rear to the '*Sammellazarett*' Hermies where he appears to have undergone some dental work probably as result of the facial wound he had received. Writing in 'Germany's Hitler' Heinz A. Heinz affords us a fairly accurate account of the next chapter of the war as provided by Ignatz Westenkirchner which veers suspiciously close to the version of events described in '*Mein Kampf*'.

'For two long years he had been at the Front: here, for the first time in all that while, he heard a German woman's voice again. It was that of the Sister at the Base Hospital. It gave him quite a shock. But he went on in the Ambulance Train, through Belgium, back home to Germany – after two years! It was amazing at last to find himself, clean, and lying in a soft white bed in hospital at Beelitz near Berlin. He had become so unused to all this refinement! It took him quite a while to get accustomed to these new surroundings. The thing, though, that struck him most, back there at home in hospital, was the demoralisation that seemed to have got hold of the men. There were chaps there making a boast of how they'd purposely maimed themselves to get out of the fighting line, and, what was a jolly sight worse, no one in authority took notice of it, no one seemed to think the less of them for it. What they said was 'Better to play the coward for a minute than to be dead for eternity.' Everybody was grousing over the beastliness of the Front, and the uselessness of the war in general. Hitler could hardly believe his ears. It might have been true, but it was unworthy and unsoldierly.'

Hitler was ill at ease in hospital and he sent a number of postcards to his colleagues at the front complaining of the tribulations caused by his dental treatment. We are fortunate to have a glimpse of his sense of humour in the post card which he sent to Balthasar Brandmeyer.

'Am suffering from hunger-induced typhus, because I cannot eat bread; additionally, I am adamantly denied any sort of jam.'

Ignatz Westenkirchner followed Hitler's progress and was later able to recall the events for Heinz A. Heinz. He picks up the narrative as Hitler is once again becoming mobile:

'Then one day, when he was fairly convalescent, he got leave to go to Berlin. Everything there looked baddish, he thought; poverty and hunger and anxiety were stamped on every face. He went into one or two of the Soldiers' Homes, but found the chaps there much in the same frame of mind as in the hospital, only worse. The grousers seemed to have it all their own way. Hitler felt pretty sick I can tell you....'

Once he had recovered from his wound, Hitler was posted to a replacement battalion away from the trenches. He hated the time spent in Munich which was the city which Hitler now called home. His period of rest was a shock and he was dismayed by the lack of popular support for the war. Hitler's wound may well have saved his life. He spent one of the most difficult and testing times in the entire history of the regiment in a rear area hospital. The Battle Of The Somme was to prove one of the most difficult ordeals in the long litany of misery for the List Regiment. By 1917, when Hitler had fully recovered, the List Regiment had served its time on the Somme and Heinz A. Heinz recorded the undimmed enthusiasm of Adolf Hitler as he returned to duty in the months which would see the build up to the Battle Of Arras. It is interesting to note that the 1937 English translation of 'Germany's Hitler' correctly avoids describing Hitler as a corporal and translates *Gefreiter* as Lance-Corporal.

'Lance-Corporal Adolf Hitler (as he was now) had, indeed, come back from the Front (as he was to emerge from the War at the end), with all his ideals and loyalties intact. He had gone from the high untried courage of the beginning through shock and horror and exhaustion to admitted cowardice and fear, but this in turn he had conquered and steeled to dogged endurance. It had never yet entered his head to start malingering; or to question the obvious tightness of the War. He was utterly disgusted by all this, back in Berlin.

When he was fit for discharge, the "iron train", which carried men on leave, took him to his Reserve Battalion in Munich. Here things were no better than in Berlin. Glowering faces, grumbling speech, and incessant invective against Prussians and militarism were to be noted on every hand. Hitler couldn't make it out how all this seemed to have got up, and got up so suddenly. He found out, however, that a lot of newspaper men having gone to the Front, their places had been taken by Jews, and that these men were using their opportunity to foment discouragement and disunion. Everything tracked to a nicety with the enemy propaganda in the trenches. If the Bavarians and the Prussians could be brought to loggerheads, so much the better for those who would like to see both go under.'

It is apparent that by 1917 the home situation was so desperate and gloomy that Hitler would do anything to escape that dismal state of affairs and return to the front where he would still at least be fighting for Germany. Hitler was clearly very unhappy to be away from the Front, he had made a place for himself in that world. He was valued and respected and he had no other desire in life than to return to his comrades. In a badly spelt postcard dated 19 December 1916, from Hitler to his regimental comrade Karl Lanzhammer, who at this time was a bicycle courier at regimental headquarters of the 16th Bavarian Reserve Infantry Regiment, he informed Lanzhammer that he was now with the Reserve Battalion, and was still undergoing dental treatment and would as soon as possible voluntarily report back to the field. In the brief text, Hitler reveals some of his characteristic spelling difficulties by rendering the German word for immediately (*sofort*) with double f – '*soffort*':

'Dear Lanzhammer, I am now in Munich at the Reserve Battalion. Currently I am under dental treatment. By the way I will report voluntarily for the field immediately.

Kind regards A. Hitler'

- CHAPTER 12 -
THE KAISERSCHLACHT

THE SPELL IN the trenches around Hochstadt, near Muhlhausen was a blessing for the men of the 16th RIR, they could take the opportunity to rest, build up their strength and gather their energies for the renewed challenges ahead. This much needed period of respite in a quiet sector was to prove disappointingly short. The List Regiment had only a couple of months rest before they went into the line again near Lizy on the Aisne.

The fighting here was dogged and obstinate and lasted practically all that winter as the months dragged round from 1917 into 1918. At the end of January 1918, however, there was at last some good news, and the 16th RIR was withdrawn to Gommines for another spell of rest. Balthasar Brandmayer joyfully recalled the much needed period of rest which was relished by the exhausted men:

'What a wonderful time! Misery and need are quickly forgotten. Anxiety and fear, through the long war years, have become unknown conceptions. So the visits, each day, of aviators dropping bombs does not disrupt in the least our royal Bavarian rest. Hitler saw a letter from my girlfiend and asked in a good-humored tone: "Brandmoari, has Trutschnelda written again?" "Good guess", I retorted. "Have you never wanted a girl?" I asked. "Look Brandmoari, I've never found time for such a thing," Hitler replied. "And I don't want to," he continued. "You're a strange one, Adi! I'll never understand you," I replied. "There's no hope for you." "How would it be if I found a mam'selle for us?" someone asked… "I'd kill myself from shame rather than make love to a French woman", Hitler leapt excitedly into the discussion. The effect of the moment was raucous laughter. "Listen to the monk!" cried one. Hitler's face became serious. "Don't any of you feel your honour as a German any more?"'

Despite the odd moment of tension among the runners, for once there was good news on the military front too. There were stunning German successes to report from the Italian front and there was even better news as Tsarist Russia collapsed and descended into revolution. On 3 March 1918, the Treaty of Brest-Litovsk marked the exit of Russia from the Great War. These strategic developments would allow the German High Command enough resources to make one last throw of the dice on the Western Front and it would involve the List regiment in some of the hardest fighting of the whole war. Ignatz Westenkirchner recalled how Adolf Hitler remained in tune with the bigger strategic picture:

'Hitler's interest in things in general never dwindled away to just concern for nothing more than what the day brought forth. That winter of 1917 the Russian Front buckled up, which was an immense thing for us, and so did the Italian; but then came the munitions strike at home. For three long years we'd held the Russian hordes at bay on the east. Endless columns of Russian prisoners swarmed over the high roads in Germany and yet there seemed to be illimitable numbers yet to come. It seemed almost laughable to us that the German Army, strung out on half a dozen fronts, should hope to resist this perennial flood. It held out successfully until the events of this winter allowed us to concentrate on the west. For the first time it almost looked as though we could change over from a war of defence to one of attack. The spirits of the men went up, and one even heard snatches of song again in the trenches. We got the idea that the enemy was losing heart: it could only now be a matter of one last terrific effort, before they, too, collapsed like Russia. As the spring advanced it was pretty plain they were jumpy and uneasy in those opposite trenches.

Then came the munitions strike at home, the most incredible bit of treachery and knavery the world has ever seen. The German Army was knifed in the back. The lives of hundreds and thousands of our men yet to be slaughtered were to lie at the doors of those who fomented and engineered this monstrous treason. Although the strike was called off too soon for the effects of it, as far as armaments were concerned, to

be much felt at the Front, the consequences on our morale were deadly.
Everyone began to ask what was the good of our carrying on out here
if the people at home had thrown up the sponge? The Army began to
be divided against itself. The enemy wasn't slow to take advantage
of all this. They peppered our lines again with propaganda leaflets:
'Germany in the throes of a general strike,' 'Give it up: we've won.'
Nevertheless, somehow, we fought on.'

The Imperial German Army did indeed fight on, and reinforced by
the influx of men from the Russian front there was just about enough
manpower for a last desperate lunge at her enemies. This was the
Kaiserschlacht, the great spring offensive of March 1918, and initially,
at least, the German Armies advanced with their morale raised at the
prospect of a war-winning attack. Balthasar Brandmayer recalled the
new found mood of optimism.

'We all felt within us the approach of the long-desired peace. Peace
– the tug of the homeland – already these thoughts in themselves gave
us courage and the confidence to endure patiently the few months
that the war on the battlefields of France would perhaps still last.
With songs of home on their lips again, for the first time in years, the
fighting battalions of the glorious List Regiment pushed on.'

This last desperate effort began when the German armies once more
gathered their strength to take the offensive. Ignatz Westenkirchner
served alongside Hitler during those tumultuous months of the
Kaiserschlacht which saw the Germans seize the initiative and break
the British and French lines. By 1918, the armies on both sides were
unaccustomed to having to advance over long distances and although
Hitler was noted for his physical endurance anyone would be taxed to
the limit by the demanding marches described by Westenkirchner:

'On 15 March 1918 our big offensive opened in Champagne
and we succeeded in retaking a good slice of the country from the
enemy. The battle was waged without cessation day or night; from
a huge defensive action between Soissons and Reims it gradually
involved the whole Front from the Marne to the Aisne. The barrage
was unintermittent. For fourteen days shot and shell rained on the

trenches. We crouched in a veritable hell of fire and flying iron. We List fellows evacuated our old position on the Oise-Aisne sector, and pushed forward on a four-day long march which I shall never forget. Forty miles covered, every day of it, and this over roads you couldn't call roads any longer, they were so ploughed and shot to pieces. We had to make way all along the march for endless trains of munition waggons, and the incessant struggling forward of heavy artillery. Every now and again the whole advance would be held up by some heavy trench mortar having got stuck in a shell-hole. Horses had to be taken from the limbers of the other guns to try and haul it out, and masses of men turned to lend a hand. A dozen or so gunners hauling on long ropes, a grey coil of exhausted men, would bow forward at the word of command, 'Heave,' and strain till the sweat poured down their powder-blackened faces, while the horses floundered up to their bellies in the mud. If at last the monster at which they pulled reared itself by degrees out of the hole, there might be some chance of getting forward again. In silence and haste we struggled forward, our wide coats flapping and waving, with the belts unfastened, the covers of our helmets all in rags. By evening, one day, we reached Fourdrain. We camped three nights in the open air and did fifty miles at a stretch. The horses of the batteries ahead went down literally in dozens, and had to be summarily put out of their misery. We marched on through heaps of unrecognizable ruins, once villages, past La Fere, Vouel and Noyen, themselves nothing but burnt and shattered shells. On the third day we came to Lassigny and Amy. The farther ahead we pushed the more cumbered grew the way with the corpses of shot horses and the wreckage of heavy ordinance.

The French made terrific efforts to hold Montdidier; they hurled their coloured troops into the battle here. After indescribable struggles on 28 March 1918 we reached Fontaine, about five kilometres west of that place. Here we went into the line again for about three weeks. The whole Front was in an unceasing uproar day and night. It blazed and roared and quivered with incessant explosions. The air was for ever filled with the screaming and the whistling of the *shells, the flash and thunder of explosives and their sickly smell. If this wasn't enough, we were on starvation rations now, and suffered agonies from thirst. The baggage waggons and the field kitchens got held up and hopelessly stuck in the wrecked roads to the rear, or came within range of the enemy guns, so that we were cut off even from such supplies as there were. One whole week we got practically nothing. I remember how Hitler and I sometimes, on an extra black night, would crawl out of the trench to scrounge round for something to eat. He'd have an empty petrol can, and I'd have a knife. We hunted round where they'd been slaughtering the horses, and if we could hit on some poor shot beast which didn't stink too badly as yet, we'd slice a bit off his quarter. Hitler'd fill the can with shell-hole water, and, stumbling back again to the dug-out, we'd deliver this booty to the cook! We were a crew of scarecrows, I can tell you, when at last we were relieved, half-starved and with the sore, red eyes of men who haven't had what you could call one decent sleep for nearly a fortnight! We were nothing but a handful of tramps, mud from top to toe, not a whole tunic amongst us. We came out of the line over twelve hundred fewer than we went in.*

They marched us another two or three days to rest billets at Ghery les Poully. For weeks we'd never had our clothes off – now, first to sleep, and then to eat! After that we had a clean-up, if our bits of once-upon-a-time shirts, or remnants of once-upon-a-time boots were yet worth the time and trouble. In the middle of it, though, the alarm was sounded; we were to be rushed to a sector, Anizy-Lizy. Grousing and swearing we limped off again towards the trenches. The Front was roaring and blazing away in full blast. We were only a few hundred strong now, and were sent to hold a line some four miles long, for ten days and nights. We spent hours sheltering in shell-holes, battered with flying clods of earth – when not directly hit by shot and shell – which hit like fists and knocked a man's breath out of his bellows.'

By 26 April 1918, it was obvious that the last great German offensive had already begun to run its course and the 16th RIR, instead of advancing, was now doggedly holding on to defensive positions where it was subject to increasingly heavy artillery barrages. Balthasar Brandmayer later recalled this terrifying period in the history of the 16th RIR:

'After a few days, not one house remained standing in the fire-zones, here and there were piles of rubble, mute testimony to the bloodiest events that had ever taken place on the face of the earth. On bright moonlight nights, the ruins loomed ghostlike over the wide battlefield, reaching heavenwards, as though in mourning for their former splendour.

Dispatch runners lay in the cellar of a badly damaged chateau.... Supplies now so inadequate, that a real famine broke out after eight days. Our group had to make do with a loaf of bread a day between us. Hitler and I often crept out at night and reached the terrain for livestock. Pieces were cut from the cadaver of a horse that was no longer fresh, and with overflowing hearts, handed to our culinary artist. Rain puddles supplied useful water to some extent. And if this made us sick, then it at least suppressed our hunger. The men were becoming jittery. After 26 days, it is high time we were relieved.'

The dejected state of the men of the List Regiment was reflected throughout the army. By May 1918, the Imperial German Army was reaching the very last reserves of its strength. The influx of manpower which had made the great offensive possible had long since been expended and the men were worn down by malnutrition, disease, fatigue and enemy action. The decision to pull the List Regiment out of the line did not come a moment too soon for the wretched survivors who had begun the great push in such high spirits. Ignatz Westenkirchner again takes up the story:

'Then at last, on 15 May 1918, when the 6th Division was relieved, the strength of the List Regiment had dwindled to that of a single company. Many of the chaps had to be carried on stretchers, or helped along somehow, or they couldn't have made the retreat. Two of us messengers were senseless, and the rest were ghosts rather than men. We filed out of the trenches, as usual, before the greying of the dawn.

*Muddy and sunken-eyed came the pitiable line of stumbling figures,
lots of them with flapping empty sleeves, unbuttoned tunics, and
blood-soaked rags bound round head or arm or hand. Others came
two by two, leaning on each other, dragging, limping. The stretchers
got knocked about over the broken ground. Single figures brought up
the rear with rifles and equipment, packs, buckets, and gear of every
indescribable description.'*

The Imperial German Army was down but not yet out, somehow it
still was able to re-group and scrape together sufficient forces for a last
series of attacks which initially met with a measure of success. On 30
June 1918, the 16th RIR was ordered to join German forces successfully
advancing on the Marne, near Chateau-Thierry. In this last great surge
forward the victorious German forces once again tasted a measure
of success and advanced 32 miles in just three days, and now came
within 50 miles of Paris. The fighting was once more severe and the
List Regiment lost 59 men on the first day of fighting, alone. Balthasar
Brandmayer again recorded his impressions of the last successful action
of the war.

*'The enemy is scarcely able to defend himself. Up-hill, down-
dale, through thick and thin, we follow on behind his fleeing heels.
Trench warfare seems to have been overtaken in full flood by a war
of movement. With Hitler, I search for companies that are advancing
surprisingly quickly. Searchlights start up and plunge path and wood
into an abundance of glaring light. The Froggie had, in between
times, reassembled. He desperately resists our assault. We run through
a raging fire. Fragments of exploding shells scatter among us. Their
flat trajectories drive us to distraction.'*

Despite these scattered advances, as 1918 wore on into autumn it was
clear that the offensive strategy of 1918 was not working any better than
the defensive strategy of 1917. Germany was finished, allied victories
outweighed the German advances and the losses were irreplaceable, but
despite the signs of impending disaster on the home front and in the
field the High Command were intent on trying to attack with the last
vestiges of its strength. It was clear that the Imperial German Army was

straining every last sinew in the attempt to continue to resist the allied steamroller. There was no time to properly rest and rehabilitate the men who had given so much in the great push. Every unit was required at the front and the men of the List Regiment were soon plunged back into combat.

It was at this juncture that, according to Ignatz Westenkirchner, Hitler demonstrated his courage and skill as a soldier by capturing a party of French soldiers. Some of Westenkirchner's words undoubtedly ring true, but his description of the episode, complete with Hitler's inner dialogue helpfully set out in detail, does smack of more than a touch of hyperbole:

'On 26 May 1918 our artillery began a fresh attack on the French trenches. Gas followed. The enemy was completely overborne on the Soissons-Fismes sector. We List found ourselves in Juvigny. Then we marched without pause to Epagny. We remained a good long time in trenches between Vezaponin and Nouvron, and spent the first part of June reconnoitring in that region. Then a queer thing happened. It was still day, 4 June, as a matter of fact, and the firing had died down for the nonce. The sun was hot. Men were sitting about, silent, weary, unsociable, sleepy, reading letters and writing home. Hitler had gone off by himself and must have been half a mile away. He had just surmounted a slight rise in the apparently vacant landscape when suddenly he heard the whirring of a machine-gun and bullets peppered all the air about him. He flung himself face downwards on the ground. The gun ceased fire. Gingerly Hitler essayed to move. Instantly it spat again, lead and fire. At length, however, he managed to worm his way to the next hole, 'Evidently a French ambush,' he thought, 'with a camouflaged gun,' and paused, and thought things over. 'Quite a number of men,' he supposed, and rightly. For within the next ten minutes or so, at least half a dozen of them, fully armed, appeared climbing over the top of the trench. 'One, two, three – five – eight – Donnerwetter!' he thought, 'however many more?' Then like a flash, he leaped to his feet, dragged his revolver from his belt, and levelling it at the enemy, shouted at them to surrender.

'Whichever of you budges, he's a dead man!' Whether the Frenchmen understood what he said or not, they understood what he meant and promptly fell into line as ordered. 'You're my prisoners! March!' Hitler signalled the way. Off they went, Hitler in the rear. Perhaps they'd covered a hundred metres this way, perhaps two, when the whole twelve of them began to wonder where the rest of the German detail might be which had captured them. Another hundred metres they plodded silently forward without a single enemy more showing up than this fellow with the revolver. 'Sacre Nom!' – exclaimed one of them – but got no farther. He found himself directly menaced by that shining barrel. Forwards! Half a mile farther and they came to the German trenches, when Hitler turned the lot over to the company, amid roars of laughter. 'Heavens! If we'd only known!' muttered the prisoners, 'but the blasted blighter carried the thing off so mighty high handed!'"

If there is even a streak of truth in this account it should come as no surprise that, in August 1918, Hitler was finally awarded the Iron Cross First Class. The award of this medal to a member of the rank and file was highly unusual, this decoration was normally the preserve of the Officer Corps. There are a number of sceptics in the body of historians, most notably Thomas Weber, who maintains that Hitler obtained the award merely because his face fitted in at Regimental H.Q., but if Westenkirchner is to be given any weight at all then we must give strong credence to the fact that Hitler certainly did deserve the award for his conduct in the field. However, despite the unusual circumstances, Hitler made a typically obdurate decision not to wear the decoration which was so highly coveted by almost every German soldier. He perversely continued to sport the ribbon of Iron Cross Second Class on his tunic and later explained his reasoning during one of his tabletalk sessions on 15 May 1942:

'During the first World War, I didn't wear my Iron Cross, First Class, because I saw how it was awarded. We had in my regiment a Jew named Guttmann, who was the most terrible coward. He had the Iron Cross, First Class. It was revolting. I didn't decide to wear my

decoration until after I returned from the front, when I saw how the Reds were behaving to soldiers. Then I wore it in defiance.'

Hitler's bravery had been recognised by his superiors and he was certainly regarded as a first class soldier by his contemporaries. There were ample opportunities for a bold individual such as Hitler to gain such recognition as the 16th RIR was involved in fierce fighting which continued into July 1918, and Ignatz Westenkirchner was able to recall the details for his interview with Heinz A. Heinz:

'After that, the fighting between the Oise and the Marne was stubborn and bitter beyond description. Step by step we were forced back by overwhelming numbers. We made a stand along the line Aisne-Marne, however, from 1 July to 14 July 1918, from which the enemy failed to dislodge us. We were relieved on 30 July 1918. They brought us out on the line to go through a ten-day course of instructions, of which interval we took advantage to get back somewhat to the semblance of ordinary mortals.'

In the middle of August 1918, the List Regiment once more entrained for the Somme region where they took part in the defence of the sector between Arras and Albert. The men of the 16th RIR and its parent formation, the 6th Bavarian Reserve Division, steadfastly held on to their trenches in a line which ran from Monchy to Bapaume. They doggedly held their ground against a series of savage onslaughts, all of which failed to dislodge the resolute defenders. The Listers remained in the vicinity of Bapaume and fought on there until the end of August 1918, and it was no doubt a great relief when they were ordered to march north east towards the frontier between Belgium and Holland. Not far from Bruges the 16th RIR put in a spell of guardwork on the frontier which included a brief excursion to Ostend.

This welcome visit gave Hitler a respite from the trenches and also the chance to view the Marines who guarded the port. One little known episode took place at this time when Hitler accepted the opportunity to take a tour aboard a U-boat. Over twenty years later on 12 August 1942, during one of Hitler's rambling tabletalks he turned to Admiral Krancke and recalled the work of Schröder, who had already retired, but who had nonetheless received the order to join up and raise corps of Marines and who rose magnificently to the occasion:

'What we accomplish today is child's play in comparison with the efforts we were called upon to make then. Schröder had absolutely nothing! But in no time he was leading his corps to battle. I myself saw these Marines in action for the first time at the Battle of the Somme; and compared with them, we felt we were the rawest of recruits. We then received orders to march to Ostend for a rest. The Regiment arrived there in a most deplorable state. Any Russian regiment, after a five-hundred-mile retreat, would have looked like the Brigade of Guards in comparison. While in Ostend I had the chance of going for a short trip on a submarine, and the sailors, smart, efficient, turned out always as if for a review, were magnificent! It made one ashamed to be seen in their company. I suppose this accounts for the slight inferiority complex which the land forces feel in the presence of the Navy. We had to cut up our great-coats in order to make puttees, and we looked like a bunch of tatterdemalion ballet-dancers! They, on the other hand, looked frightfully smart in their belts and gaiters; and we were not sorry when we escaped to the decent obscurity of our trenches once more.'

The long running saga of the war in the trenches was now rapidly drawing to a close, but for the 16th RIR there was still hard fighting to be done. By September 1918, the brief and merciful respite at Ostend and the Dutch Border was over, and Hitler along with the rest of the Listers found himself in the middle of the last of the fighting which he and Westenkirchner were to see together. For the third time the List Regiment was ordered back to the familiar vicinity of the Ypres salient and, even in the quiet spells, the monotonous bouts of allied shelling continued as grim and unrelenting as ever. By now however, time was running out for Hitler and Westenkirchner later recalled Hitler's last action of the Great War which was played out in the Ypres salient where the whole adventure had begun:

'For the third time we were back on the old ground fought over in 1914. Now we had to defend it, inch by inch, all over again.

We were in the neighbourhood of Gommines; dazed and bewildered with the ceaseless flash and thunder of explosives. Fiercer and fiercer grew the firing. On the night of 13-14 October 1918 the crashing and howling and roaring of the guns was accompanied by something still more deadly than usual. Our company lay on a little hill near Werwick, a bit to the south of Ypres. All of a sudden the bombardment slackened off and in place of shells came a queer pungent smell. Word flew through the trenches that the English were attacking with chlorine gas. Hitherto the List hadn't experienced this sort of gas, but now we got a thorough dose of it. As I stuck my head outside the dug-out for a quick look round I found myself confronted by a hideous lot of bogies. In the place of men were creatures with visages of sheer horror. At that I shot into my own gas-mask! For hours we lay there with this foul stuff poisoning every gulp of air outside. Suddenly one of the chaps could stand it no longer. He sprang up, wrenched the mask from his head and face, gasping, only to encounter a waft of the white-green poison. It caught him by the throat and flung him back choking, gurgling, suffocating, dying. The gas let off by morning and the shelling began again, to our unbounded relief. Better the deadliest bombardment than that poisoned drowning stifling. How we tore off those masks, and gulped in the air! It was still stinking of the stuff, and reeked again of high explosive, but to us it was the very breath of Heaven. Every now and then the enemy still sent a gas bomb over together with the rest. A man would shriek, throw up his arms, and fling them across his eyes. There was nothing for it but to clap the filthy masks over our heads again. The ferocity of the attack increased. Hour after hour of this inferno went by. It seemed as though that paling in the east which heralded the longed-for dawn would never come again. We chaps just hugged the ravaged and shattered ground, lying, indistinguishable lumps of filth and earth ourselves, within the sheltering lip of the water-filled craters torn up by previous shelling. We were practically finished. Only a handful of us yet remained. Most of us lay there, black bundles, never to move again.

As for me, I was at my last gasp. I began vomiting into my own face – wrenched the gas-mask off – and knew no more.

About seven next morning Hitler was despatched with an order to our rear. Dropping with exhaustion, he staggered off. It was useless by now to count up how many days and nights we'd gone without sleep. His eyes were burning, sore, and smarting – gas, he supposed, or dog weariness. Anyhow, they rapidly got worse. The pain was hideous; presently he could see nothing but a fog. Stumbling, and falling over and over again, he made what feeble progress he could. Every time he went down crash, it was harder and harder to drag himself to his feet again. The last time, all his failing strength was exhausted in freeing himself from the mask... he could struggle up no more... his eyes were searing coals... Hitler collapsed. Goodness only knows how long it was before the stretcher bearers found him. They brought him in, though, at last, and took him to the dressing-station. This was on the morning 14 October, 1918 – just before the end.'

Even Lucky Linzer couldn't hope to outrun the carnage of the Great War. On 13 October 1918, his store of good fortune had finally run out and, less than a month before the Armistice, Hitler was again admitted to a field hospital. He had been temporarily blinded, not by chlorine gas as Westenkirchner believed, but by a British mustard gas attack. During the night of 13-14 October, the British had opened an attack with gas on the front south of Ypres using a new strain of the yellow gas whose effect was unknown. Hitler was destined to experience it that very night. On that low hill south of Werwick, in the evening of 13 October, Hitler and his comrades were subjected for several hours to a heavy bombardment with gas bombs, which continued throughout the night with more or less intensity. About midnight a number of Hitler's comrades were put out of action, some forever. Towards morning Hitler also began to feel pain. It increased with every quarter of an hour; and by about 7 A.M. his eyes were scorching and he staggered back and delivered the last dispatch he was destined to carry in the Great War. The terrible effect of the gas continued and Hitler vividly recalled its effects:

'*A few hours later my eyes were like glowing coals and all was darkness around me. I was sent into hospital at Pasewalk in Pomerania, and there it was that I had to hear of the Revolution.*'

In the hospital at Pasewalk Hitler, to his intense relief, was soon beginning to experience signs that he might recover his sight. The burning pain in his eye-sockets had become less severe. Gradually he was able to distinguish the general outlines of his immediate surroundings and the first glimmers of hope arose that he would regain his sight.

Hitler had some reason for optimism in his private world, however the wider pictured remained gloomy and the spectre of revolution now loomed over Germany. For some time there had been something in the air which only Hitler failed to recognise as the indefinable hint of insurrection. Although Hitler did not recognise the signs, Germany's strategic situation was becoming unbearable, the tensions were obvious, widespread industrial unrest had led to a munitions strike similar to the spring of 1918, rationing was growing even more strict and something was bound to give within the next few weeks. Rumours were constantly coming from the Navy, which was now in a state of ferment. Hitler later recalled how his fellow patients in the hospital were constantly talking abut the end of the war and hoping that this was not far off. No doubt this would have triggered one of Hitler's trademark harangues against defeatism especially when faced with three Jewish soldiers who were suffering from venereal disease which was considered a self inflicted wound:

'*A few Jew-boys were the leaders in that combat for the 'Liberty, Beauty, and Dignity' of our National Being. Not one of them had seen active service at the front. Through the medium of a hospital for venereal diseases these three Orientals had been sent back home. Now their red rags were being hoisted here.*'

Throughout November 1918, the general tension increased. Finally Hitler recalled how one day in November 1918, the outside world suddenly broke in upon the closed world of the hospital. Sailors came in motor-lorries and called on the patients to rise in revolt. Hitler scornfully recalled those startling events as he first thought that this outbreak of high treason was only a local affair. He recalls how he tried to enforce this belief among his wounded comrades. Hitler's Bavarian hospital mates, in particular, were readily responsive. Their inclinations were not revolutionary and Hitler deemed that their loyalty to the Bavarian House of Wittelsbach was stronger than the will of 'a few Jews'. Hitler clung to the belief that this was merely an isolated revolt in the Navy which would suppressed within the next few days.

Hitler was in for a shock. Within the next few days came the most astounding information that was in reality a general revolution. In addition to this, from the front came the shameful news that the army wished to capitulate. On 10 November 1918, the local pastor visited the hospital for the purpose of delivering a short address. It was in this way they came to know the whole shocking story. Kaiser Wilhelm II had abdicated and fled to the Netherlands. A republic had been hastily proclaimed on 8 November 1918, by Social Democrat Philipp Scheidemann in order to prevent a Communist revolution. Hitler was in a fever of excitement as he listened to the address:

'The reverend old gentleman informed the patients that the Prussian House of Hohenzollern would no longer wear the Imperial Crown, that the Fatherland had become a Republic.'

Hitler recalled how a feeling of profound dismay fell on the people in that assembly, and how he broke down completely with the realisation that the war was lost, he said, and Germany was now at the mercy of the victors. Hitler was made painfully aware of the fact that his beloved Fatherland would have to bear heavy burdens in the future. Germany was nonetheless forced to accept the terms of the Armistice and trust to the magnanimity of her former enemies. It was impossible for Hitler to stay and listen to any more of the address. He recalled how darkness surrounded him as he staggered and stumbled back to his ward and buried his aching head between the blankets and pillow. Hitler had not cried since the day that he stood beside his mother's grave but, now, we are told, he wept floods of tears.

'During all those long years of war, when Death claimed many a true friend and comrade from our ranks, to me it would have

appeared sinful to have uttered a word of complaint. Did they not die for Germany? And, finally, almost in the last few days of that titanic struggle, when the waves of poison gas enveloped me and began to penetrate my eyes, the thought of becoming permanently blind unnerved me; but the voice of conscience cried out immediately: Poor miserable fellow, will you start howling when there are thousands of others whose lot is a hundred times worse than yours? And so I accepted my misfortune in silence, realizing that this was the only thing to be done and that personal suffering was nothing when compared with the misfortune of one's country.'

Heinz A. Heinz, writing in 'Germany's Hitler', took up the narrative of Hitler's journey into despair and it provides an interesting glimpse into the histrionic style of Nazi propaganda in the thirties.

'It was in hospital at Pasewalk, in Pomerania, that Adolf Hitler heard of the Revolution, the flight of the Kaiser, and the collapse of the Fatherland.'

His description so closely follows the passage in *'Mein Kampf'* that we must assume Heinz refreshed his memory from Hitler's account:

'He had not wept since he stood by his mother's graveside. Now, however, with the gas still "ravening" on his eyes, and threatening him with their total loss, he weeps again. He stumbles away, falls down on his hospital cot, and cries out in anguish all the sacrifice had been in vain! Would not the graves open of all the hundreds and thousands of those who had left the Fatherland full of high belief and hope, never to return…'

Hitler now had to face the unpalatable truth that it had all been in vain. In his anger and despair he instantly formed the view that, what he described as, a gang of despicable criminals, had somehow gotten their hands on the Fatherland. This was to become known as the *Dolchstoss legende*, the belief that the Imperial German Army had been betrayed and had suffered a stab in the back which delivered Germany into the hands of her enemies.

Inevitably Hitler came to lay the blame at the door of the Jews and in a chillingly prophetic passage from *'Mein Kampf'* he outlined what his own solution would have been; it involved the massacre of fifteen thousand Jews by poison gas. It is sobering to realize that within sixteen years from the date on which this passage was written, under the direction of Heinrich Himmler, the actions which Hitler advocated so fervently were being turned into reality on an unimaginable scale:

'At the beginning of the War, or even during the War, if twelve or fifteen thousand of these Jews who were corrupting the nation had been forced to submit to poison-gas, just as hundreds of thousands of our best German workers from every social stratum and from every trade and calling had to face it in the field, then the millions of sacrifices made at the front would not have been in vain. On the contrary: If twelve thousand of these malefactors had been eliminated in proper time probably the lives of a million decent men, who would be of value to Germany in the future, might have been saved.'

It was not just the Jews who bore the brunt of Hitler's pent up wrath. In the pages of *'Mein Kampf'* Hitler reacted with typical psychotic venom to what he imagined was a fully fledged press conspiracy. The more Hitler tried to glean some definite information of the terrible events that had happened, the more his head became aflamed with rage and shame. The following days were terrible for a zealot like Hitler to bear, and during the long nights in Pasewalk his hatred increased for those he perceived to be the originators of the dastardly crime. Finally, the grand scheme of events became clear to Hitler and he reasoned that Emperor William II was the first German Emperor to offer the hand of friendship to the Marxist leaders, not suspecting, of course, that they were scoundrels without any sense of honour. Hitler envisaged that while they held the Imperial hand in theirs, the other hand was already feeling for the dagger. From that conclusion he moved swiftly on to a new and ominous conclusion. 'There is no such thing as coming to an understanding with the Jews. It must be the hard-and-fast 'Either-Or'.' From that moment onwards it seemed that Hitler decided that he would take up a political career.

Hitler's role in the creation of the Nazi party is well documented and is outside the scope of the present volume, but the story of Ignatz

Westenkirchner is less well known and his life after the Great War makes an interesting epilogue which touches upon the misery endured by many former soldiers during the postwar years of depression and paints a gritty counterpoint to Hitler's glittering rise to fame. His saga was related to Heinz A. Heinz who recorded the story for posterity:

"After that hideous night in Flanders in 1918 when he got gassed," said Westenkirchner, "I never bumped up against Hitler again until we ran across each other here in Munich, in the Sterneckerbrau. That was in the beginning of 1920. I belonged to the Green Police just then – I'd enrolled just after the great bust-up of the Revolution. We old comrades of the List Regiment foregathered at the Sterneckerbrau: Hitler used the place regularly. But in the March of that year I left the police and went home to my own town not far from Munich. Hitler was against it. He did all he could to persuade me to stop where I was. He said he was dead certain he would himself succeed over his own plans and political ideas, and that if I'd only hang on, he would give an eye to me as well. But I wasn't to be turned aside. After a year or two I got into difficulties – couldn't make a go of it – and found myself among the workless and the unemployed. I decided to clear out, family and all, to the U.S.A. At first it wasn't too bad, but things were none too cheerful even over there, and by the beginning of '33 I was as poorly fixed as ever, and out of a job. Anyhow I'd kept up with some of the old List comrades and in the autumn of that year one of them sent me word that Hitler'd like a line from me from time to time. I wrote straightaway to him in Berlin, but got no answer. So I had another shot at it and wrote to his sister at Obersalzberg. And she sent him my news. Not particularly good news, mine! Then, suddenly, one day at Reading in Pennsylvania, where I happened to be living, I got a telegram from a German shipping office informing me that the Führer, Adolf Hitler himself, had defrayed all the expenses of my return with my family to Germany, and that I could set out to come home just as soon as I liked. Overjoyed, the whole lot of us set sail early in December. We reached Hamburg and went on straight to Berlin. I just longed to see my old comrade again – Reichskanzler

though he be – and thank him from the bottom of my grateful heart for having come so splendidly to our rescue.

I got to the Chancellery and found him just the same as ever. His greeting was as warm as man could wish. He spoke, too, in our local dialect, 'Jolly glad to see you back, Westenkirchner! Suppose you just sit yourself down and tell me all the yarn.' We had a good old talk, as you may imagine, and he wound up by saying he'd got a job for me on the party paper here in Munich. Wouldn't hear a word of thanks. I just tried to tell him what I felt and what I thought of him, but laughingly he waived it all aside, 'Take it as read! Take it as read,!' he said, and so I had to.'

- CHAPTER 13 -

HITLER - THE POLITICIAN

A MAELSTROM OF political strife and turmoil marked the immediate aftermath of the Great War in Germany as multiplicity of parties and competing ideas contested for power. Matters were further confused by the federal structure of the new order which produced a chequerboard pattern of regional political allegiances making any form of national cohesion extremely difficult.

In Bavaria the political foment had succeeded in producing a revolutionary government by workers council the *Räterrepublic* (The Council's Republic). It was this development which was to provide the first fatal steps towards the National Socialist era. Towards the end of November 1918, Hitler returned to Munich and reported to the depot of his beloved List regiment only to find it was now in the hands of the 'Soldiers' Councils'. Hitler would no doubt have been incensed to discover the man behind the Munich foment was a Jew named Kurt Eisner.

He had joined the Independent Social Democratic Party of Germany in 1917, at the height of the war and was convicted of treason in 1918, for his role in inciting a strike of munitions workers. He spent nine months in Cell 70 of Stadelheim Prison after which he was released during the General Amnesty in October of that year. Following his release from prison, Eisner organised the revolution that overthrew the Witelsbach monarchy in Bavaria. On 8 November 1918, while Hitler was still in hospital, it was Eisner who declared Bavaria to be a free state and republic, becoming the first republican premier of Bavaria. Hitler was later able to point to Eisner as an example of Jewish perfidy as Kurt Eisner was not his real name. He was in fact born in Berlin on 14 May 1857, of Jewish parents and his name (which was never officially changed) was Kamonowsky. Eisner was the name he took when he began to write and was also name he adopted in his work for Social-Democracy.[27]

Kurt Eisner was diametrically opposed to Hitler in every conceivable way, he was always an open Republican as well as a Social-Democrat and fought actively for political democracy. Under his alias he became editor of the left wing magazine *'Vorwärts'* after the death of Wilhelm Liebknecht in 1900, but was subsequently called upon to resign from that position. After his withdrawal from *'Vorwärts'*, his activities were confined in the main to Bavaria, though he toured other parts of Germany.

Like Hitler, he was in Munich when the war broke out. At first he leaned towards the view of the Majority and was in support of the war. He soon took the side of the Minority, and became a leading figure among the Independents. Once convinced that the German Government bore the main responsibility for the outbreak of war, Kurt Eisner voiced his opinions in speeches and in print. He was condemned for his activities and suffered imprisonment, from which he was released on 7 November 1918. He immediately returned to Bavaria and threw his heart and soul into the German Revolution, his vigour was one of the factors which forced the immediate abdication of the Wittelsbach dynasty from the throne of Bavaria. This was after the great meeting that he addressed in Munich's Theresienstrasse on 10 November 1918. Appointed as Premier of Bavaria after the Revolution, his few months of power were, for him, one incessant struggle against the reactionaries on the one hand, and Majority Social-Democratic leaders, whom he thoroughly distrusted, on the other. Whilst not going so far towards Soviet politics as the *Spartacists*, nevertheless he wanted a Revolutionary Government composed of Socialists who knew their own minds, and who would pursue a thoroughgoing Socialist policy so as to remove the old regime as quickly as possible. The results of the election, both for the National Assembly and the Bavarian Constituent Assembly therefore

---

27. 'Justice', the Weekly Newspaper of British Journal of Social Democracy – 27 February 1919.

came as a bitter disappointment revealing the political weakness of the Independents.

Eisner embodied for Hitler the idea of the *Dolchstoss* as Eisner was very open in expressing his opinion that Germany had a heavy guilt for bringing about the Great War and had to bear the burden of war reparations in order to repay her debts to the international community and go forward on the way to Socialism. Eisner declared that it was impossible to shake hands with other countries until responsibility for the war had been clearly established, and accordingly he demanded the publication of state documents despite the fact that he knew they would add substantially to Germany's burden; in response to the resultant criticism Eisner simply stated that the world must have the truth at all costs.

Understandably the new Eisner administration was anathema to Hitler and he resolved to leave the uncongenial atmosphere of Munich as soon as he possibly could. In company with his faithful war-comrade, Ernst Schmidt, Hitler arranged to be transferred to the more politically congenial atmosphere of the prisoner of war camp for Russian soldiers at Traunstein which was then in the process of being decommissioned. He remained there until the camp was broken up in 1919.

Eisner's Independent Social Democrats were narrowly defeated in the January 1919 election by the Bavarian People's Party and events took a turn for the worse when Kurt Eisner was assassinated in Munich by German nationalist Anton Graf von Arco auf Valley who shot Eisner in the back on 21 February 1919. Ironically Eisner was actually on his way to present his resignation to the Bavarian parliament. Eisner's assassination had the opposite effect to that intended by Graf von Arco auf Valley and precipitated the left wing revolt which directly resulted in the establishment of the Bavarian Soviet Republic following the flight of the elected Bavarian government.

In March 1919, Hitler was back again in Munich. A temporary military *organisation* existed under a *Reichstag* law of 6 March 1919. However, the situation there was confused and explosive. For many it looked as if there might be a further extension of the Red revolution.

Eisner's death served only to hasten this development and finally led to the dictatorship of the Councils or as Hitler perceived it, a 'Jewish hegemony', which turned out to be transitory but which was the original aim of those who had contrived the revolution.

At this juncture Hitler claims to have formed innumerable plans only to be thwarted as every project had to give way before the hard fact that he was quite unknown and wielded no political power of any kind. He lacked even the first pre-requisite necessary for effective action and could not decide to join any of the parties then in existence.

As the new Soviet Revolution began to run its course in Munich it was clear that Corporal Hitler was a staunch and vocal opponent as a result of his widely known stance. In the early morning of 27 April 1919, Hitler was to have been arrested by order of the Central Council; but if the version as detailed in *'Mein Kampf'* is to be believed, the three soldiers who came to arrest him did not have the courage to face down Hitler and withdrew empty handed. Fortunately for Hitler the Red revolution soon faltered and there was to be no further attempt to arrest him. In early May 1919, Munich was retaken by the *Freikorps* and following an intense and bloody bout of street fighting which saw machine guns, flame throwers, artillery and even armoured cars deployed in the streets of Munich as power was finally wrested from the hands of the Soviets.

Otto Strasser was a member of the Nazi Party from 1925 onwards. Together with his brother Gregor, Strasser was to become a leading member of the party's left-wing faction. He later broke from the party due to disputes with the *'Hitlerite'* faction. Following the murder of his brother, Strasser was destined to become a fierce and unyielding critic of Hitler, he knew Hitler intimately and had by 1940, countless reasons to hate Hitler, but his 1940 account of Hitler's actions during the turbulent year of 1919 bear the stamp of truth. For his opponents such as Strasser, the fact that Hitler had not seen fit to join any of the *Freikorps* was a glaring omission. Hitler was obviously a man of action with conservative credentials who, lacking family commitments and a regular trade, evidently had the opportunity to serve in such an overtly German nationalist movement:

'The soldiers returned from the front. One-and-a-half million men were withdrawn from occupied Poland, and three hundred thousand officers and seven or eight hundred thousand non-commissioned officers led aimless and hopeless lives in Berlin and the other big cities of Germany. The heroes of the fighting in the Baltic, where Germany defended Finland against the Russians, returned under the leadership of von der Goltz, Captain Stenes and Lieutenant Rossbach. If there is anyone today still naive enough to believe in Adolf Hitler's good faith, at least in so far as the ideals of the German people are concerned, let him think of the sacrifices of the German soldiers in that struggle, and then let him consider the Führer's attitude in the Russo-Finnish conflict. Moreover, Hitler failed to participate in the spontaneous battles that the Germans fought after the War, for their lives and for their honour. He was not a member of the armed force led by General von Epp which overthrew the Red dictatorship of Kurt Eisner in 1919, nor was he among the men of von der Goltz. When bloodthirsty fighting broke out in Upper Silesia, where German Freikorps defended the frontiers of Germany against the Poles, Hitler, addressing a band of Austrian volunteers, tried his hardest to dissuade them from fighting. His eloquence failed to convince them or to restrain them, and he stayed at home, meditating the diabolical plan which, despite all his treachery and double-dealing, was to lead him to power.'

The most prosaic reason for the fact that Hitler did not join the *Freikorps* is more likely to have stemmed from the simple fact that he was determined to remain in the army and the army was not directly involved in the fighting. During the turbulent days in the immediate aftermath of the Great War he still lacked direction. He had not yet decided on a life in politics and he clung on to his place in the army as the only alternative to a life of a drifter. A few days after the liberation of Munich, Hitler was ordered to appear before the Inquiry Commission which had been set up in the 2nd Infantry Regiment for the purpose of surveying revolutionary activities. Hitler was accepted as being useful as someone who could plausibly infiltrate extremist political parties and act as an informant. This was to be Hitler's first incursion into the political field.

While the fighting was still going on in Bavaria, the new National Assembly met at Weimar and sat from 6 February to 11 August 1919. The assembly drew up a new constitution for a new Germany which was soon named the Weimar Republic. The new constitution created a strong central government controlling all taxation and military forces; its laws overrode those of the seventeen *Länder*, or states. The states were still represented in the *Reichsrat*, but this chamber was subordinate to the *Reichstag*, to which alone the chancellor and his government were responsible. In the wake of the Great War, the German army was strictly limited in line with the draconian provisions of the Treaty of Versailles signed by the Weimar politicians on 28 June 1919. The army of the new Weimar Republic was to total no more than 100,000 men, including 4,000 officers. Chancellor Ebert called upon *Generalleutnant* Hans von Seeckt to head a commission to study the matter and submit recommendations on which the organisation of the postwar force could be based.

On being accepted for his new role Hitler received orders to attend a course of lectures which were being given to members of the army. This course was designed to inculcate certain fundamental principles on which the soldier could base his political ideas. For Hitler the advantage of this organisation was that it gave him the chance of meeting fellow soldiers who held similar values. Hitler and his confidants were by now firmly convinced that Germany could not be saved from what they perceived to be imminent disaster by those who had participated in the November treachery; that is to say, the Centre and the Social-Democrats. Hitler was of the view that bourgeois championed *völkisch* and nationalists groups could not make much headway as they lacked popular support. Hitler and his small circle therefore discussed the prospect of forming a new party which would appeal to the mass of the people and chose the name 'Social-Revolutionary Party' because the social principles of the new organisation were indeed revolutionary. It is typical of Hitler to look to the past for inspiration. Encouragement was drawn from the great statesmen who were also great reformers. Frederick the Great was the key figure for Hitler and despite his own Roman Catholicism, Hitler also revered Martin Luther. Rather predictably he also cited the influence of Richard Wagner.

Gottfried Feder lectured Hitler and his comrades on 'The Abolition of the Interest-Servitude', and Hitler understood immediately that here was a 'truth' which he considered to be of transcendental importance for the future of the German people. The absolute separation of stock-exchange capital from the economic life of the nation would make it possible to oppose the process of internationalization in German business without at the same time attacking capital. In Feder's speech, Hitler found an effective rallying-cry for his coming struggle. Thus the judgement arrived at by Gottfried Feder convinced Hitler to make a fundamental study of a question with which he had hitherto not been very familiar. Hitler began to study the substance and purpose of the life-work of the Jew, Karl Marx.

Besides the study of economics the Jewish question also raised its ugly head. One day Hitler put his name down as wishing to take part in the discussion. Another of the participants spoke on behalf of the Jews and entered into a lengthy defence of them. This aroused Hitler's heated opposition. With the prevailing culture of anti-Semitism, an overwhelming number of those who attended the lecture course supported Hitler's views. The consequence of his popular victory in debate was that, a few days later, Hitler was assigned to a regiment then stationed at Munich and given a position there as 'instruction officer'.

Hitler recalled that at that time the spirit of discipline was rather weak among those troops. The army was still suffering from the after-effects of the period when the Soldiers' Councils were in control and real military discipline and obedience had to be re-introduced in place of 'voluntary obedience', a term which had been used to express the ideal of military discipline under Kurt Eisner's short lived regime.

Hitler was much more happy with the new government which had been introduced following the victory won by the *Freikorps*. He was in favour of the idea that the soldiers of the new Weimar Republic were once again to be taught to think and feel in a national and patriotic way. Hitler was naturally delighted to be given this brief and took up his work with the greatest delight and devotion.

It was now that Hitler's gifts as an orator came to the fore. In the course of eight years he had progressed from the speeches addressed to Kubizek as the lone member of his audience to impromptu speeches addressed to small groups in the men's hostels and trenches, but that was hitherto the limit of his political experience. Hitler was, for the first time in his life, presented with the opportunity of speaking before large audiences. He rose effortlessly to the challenge and in doing so he was able to confirm to himself something that he had always suspected, namely, that he had a genuine talent for public speaking. With practice his voice soon strengthened as he became accustomed to making himself heard and understood in all parts of the small halls where the soldiers assembled.

No task could possibly have been more pleasing to Hitler than this one and there can be little doubt that his talks were successful in converting the bulk of his audiences to the cause of pan-German nationalism. Hitler claims to have 'nationalised' these troops and by so doing helped to restore general discipline. Here again Hitler made the acquaintance of several like minded comrades whose thoughts ran along the same lines as his own and who later became members of the first group out of which the National Socialist new movement developed. According to his 'Mein Kampf' account it was at this time that Hitler became convinced the purpose of his life was to 'save Germany.'

On returning to his regiment in Munich, Hitler had emerged into a very different army from the old Imperial war machine. The negotiations surrounding the treaty of Versailles were concluded by the signatures of the German Delegation on the document dated 28 June 1919. There was little else the delegates could have done, the allies held all the aces in the negotiations and ruthlessly exploited their position of strength. In consequence, the terms of the peace treaty were ridiculously harsh. In addition to humiliating territorial losses, Germany learned formally the fact that she was to be made responsible for the war. By the insertion of Article 231 in the treaty Germany and its allies were unequivocally held responsible for all losses and damages suffered by the Allies. On 27 April 1921, the Allied Reparations Commission finally fixed the total to be paid by Germany at 132 billion gold Marks, an enormous sum for a stagnant economy wracked by the legacy of four years of war. In order to prevent a rapid programme of clandestine military training the Allies had decreed non-commissioned officers and privates were to be enlisted for 12 years, officers were to be required to serve for a period of 25 years. A further stipulation by the Allies meant that no more than five per cent of the officers and enlisted personnel could be released yearly. This ensured that opportunities to gain military experience and knowledge was strictly limited. One other humiliating provision was that the detailed organisation and proposed armament of all German units formed had first to be approved by the Allies. The Navy was authorised 15,000 men, including 1,500 officers. Six obsolete battleships, 6 light cruisers, 12 destroyers, and 12 torpedo boats were permitted the fleet, with 2 battleships, 2 cruisers, 4 destroyers, and 4 torpedo boats in reserve. The building of ships displacing over 10,000 tons was prohibited. A further restriction limited naval guns to a maximum of 11 inches.

Arms and munitions industries and factories producing military equipment were reduced in number to the minimum essential to maintain authorised stocks. No troops were to be permitted in a demilitarised zone extending 50 kilometres (approximately 31 miles) east of the Rhine. Allied control commissions were to be allowed to inspect factories and the Army and Navy for compliance with the treaty and the Reich defence laws enacted in conformity with its provisions.

The harsh conditions of the Versailles treaty led to the creation of a large number of well armed and well trained paramilitary units – these were the *Freikorps*. Initially the *Freikorps* served as an armed auxiliary force assisting the hard pressed army in Germany itself to deal with armed insurrection by leftist elements. In early 1919, the strength of the *Reichswehr*, the regular army, had declined rapidly from its war time establishment and was estimated at 350,000. There were in addition more than 250,000 men enlisted in the various *Freikorps*. Under the terms of the Versailles Treaty, Germany was required to reduce its armed forces to a maximum of 100,000. *Freikorps* units were therefore expected to be disbanded. The infighting which followed led directly to the Kapp Putsch of 1920. In March 1920, orders were issued for the disbandment of the *Marinebrigade* Ehrhardt. Its leaders were determined to resist dissolution and appealed to General Walther von Lüttwitz, commander of the Berlin *Reichswehr*, for support. Lüttwitz, an organiser of *Freikorps* units in the wake of World War I, and a fervent monarchist, responded by calling on President Friedrich Ebert and Defence Minister Gustav Noske to stop the whole programme of troop reductions. When Ebert refused, Lüttwitz ordered the *Marinebrigade* Ehrhardt to march on Berlin. It occupied the capital on 13 March. Lüttwitz, therefore, was the driving force behind the 1920 *putsch*, even though its nominal leader was Wolfgang Kapp, a 62-year-old East Prussian civil servant and fervent nationalist.

At this point Noske called upon the regular army to suppress the *putsch*. He encountered a blank refusal. The *Chief der Heeresleitung* General Hans von Seeckt, one of the *Reichswehr's* senior commanders, told him: '*Reichswehr does not fire on Reichswehr.*' The government, forced to abandon Berlin, moved to Dresden, where they hoped to get support from *Generalmajor* Maercker. When they realised that Maercker did not want to take a clear stance they moved further to Stuttgart. The Cabinet issued a proclamation calling on Germany's workers to defeat the *putsch* by means of a general strike. The strike call received massive support and although the resultant struggle claimed numerous victims among workers the country was effectively paralysed and the *putsch* soon collapsed. Faced with the state of national paralysis Kapp and Lüttwitz, now totally unable to govern, gave up the fight and fled to Sweden.

There were two main reasons why the Weimar Republic survived in 1920. Firstly, the working classes rallied to its defence. Secondly, most of the leading *Freikorps* commanders refused to join the *putsch*, perhaps because most had formed the view that it was premature.

Otto Strasser was a contemporary of Hitler's who was to later become a member of the Nazi party. In his 1940 memoir Strasser described how he had fought against the *Friekorps* forces supporting the Kapp Putsch:

'Six months earlier the celebrated Kapp Putsch had taken place in Berlin, on which occasion I had fought boldly for the Weimar Republic. I had led three squads of Berlin working-men against Colonel Erhardt's Brigade and General Luttwitz's Regiment. Erhardt and Luttwitz had wished to seize power and set up a reactionary government. Militarily our forces (we were known as the 'Reds' to distinguish us from the reactionary 'Whites') had been defeated. Erhardt had marched triumphantly into Berlin by the Brandenburg Gate, and, with the capital at his feet, had said to Kapp, former governor of East Prussia and the civil leader of the insurrection, 'I have put your foot in the stirrup, and now it is up to you to govern.'

The legal Government had fled to Stuttgart, and for three days the putschists were able to enjoy their ephemeral victory. A general strike was immediately declared and was followed by rioting in the streets. Bloody fighting took place in the neighbourhood of Wesel in the Ruhr. General Luttwitz, Colonel Erhardt and Governor Kapp fled to Sweden. The Socialists, of whom I was one, declared themselves ready to lay down their arms, subject to terms, which included the purging of the Army and the socialization of heavy industry, and they signed the Bielefeld Agreement with the Minister, Herr Severing. The Communists, however, did not lay down their arms, and carried on a bloodthirsty struggle. In order to suppress them the Weimar Government did not hesitate to use the decapitated and defeated troops of Luttwitz and Erhardt. As soon as the Communists were crushed the treacherous Government repudiated its promises to the Socialists and announced that Severing had no authority to sign any agreement with us.

It was as a consequence of this shocking state of affairs that I left the Socialist Party. I was disheartened by the outcome of events in Germany, and felt like a ship without a rudder. I was a young student of law and economics, a Left Wing student leader, and a leader of ex-soldier students.

However the military life had become addictive the *Freikorps* also fought outside of the borders of the Republic. On the fringes of the former Second Reich where territory had been ceded to Poland the treatment of ethnic Germans was harsh and the events of the Upper Silesian crisis of 1921 were to have wider consequences in the immediate post war period. The forces of law and order in the new Polish state, it appeared to many ethnic Germans, turned a blind eye to the widespread brutalities which occurred as old scores were settled and a new order introduced. This unhappy situation eventually resulted in the 1921 crisis in Upper Silesia. The hastily formed *Freikorps* unit the *Selbschtuz Oberschleisen* took the field against the regular Polish army and managed to hold their own in the early fighting.

Fettered by the Treaty of Versailles and tarnished by the spectre of defeat the *Reichswehr* (the regular German army) could not act in support of the ethnic Germans, but one possible solution did present itself in the form of the *Freikorps*. These nationalist paramilitary units were drawn from the ranks of battle hardened World War One veterans. They had successfully countered the communists in Germany during 1920, and would prove highly efficient against the Bavarian Soviet Republic in 1921, and were pledged to defending the interests of the Greater German Reich, as they themselves interpreted those interests. Three battalions of these tough auxiliaries in the form of the *Oberland Freikorps* were sent to the aid of the local *Selbstschutz Oberscleisen* which, in 1921, was engaged in fighting the Polish regular army. The very existence of the *Freikorps*, which was clearly an auxiliary military force, was highly questionable under the terms of the Versailles treaty and unwelcome questions were immediately raised by the Allies. Oblivious to the political machinations the *Freikorps* got on with the job in hand. These were ideologically motivated warriors who were hard-nosed veterans of the Great War. Their whole *raison d'être* was to fight in the cause of German interests and honour. A notable victory was gained by these irregular but highly effective troop over Polish regular forces at Annaberg in May 1921. As the shock news of the Polish defeat spread political pressure mounted and the first inklings of that pressure came in the form of a threat from

France that they would withdraw their peace keeping forces from Silesia, leaving the ethnic Germans totally at the mercy of the Poles. Despite the effectiveness of their military contribution the political tide in Germany soon began to run against the activities of the *Freikorps* in Poland who were dismissed as 'gangs of thugs'. Nonetheless the *Freikorps* continued to fight on. Further victories in the field around Ratisbon eventually forced the Poles to bow to British pressure and evacuate Upper Silesia on 5 July 1921.

These gains were to prove in vain however. The obvious breach of the Versailles treaty was too great to ignore and this eventually forced the embarrassed Weimar Republic to order the withdrawal and disbandment of the *Freikorps*. This order was obeyed after a fashion although many weapons were buried rather than surrendered and a large portion of the *Freikorps* remained behind in Upper Silesia where, in anticipation of further trouble, they worked undercover posing as agricultural labourers and forestry workers. Despite heated German protests which received strong British support for Germany over what was obviously a reciprocal Polish breach of the terms of the Treaty of Versailles, the areas seized by the Poles by force from Germany were nevertheless incorporated into Poland.

On returning to Germany the *Freikorps* veterans loudly proclaimed that there had been a repeat of the *dolchstosslegende*, that they had been 'stabbed in the back' by the representatives of a state whose interests they had sought to protect. As these Great War veterans already considered themselves to have been betrayed once before, the wounds were beginning to run deep. An embittered sense of alienation and an overriding desire for revenge fuelled their nationalist ambitions which centered around a crusade to restore the lost honour and power of the Reich. Among the ranks of the departing *Freikorps* was the notorious Sepp Dietrich. From the evidence of the fact that he was awarded the Silesian Eagle First Class, a decoration which was only presented to veterans in recognition of six months field service in Silesia, it appears that Dietrich was one of those who remained behind in anticipation of further flare ups. He seems to have slipped back into Germany in October 1921, some three months after the disbandment of the *Freikorps*. Dietreich was one of many *Freikorps* veterans who felt he had a score to settle and he would return to Poland seventeen years later in more sinister form as a battalion commander in the ranks of the *SS Verfüngungstruppe* (SS Special Purpose Troops), the forerunners of the fearsome *Waffen SS*.

It was now the task of the new German Republic under President Ebert to create as effective an armed force as possible within the framework of the restrictions imposed by the Allies. Hitler was intent on remaining in the small postwar army, it was here that he had found real purpose to his life. Hitler was a political animal and having succeeded in being appointed to the Intelligence/Propaganda section he continued with his political training. His activities increasingly involved making speeches to the troops advocating German nationalism and anti-left wing activities. He also acted as an army informer, spying on small political parties. One of these was a tiny group known as the *Deutsche Arbeiter-Partei* (DAP) (the German Workers' Party). The DAP was founded in Munich in the hotel 'Fürstenfelder Hof' on 5 January 1919 by Anton Drexler, a member of the occultist Thule Society. The party had developed out of the *'Freien Arbeiterausschuss für einen guten Frieden'* (Free Workers' Committee for a good Peace) which Drexler had also founded and led. Its first members were mostly colleagues of Drexler's from the Munich rail depot. Drexler was encouraged to found the DAP by his mentor, Dr. Paul Tafel, a leader of the *Alldeutscher Verband* (the All Germany Union), a director of the *Maschinenfabrik Augsburg-Nürnberg*, and a member of the Thule Society and his wish was for a party which was both in touch with the masses and nationalist, unlike the middle class parties. The initial membership was about forty people.

On 24 March 1919, Karl Harrer, a sports journalist and also a member of the Thule Society, joined the DAP. His ambition was to increase the influence of the Thule Society over the DAP's activities, and the party name was at one point changed to the 'Political Workers' Circle'. The membership remained as scarce as the original list and the name was reinstated but meetings were still held in the small local beer houses.

Hitler had by now received a direct order from his superiors to investigate the nature of this tiny association which was apparently political and potentially left leaning. Hitler soon learned that the DAP was to hold a meeting at which Gottfried Feder would speak. Hitler was ordered to attend this meeting and report on the situation.

The intense spirit of suspicion with which the army authorities then regarded political parties can be very well understood. The revolution had granted the soldiers the right to take an active part in politics and many availed themselves of this right. Soon however, the Centre and the Social-Democratic parties sensed that the sympathies of the soldiers were skewed to the right and towards the nationalist movement in particular, and steps were later taken to withdraw from the army the right to vote and eventually to forbid it all political activity of any description.

In the pages of 'Mein Kampf' Hitler wrote a detailed account of that meeting and tells how when he arrived at the guest room of the former Sternecker Brewery he found approximately 20-25 people present, most of them belonging to the working classes. The theme of Feder's lecture was already familiar to Hitler as he had heard it in the army lecture course and could therefore concentrate his attention on studying the society itself. The impression it made upon Hitler was neither good nor bad. He felt that here was just another one of these many new societies which were being formed at that time. Hitler recorded with displeasure how 'in those days' it seemed as if everybody felt called upon to found a new Party whenever he felt displeased with the course of events and had lost confidence in all the parties already existing.

Hitler's initial opinion of the DAP was not very different after he had listened to their proceedings for about two hours. He was glad when Feder's all too familiar speech finally came to a close. He felt he had observed enough and was just about to leave when it was announced that anybody who wished was free to open a discussion. Thereupon, Hitler decided to remain. It was to prove an ill fated choice which changed the course of human history. The discussion seemed to proceed without anything of vital importance being mentioned, when there suddenly commenced to speak a man whom Hitler facetiously described as a 'professor'. According to Hitler the man opened by throwing doubt on the accuracy of what Feder had said, and then, after Feder had replied very effectively, the 'professor' suddenly took up his position on what he called 'the basis of facts', but before this he recommended the young party most urgently to introduce the secession of Bavaria from Prussia as one of the leading proposals in its programme. Hitler recalled how, in the most self-assured way, this man kept on insisting that German-Austria would join Bavaria and that the peace would then function much better. At this juncture Hitler felt bound to ask for permission to speak and to give the learned gentleman the benefit of his pent up opinions. The result, according to Hitler's self laudatory account, was that the honourable gentleman who had last spoken slipped out of the place, 'like a whipped cur', without uttering a sound. While Hitler was speaking he claims to have noticed that the audience listened with an expression of surprise on their faces. When Hitler was just about to say good-night to the assembly and to leave, Anton Drexler came after him quickly and introduced himself. Hitler did not grasp the name correctly; but Drexler placed a little book in Hitler's hand, which was obviously a political pamphlet. Hitler recalled how Drexler had asked him very earnestly to read it. This innocuous exchange was to prove one of the turning points of the 20th Century.

Hitler was initially quite pleased to have Drexler's pamphlet because in this way, he could now produce a report on this association without having to attend its tiresome meetings. Moreover, Drexler clearly had the appearance of a workman, and therefore made a good impression on Hitler who admired artisans. Nonetheless Hitler simply turned and left the hall without giving Drexler the assurance he sought.

At the time he met Drexler, Hitler tells us he was living in one of the barracks of the 2nd Infantry Regiment. He had a little room which still bore the unmistakable traces of the revolution. During the day he was mostly out at the quarters of Light Infantry No. 41 or else attending meetings or lectures, held at some other branch of the army. Hitler spent only the night at the quarters where he lodged. Since Hitler usually woke up about 5 A.M. every morning he had gotten into the habit of amusing himself with watching the little mice which played around in his small room. Hitler was in the habit of placing a few pieces of hard bread or crust on the floor and watch the little beasts playing around and enjoying themselves with these delicacies. Hitler tells us that he felt that he had suffered so many privations in his own life that he well knew what hunger was and could only too well picture to himself the pleasure these little creatures were experiencing.

It was for this reason that on the morning after the meeting, it so happened that about 5 A.M. Hitler lay fully awake in bed, watching the mice playing and vying with each other. He was not able to go to sleep again and he suddenly remembered Drexler's small pamphlet given to him at the meeting. In his little book Drexler the railway worker described how his mind had thrown off the shackles of the Marxist and trades-union phraseology, and had come back to nationalist ideals. He had entitled his little book describing his journey: 'My Political Awakening'. The pamphlet secured Hitler's attention the moment he began to read, and he read with interest to the end of the short tome. To Hitler, the process Drexler described was uncannily similar to that which Hitler had experienced ten years previously. Unconsciously Hitler's own experiences began to stir again in his mind. During that day Hitler's thoughts returned several times to what he had read, but despite being interested Hitler finally decided to give the matter no further attention.

A week or so later, however, Hitler received a postcard which informed him, to his astonishment, that he had been admitted into the DAP. Hitler was asked to answer this communication and to attend a meeting of the Party Committee on Wednesday next. Hitler was indignant: he had a highly developed sense of protocol and this unorthodox and rather presumptuous manner of recruiting members seems to have offended his pompous self importance. Hitler claims that he did not know whether to be angry or laugh at the invitation. Hitherto Hitler had not entertained the idea of entering a party already in existence but had hoped to found one of his own. Such an invitation as he now had received, appeared out of the question. Hitler was about to send a written reply rejecting the offer when his curiosity got the better of him, and he decided to attend the gathering at the date assigned. If nothing else he could give the presumptuous little crew a piece of his mind.

Wednesday arrived and Hitler duly attended the tavern in which the meeting was to take place. This was the Alte Rosenbad in the Herrnstrasse, into which apparently only an occasional guest wandered. Hitler had never before heard of this restaurant but this was not very surprising in the year 1919, when the bills of fare even at the larger restaurants were only very modest and scanty in their pretensions.

Hitler went through the badly-lighted guest-room, where not a single guest was to be seen, and searched for the door which led to the side room; and there came face-to-face with the 'Congress'. Under the dim light shed by a grimy gas-lamp Hitler could see four young people sitting around a table, one of them Hitler recognised as Drexler, the author of the pamphlet. He greeted Hitler cordially and welcomed him as a new member of the German Labour Party.

Hitler was taken somewhat aback on being informed that actually the National President of the Party had not yet come, so he decided that he would keep back his own exposition on good manners for the time being. Finally, the President appeared. Hitler noted that this was Karl Harrer, the man who had been chairman of the meeting held in the Sternecker Brewery, at which Feder had spoken. Hitler's curiosity was stimulated anew and he sat waiting for what was going to happen.

It was to prove a less than thrilling experience. The minutes of the previous meeting were read out and a vote of confidence in the secretary was passed. Then came the treasurer's report. The Society possessed a total fund of seven Marks and fifty pfennigs, whereupon the treasurer was assured that he had the confidence of the members. This was now inserted in the minutes. Then the real business of the evening began as the members considered letters of reply which had been written by the chairman to the three letters which had been received the previous week. The first was a reply to a letter received from Kiel, then to one from Düsseldorf and finally to one from Berlin. All three replies received the approval of all present. Then the incoming letters were read. Hitler grew weary as three letters were produced again; one from Berlin, one from Düsseldorf and one from Kiel. The reception of these letters seemed to cause great satisfaction among the members. This increasing bulk of correspondence was taken as the best and most obvious sign of the growing importance of the German Workers' Party. There then followed a long discussion of the replies which would be given to these newly-received letters.

Hitler acknowledged that it was all very awful. This was the worst kind of club life, and Hitler was supposed to become a member of such a club? The question of new members was next discussed: that is to say, the question of catching Hitler in what he described as 'the trap'. Hitler now began to ask questions and soon found that, apart from a few general principles, there was nothing of substance, no programme, no pamphlet, nothing at all in print, no card of membership, not even a party stamp, nothing but what Hitler described as 'obvious good faith and good intentions'.

He sensed the common feeling of frustration which had induced those few young people to join in what seemed such a doomed enterprise and like them he believed that the whole party system as it existed was not the kind of force that could restore the German nation or repair the damages that had been done to the German people by the treaty of Versailles. Hitler quickly read through the list of principles that formed the platform of the party. These principles were stated on typewritten sheets. Here again he found evidence of the spirit of longing and searching, but no sign whatever of a knowledge of the conflict that had to be fought. Hitler had experienced the feelings which inspired those people. He described it as the longing for a movement which could be more than a party.

When he returned to his room in the barracks that evening Hitler had still not formed a definite opinion on this association and was facing what he described as 'the most difficult problem of my life'. Should he join this party or refuse? From the side of the intellect alone, every consideration urged Hitler to refuse; but he was troubled. The more he tried to prove to himself how senseless this club was, in typical Hitler fashion, the more his inner feelings inclined him towards the contrary. During the following days, Hitler records that he was restless. He began to consider all the pros and cons of membership of the tiny party. After all, he reasoned he had long ago decided to take an active part in politics. The fact that he could do so only through a new movement was quite clear in his own mind; but Hitler had hitherto lacked the impulse to take concrete action.

In the wake of the invitation to join Hitler reasoned that Fate now seemed to supply the sign-post that pointed out the way. Hitler decided he could never have entered one of the big parties already in existence. This ludicrous little formation, with its handful of members, seemed to have the unique advantage of not yet being fossilised into an 'organisation' and still offered a chance to mould the outcome by real personal activity on the part of the individual. Hitler reasoned here it might still be possible to do some effective work; and, as the movement was still small, Hitler could all the easier give it the required shape. Here it was still possible to determine the character of the movement, the aims to be achieved and the road to be taken, which would have been impossible in the case of the big parties already in existence.

Hitler records that the longer he reflected on the problem, the more his opinion developed that just such a small movement would best serve as an instrument to prepare the way for the national resurgence, and that this could never be done by the political parliamentary parties which were too firmly attached to obsolete ideas or had an interest in supporting the new regime. What had to be proclaimed here was a new *Weltanshauung*, a world view, and not merely a new election cry.

It was, however, infinitely difficult to decide on putting the intention into practice. Hitler questioned the qualifications which he could bring to the accomplishment of such a task? The fact that he was poor and without resources could, in his opinion, be the easiest to bear. But the fact that he was utterly unknown raised a more difficult problem. Another difficulty arose from the fact that he had not gone through the regular school curriculum. Hitler was concerned that the so-called 'intellectuals' still looked down with infinite superciliousness on anyone who had not been through the prescribed schools. After two days of careful brooding and reflection Hitler became convinced that he must take the contemplated step. 'It was the most fateful decision of my life. No retreat was possible.'

Hitler had finally declared himself ready to accept the membership tendered him by DAP and received a provisional certificate of membership. Hitler claims that his card was numbered seven although this claim has been proven to be misleading. Hitler accepted the invitation, joining in late September 1919. At the time when Hitler joined the party, there were no membership numbers on cards. It was not until January 1920, that a system of numeration was introduced. Members were listed in order, Hitler received the number 555. In reality he had been the 54th member of the party, but the counting started at the number 501 in order to make the party appear larger. Hitler's claim in *'Mein Kampf'* that he was party member number seven and therefore one of the founding members, is widely dismissed; it is more likely that he was referring to the committee of which he was most probably the seventh member.

Regardless of his party number, Hitler had finally agreed to join the tiny *Deutsche Arbeiterpartei* (German Workers' Party), an extreme anti-communist, anti-Semitic right wing organisation. The DAP had its roots in the mystical *Thule-Gesellschaft* (Thule society). The connection between the DAP and the Thule can easily be overstated however and a highly imaginative mythology has grown up around the scope of the influence of the Thule within both the DAP and later the National Socialist Party. This semi-masonic *völkisch* group, one of hundreds in Germany at the time, was founded on 17 August 1918, by Rudolf von Sebottendorff. The original name of the Thule Society was *Studiengruppe für Germanisches Altertum* (Study Group for Germanic Antiquity), but it soon moved beyond this particular sphere and started to disseminate anti-republican and anti-Semitic propaganda. It is certainly true that in January 1919, Dietrich Eckart, a member of The Thule Society, was instrumental in the foundation of the DAP. Furthermore, the *'Münchener Beobachter'* (Munich Observer), owned by Sebottendorff, was the press organ of another small nationalist party and later became the *'Völkischer Beobachter'* (People's Observer). Friedrich Krohn, a Thule member, is often cited as the 1919 designer of the original version of the Nazi *Hakencruz* or swastika. Krohn, a dentist from Starnberg, had indeed submitted his design of a flag which had been used at the founding meeting of his own local party: a swastika against a black-white-red background. The swastika, for long time a symbol of the Teutonic Knights, had been in use by Lanz, the Thule Society and a number of *Freikorps* units. Hitler gives his own account of seeing the dentist's design for the first time:

> *'Actually, a dentist from Starnberg did deliver a design that was not bad after all, and, incidentally, was quite close to my own, having only the one fault that a swastika with curved legs was composed into a white disk.'*

During the initial phase of the DAP, Hitler soon recognised that the greatest handicap was the fact that none of the members were known and their names meant nothing, a fact which then seemed to some to make the chances of final success problematical to say the least. Hitler recalled that his most difficult task then was to make the members firmly believe that there was a tremendous future in store for the movement and to maintain this belief as a living faith. The dispiriting truth, according to Hitler's own account, was that at that time on occasion only six, seven or eight persons came to hear the speakers, hardly a promising platform from which to launch a mass movement.

Hitler acknowledged that the tiny group would have been very pleased to have been verbally attacked or even ridiculed. The most depressing fact was that nobody paid any attention to the party whatever. This utter lack of interest caused Hitler a great deal of embarrassment at that time. The initial picture was indeed quite depressing and discouraging. There was nothing, absolutely nothing at all. There was only the name of a party. Hitler recorded that the committee consisted of all of the party members and Hitler recalled in frustration how this small circle engaged in interminable discussions as to the form in which they might answer the letters which they were delighted to have received.

Needless to say, the public knew nothing of all this. In Munich, nobody knew of the existence of such a party, not even by name. Hitler recalled how every Wednesday, what was called a committee meeting was held in one of the cafés, and a debate was arranged for one evening each week. In the beginning, all the members of the movement were also members of the committee, therefore the same all too familiar faces always turned up at both meetings.

Hitler was the catalyst who urged that the first step that had to be taken was to extend the narrow limits of this small circle and get new members, but the principal necessity was to utilise all the means at their command for the purpose of making the movement known.

'We chose the following methods: We decided to hold a monthly meeting to which the public would be invited. Some of the invitations were typewritten, and some were written by hand. For the first few meetings we distributed them in the streets and delivered them personally at certain houses. Each one canvassed among his own acquaintances and tried to persuade some of them to attend our meetings. The result was lamentable.

I still remember once how I personally delivered eighty of these invitations and how we waited in the evening for the crowds to come. After waiting in vain for a whole hour the chairman finally had to open the meeting. Again there were only seven people present, the old familiar seven.'

Faced with the continuing failure to expand the movement, and under pressure from the increasingly forthright Adolf Hitler, the small party reluctantly changed its recruiting methods. Invitations were written with a typewriter in a Munich stationer's shop and then multi-graphed to produce a more imposing and impersonal effect.

The new system introduced by Hitler worked in a modest way and the result was that a few more people attended the next meeting. Hitler recalled how the number increased gradually from eleven to thirteen to seventeen, to twenty-three and finally to thirty-four.

The next major advance came when the committee collected some money within its own circle, each of the members making a small contribution, and in that way raised sufficient funds to be able to advertise one of their meetings in Rudolf von Sebottendorff's 'Munich Observer', which although owned by a founder member of the Thule Society and therefore sympathetic to right wing causes, was still an independent paper which required payment for its advertisements.

This radical new initiative proved to be an astonishing success. Hitler had chosen the Munich Hofbrauhaus as the meeting-place. The venue was a small hall and would accommodate scarcely more than 130 people. At the time even this modest ambition loomed like a mountain for the nervous Adolf Hitler:

'To me, however, the hall seemed enormous, and we were all trembling lest this tremendous edifice would remain partly empty on the night of the meeting.'

Hitler need not have been concerned, he was about to be given his first glimpse of the power of advertising. It was a lesson he would take to heart and turn into an art form over the next twelve years. In the hands of Hitler and Goebels, advertising on posters in the press was a fearsome weapon to be wielded by master practitioners. The first humble advertisement in the 'Munich Observer' was the forerunner of an edifice which would incorporate a Propaganda Ministry controlling and manipulating all forms of mass communication. The first humble meeting was advertised at the pooled expense of the committee. It was the first success for the German Workers' Party and Hitler enthusiastically recalled the events:

'At 7 P.M., 111 persons were present, and the meeting was opened. A Munich professor delivered the principal address, and I spoke after him. That was my first appearance in the role of public orator. The whole thing seemed a very daring adventure to Herr Harrer, who was then chairman of the party. He was a very decent fellow; but he had a conviction that, although I might have quite a number of good qualities, I certainly did not have a talent for public speaking. Even later he could not be persuaded to change his opinion. But he was mistaken. Twenty minutes had been allotted to me for my speech on this occasion, which might be looked upon as our first public meeting.'

Hitler talked for thirty minutes, and soon discovered that what he had always suspected since the days when he made his one man speeches to Kubizek was absolutely true. He could make a great impact as a political speaker. At the end of the thirty minutes it was quite clear that all the audience in the little hall had been profoundly impressed by Hitler. The enthusiasm aroused among them found its first concrete expression in the fact that Hitler's appeal to those present brought donations which amounted to three hundred Marks. This was a great relief for the party at the time, as finances were so meagre that it could not afford to have its party prospectus printed, or even leaflets. Now the fledgling movement possessed at least the nucleus of a fund from which they could pay the most urgent and pressing expenses. The series of meetings which they held in late 1919 enabled the DAP to collect the financial means that were necessary to have its first pamphlets, posters and programmes printed.

The success of this first larger meeting was also important from another point of view. Hitler had already begun to introduce some young and fresh members into the committee. During the long period of his military service he had come to know and trust a large number of former comrades whom he was now able to persuade to join the party. All of them were energetic and disciplined young men who, through their years of military service, had been imbued with the principle that with enough effort almost nothing was impossible. They believed Hitler's repeated exhortation that where there was a will there was a way.

The triumph of the first public meeting strengthened Hitler's own position. The members felt encouraged to arrange for a second meeting, on an even larger scale. Sometime in October 1919, the second larger meeting took place in the *Eberlbräu Keller*. The theme of Hitler's speech was 'Brest-Litowsk and Versailles'. There were four speakers. Hitler talked for almost an hour, and he later recalled that success was even more striking than at their first meeting. The number of people who attended had grown to more than 130. An attempt by left wingers to disturb the proceedings was immediately frustrated by Hitler's comrades and the violence loving Hitler proudly recorded the event:

'The potential disturbers were thrown down the stairs, bearing imprints of violence on their heads.'

A fortnight later, another meeting took place in the same hall. The number in attendance had now increased to more than 170, which meant that the room was fairly well filled. Hitler spoke again, and once more the success obtained was greater than at the previous meeting. It was at this juncture that Hitler proposed that a larger hall should be found. After searching around for some time the party settled on another hall at the opposite end of the town, in the *'Deutschen Reich'* in the Dachauer Strasse. The first meeting at this new rendezvous was not a great success and produced a smaller attendance than the previous meeting. There were just less than 140 present. The members of the committee began to be discouraged, and those who had always been sceptical were now convinced that this falling-off in the attendance was due to the fact that the party was holding the meetings at too short intervals. This was the signal for a series of lively discussions, in which Hitler put forth his own opinion that a city with 700,000 inhabitants ought to be able not only to stand just one meeting every fortnight, but rather ten meetings every week. He held that the party should not be discouraged by one comparative setback and that the tactics he had imposed on his colleagues were correct, and that sooner or later success would be theirs if only they continued with determined perseverance to push forward on the road which Hitler had mapped out for them. The winter of 1919-20 was one continual struggle to strengthen confidence in Hitler's ability to carry the movement through to success and to intensify this confidence until it became in his words, 'a burning faith that could move mountains'.

Although there is little or no evidence that in 1919 anyone particularly cared about his minuscule organisation, according to Hitler, the Marxist leaders naturally hated the young movement which was so bitterly opposed to international Marxism and the Jewish and Stock Exchange parties. He boastfully recorded that the name 'German Labour Party' irritated those figures on the left who, in Hitler's opinion, were still intoxicated with their *Dolchstoss* triumph in 1918. Hitler was well aware that as the party grew it was inevitable that physical conflict would occur.

A number of people in the small circles of Hitler's own movement at that time showed a certain amount of anxiety at the prospect of such a conflict. They wanted to refrain as much as possible from coming out into the open, because they feared that they might be attacked and beaten. Hitler suspected that, in their minds, they fretted that their first public meetings might be broken up and they feared that the movement might be ruined forever. Hitler found it difficult to advance his own diametrically opposed position. He fervently believed that physical conflict should not be evaded but should rather be faced openly and that the party should be armed with the weapons and muscle power to provide protection against the application of brute force which would inevitably be employed by their political enemies. Hitler argued that any attempt to impose terror could not be overcome by the weapons of the mind, but only by counter-terror. In the years ahead it was to become an all too familiar refrain.

To the delight of Adolf Hitler, the next meeting in the small hall proved to be much more successful and validated the truth of Hitler's contention that a change of venue and increased advertising would result in more adherents. The audience for the meeting had increased to more than 200. The publicity effect was noticeable as word of mouth concerning the mesmeric speaker began to circulate. The effect on the party's finances were equally positive, providing a welcome injection to party coffers. No sooner had the meeting finished than Hitler immediately urged that a further meeting should be held to capitalise on the growing success. The next meeting took place in less than a fortnight, and Hitler was delighted that there were more than 270 people present. Two weeks later for the seventh time in 1919, the party invited all of its followers and their friends to attend an open meeting. The same hall was scarcely large enough for the number that came. They amounted to more than four hundred.

In March 1920, Hitler was finally discharged from the army. He was immediately immersed in the German Workers' Party and soon found a new life which provided a replacement for the comradeship he had enjoyed so much in the army. As he bustled around Munich, Hitler once again fell under the disproving gaze of Alexander Moritz Frey:

'After the end of the war in Munich, where we both lived, I often saw Hitler, although I never spoke to him again. For a long time we lived in the same neighbourhood. I often ran into him in the Maximilianstrasse. He bought his newspapers at the same newspaper stand as I did. He bought a lot of newspapers at the same time... The newspaper woman appreciated him as one of her best customers. Incidentally she complained loudly, in a very Bavarian way, about the Nazi gangs.'

Some caution needs to be exercised here in accepting Moritz Frey's account as the unvarnished truth. In the beginning of 1920, the Nazi gangs mentioned by Moritz Frey had not yet been formed. The party was still known as the DAP and would not become the NSDAP, or Nazis, for some months to come. The party was nonetheless growing in stature and Hitler felt that the party had sufficient momentum to support the idea of holding its first mass DAP meeting. On hearing his proposal, there were differences of opinion amongst the faithful. Some leading members, led by Karl Harrer, considered that the time was not ripe for such a meeting and that the result might be detrimental. However, according to Hitler the press on the left had at last begun to take notice of the DAP and the party was growing in stature to a point where it could no longer be ignored and was gradually beginning to arouse the first smouldering of wrath of the left. This was a good thing in Hitler's eyes, he believed that publicity of any description was vital, and in order to speed up the process he and his military cronies had begun to appear at certain left wing meetings where they would bellow rhetorical questions or simply contradict the speakers. The natural result of the presence of Hitler and his team at left wing meetings was that they were shouted down or forcibly ejected. Hitler argued that the DAP contingents thereby gained some of their political ends. They had managed to get themselves noticed and as the oxygen of publicity began to flow, more and more people gradually began to know of the existence of the DAP. The party was no longer an anonymous grouping and the better the opponents on the left understood the DAP the stronger became their aversion and their enmity.

Hitler correctly surmised that a large contingent of left wing firebrands might return the favour and attend the first DAP mass meeting bent on ensuring that proceedings were halted. Hitler fully realized that the meeting would probably be the target of an attempt to break it up. He argued that the time had come to face the fight. Hitler was by now well acquainted with his left wing opponents, and he knew quite well that if the DAP opposed them tooth and nail not only would they make an impression on them, they might even win some new followers. He therefore prevailed on the party to adopt an aggressive stance and obtained the agreement on a policy of active and violent opposition.

The decision to employ force required an infusion of fresh blood into the ranks of the DAP. Hitler, after only a few months of collaboration with the new members, had come to the conclusion that the management of the fledgling party required a similar overhaul. Karl Harrer, who was the founder and then chairman of the party, was a journalist by profession but as leader of the party he had one very serious handicap: he could not speak to the crowd. Though even Hitler had to concede he did his work conscientiously, it lacked the necessary driving force, probably for the reason that he had no oratorical gifts whatsoever. Anton Drexler, who at that time was chairman of the Munich local group, was a simple working man. In Hitler's judgment he, too, was not of any great importance as a speaker. Moreover, he was not a soldier. He had never done military service, even during the War. In consequence, this man who was 'feeble and diffident' by nature, had missed the only experience which, in Hitler's opinion, had any value and which he opined could transform diffident and weakly creatures such as Drexler into 'real' men.

Hitler soon formed the view that it was abundantly clear that neither of those two men were of the stuff that would have enabled them to stir up an ardent faith in the new movement and to brush aside all obstacles. Hitler reasoned that the task would require the obstinate use of force if necessary, combined with brutal ruthlessness. Such a task, in Hitler's opinion, could only be carried out by men who had been trained body and soul in those military virtues which Hitler claimed make a man 'Agile as a greyhound, tough as leather, and hard as Krupp steel.'

One man whom Hitler did have respect for was the highly influential Deitrich Eckart. Eckart was a very successful and widely revered playwright, known especially for his adaptation of Henrik Ibsen's Peer Gynt. This particular version of Peer Gynt was one of the best attended productions of the age with more than 600 performances in Berlin alone. It was this success that not only made Eckart a wealthy man, but gave him the social contacts needed to introduce Hitler to all of the important German citizens of the day. These introductions to socialites and industrialists proved to be pivotal in Hitler's ultimate rise to power.

Hitler respected Eckart for his widely acknowledged reputation as a man of letters. Eckart had triumphed in the public eye and enjoyed a wide measure of fame. Hitler listened in rapt attention as Eckart expanded upon his ideology of a 'genius superman' which in part at least appears to have been based on writings by Lanz von Liebenfels; Eckart saw himself following the tradition of Arthur Schopenhauer. Hitler later acknowledged that Eckart had the greatest significance with regard to his own personal development.[28]

Between 1918 and 1920, Eckart edited the anti-Semitic periodical *'Auf gut Deutsch'* (In Plain German), published with the help of future National Socialist luminaries Alfred Rosenberg and Gottfried Feder. A fierce critic of the Weimar Republic, Eckart vehemently opposed the Treaty of Versailles, which he viewed as treason, and was a fierce proponent of the so-called *Dolchstosslegende*, according to which Eckart proposed Social Democrats and Jews were to blame for Germany's defeat in World War I.

Eckart was involved in founding the DAP together with Gottfried Feder and Anton Drexler in 1919, he also wrote the lyrics of *'Deutschland Erwache'* (Germany Awake), which became an anthem of the Nazi party.

---

28. Timothy Ryback 'Hitler's Private Library' p30.

Eckart met Adolf Hitler during a speech he gave before party members in 1919. In the four years prior to his death in 1923, Eckart exerted considerable influence on Hitler and is strongly believed to have helped establish the theories and beliefs of the Nazi party. Few other people had as much influence on Hitler in his lifetime. It was Eckart who introduced men like Alfred Rosenberg to Adolf Hitler. Between 1920 and 1923, Eckart and Rosenberg laboured tirelessly in the service of Hitler and the party.

Although he had been discharged from the army in March 1920, at that time Hitler was still very much a soldier. Physically and mentally he considered himself polished by six years of service, four of them in the front line. Hitler claimed that this combination of dutiful service and hard won experience produced a practical and positive attitude to life. Hitler made the pompous statement that in common with his army comrades he had forgotten the meaning of such everyday civilian phrases as: 'That will not go', or 'That is not possible', or 'We ought not to take such a risk; it is too dangerous.'

For Hitler, nothing was impossible despite the fact that the whole undertaking of producing a right wing nationalist movement was of its very nature dangerous:

'At that time there were many parts of Germany where it would have been absolutely impossible openly to invite people to a national meeting that dared to make a direct appeal to the masses. Those who attended such meetings were usually dispersed and driven away with broken heads. It certainly did not call for any great qualities to be able to do things in that way. The largest so-called bourgeois mass meetings were accustomed to dissolve, and those in attendance would run away like rabbits when frightened by a dog as soon as a dozen communists appeared on the scene. The Reds used to pay little attention to those bourgeois organisations where only babblers talked. They recognised the inner triviality of such associations much better than the members themselves and therefore felt that they need not be afraid of them. On the contrary, however, they were all the more determined to use every possible means of annihilating once and for all any movement

that appeared to them to be a danger to their own interests. The most effective means which they always employed in such cases were terror and brute force.'

In the autumn of 1919, when the party was founded, Hitler claimed that there were only six members. This was patently untrue and probably refers to the number of committee members, but what does appear to be true is his claim that the party did not have any headquarters, nor officials, nor formularies, nor a stamp, nor printed material of any sort. The committee first held its sittings in a restaurant on the Herrengasse and then in a café at Gasteig. Hitler knew that this state of affairs could not last. Even before he had been discharged from the army, he took action in the matter. Hitler personally went around to several restaurants and hotels in Munich, with the idea of renting a room in one of them for the use of the Party. In the old *Sterneckerbräu* on Tal 54, he discovered there was a small room with an arched roof, which in earlier times was used as a sort of festive tavern, a drinking den where the Bavarian Counsellors of the Holy Roman Empire foregathered to discuss the affairs of the world and put matters to right over mugs of beer.

It was dark and dismal and accordingly well suited to its previous uses, though less suited to the new purpose it was now destined to serve. The little street on which its one window looked out was so narrow that even on the brightest summer day the room remained dim and sombre. Here, on 1 January 1920, the party took up its first fixed abode. The rent came to fifty Marks per month, which was then an enormous sum for the DAP. The running costs had to be very modest and the party considered itself so lucky to have premises that dared not complain even when the landlords removed the wooden wainscoting a few days after the party had taken possession. This panelling had been specially put up for the Imperial Counsellors and Hitler recorded that afterwards the place began to look more like a grotto than a political party office. Still it marked an important step forward. Eventually the fledgling party had electric light installed and later on a telephone. A table and some borrowed chairs were brought, an open paper-stand and later on a cupboard. Two sideboards, which belonged to the landlord, served to store the leaflets and placards which were at last being printed.

As time went on it turned out to be impossible to direct the course of a growing movement merely by holding a committee meeting once a week. The current business administration of the movement could not be regularly attended to except by a salaried official. The problem was that although it was growing fast the movement had still so few members that it was hard to find among them a suitable person for the job who would be content with very little for himself and at the same time would be ready to meet the manifold demands which the movement would make on his time and energy. After a long search, Hitler discovered a former soldier who consented to become the party's first administrator. His name was Schüssler, another old war comrade of Hitler's from the ranks of the List Regiment. At first, he came to the new office everyday between 6 and 8 P.M.. Later on he came from five to eight and subsequently for the whole afternoon. Finally it became a full-time job and Schüssler was soon working in the office from morning until late at night. He describes him as an industrious, upright and thoroughly honest man, who was faithful and totally devoted to the movement. Schüssler had one additional advantage. He brought with him a small Adler typewriter of his own. It was the first machine of its type to be used in the service of the party. Subsequently the party bought it from Schüssler by paying for it in installments. Hitler also recalled that the party needed a small safe in order to keep its papers and register of membership from danger of being stolen and certainly not to guard the funds, which according to Hitler did not then exist. He declared that the financial position was so miserable that he often had to dip into his own personal savings to keep things moving.

Hitler's influence on the party was growing exponentially and his wild energy was clearly beginning to pay dividends, however Karl Harrer was still chairman of the party and increasingly he did not see eye to eye with Hitler. Harrer collided with Hitler on a number of key points, in particular he wished to maintain the party as a kind of secret society similar to the Thule Society, he also disagreed as to the opportune time for the first mass meeting of the party. Hitler was increasingly strident in his demands for a mass meeting and accordingly, in January 1920, Harrer felt himself obliged to resign from the leadership of the movement. Despite their differences, Hitler accorded Harrer the plain testament that he was as an upright and honest man. Anton Drexler took Harrer's place, however Hitler kept complete control of the propaganda programme. He would not allow others to be involved in the decision making process and jealously guarded his patch reserving all control of propaganda strictly to himself and would only perform this vital work on his own terms. Hitler later admitted he would broach no compromise whatsoever and this childish trait was to become an attitude which marked his dealings with the party and later defined his whole behaviour.

At the insistence of the truculent Adolf Hitler, the DAP finally agreed on 24 February 1920 as the date for the first great popular meeting to be held under the aegis of this movement which was hitherto unknown. With Harrer out of the way, Hitler made all the preparatory arrangements personally. Hitler took full advantage of the short notice and claimed that it was suddenly necessary within twenty-four hours to decide on the stance the party should take with regard to the key questions of the day. Before holding the first great mass meeting it was now an obvious matter of necessity that propaganda material and advertising posters must be readied but also to have the main items of the DAP programme printed and ready for distribution to the eager masses.

Hitler claims he responded to the new found need for urgency by insisting that the manifesto should be drafted there and then. The resulting policies obviously needed to be incorporated into a coherent party programme to be unveiled both verbally and in print at the mass meeting. This version of events was later disputed in a letter drafted by Anton Drexler in 1941, but wisely not actually sent to the man who had by then become an omnipotent demagogue. It would appear that the manifesto was actually drafted over a period of time in 1919 and 1920, and eventually coalesced into the form of the now infamous twenty-five points. With his numbered list Hitler was consciously following the footsteps of his hero Martin Luther whose Ninety-Five Theses had triggered the reformation in 1517. The twenty-five points of the DAP Programme were certainly composed by Adolf Hitler and Anton Drexler. Given all we know about Hitler and his mania for control it must be considered likely that Hitler exercised the lion's share of the decision making process:

'The Twenty-Five Points as proposed by Hitler – 19 February 1920.

The Programme of the German Workers' Party is designed to be of limited duration. The leaders have no intention, once the aims announced in it have been achieved, of establishing fresh ones, merely in order to increase, artificially, the discontent of the masses and so ensure the continued existence of the Party.

1. *We demand the union of all Germany in a Greater Germany on the basis of the right of national self-determination.*
2. *We demand equality of rights for the German people in its dealings with other nations, and the revocation of the peace treaties of Versailles and Saint-Germain.*
3. *We demand land and territory (colonies) to feed our people and to settle our surplus population.*
4. *Only members of the nation may be citizens of the State. Only those of German blood, whatever be their creed, may be members of the nation. Accordingly, no Jew may be a member of the nation.*
5. *Non-citizens may live in Germany only as guests and must be subject to laws for aliens.*
6. *The right to vote on the State's government and legislation shall be enjoyed by the citizens of the State alone. We demand therefore that all official appointments, of whatever kind, whether in the Reich, in the states or in the smaller localities, shall be held by none but citizens.*

    We oppose the corrupting parliamentary custom of filling posts merely in accordance with party considerations, and without reference to character or abilities.

7. *We demand that the State shall make it its primary duty to provide a livelihood for its citizens. If it should prove impossible to feed the entire population, foreign nationals (non-citizens) must be deported from the Reich.*

8. *All non-German immigration must be prevented. We demand that all non-Germans who entered Germany after 2 August 1914, shall be required to leave the Reich forthwith.*

9. *All citizens shall have equal rights and duties.*

10. *It must be the first duty of every citizen to perform physical or mental work. The activities of the individual must not clash with the general interest, but must proceed within the framework of the community and be for the general good.*

    We demand therefore:

11. *The abolition of incomes unearned by work. The breaking of the slavery of interest.*

12. *In view of the enormous sacrifices of life and property demanded of a nation by any war, personal enrichment from war must be regarded as a crime against the nation. We demand therefore the ruthless confiscation of all war profits.*

13. *We demand the nationalisation of all businesses which have been formed into corporations (trusts).*

14. *We demand profit-sharing in large industrial enterprises.*

15. *We demand the extensive development of insurance for old age.*

16. *We demand the creation and maintenance of a healthy middle class, the immediate communalising of big department stores, and their lease at a cheap rate to small traders, and that the utmost consideration shall be shown to all small traders in the placing of State and municipal orders.*

17. *We demand a land reform suitable to our national requirements, the passing of a law for the expropriation of land for communal purposes without compensation; the abolition of ground rent, and the prohibition of all speculation in land.*

18. *We demand the ruthless prosecution of those whose activities are injurious to the common interest. Common criminals, usurers, profiteers, etc., must be punished with death, whatever their creed or race.*

19. *We demand that Roman Law, which serves a materialistic world order, be replaced by a German common law.*

20. *The State must consider a thorough reconstruction of our national system of education (with the aim of opening up to every able and hard-working German the possibility of higher education and of thus obtaining advancement). The curricula of all educational establishments must be brought into line with the requirements of practical life. The aim of the school must be to give the pupil, beginning with the first sign of intelligence, a grasp of the nation of the State (through the study of civic affairs). We demand the education of gifted children of poor parents, whatever their class or occupation, at the expense of the State.*

21. *The State must ensure that the nation's health standards are raised by protecting mothers and infants, by prohibiting child labor, by promoting physical strength through legislation providing for compulsory gymnastics and sports, and by the extensive support of clubs engaged in the physical training of youth.*

22. *We demand the abolition of the mercenary army and the foundation of a people's army.*

23. *We demand legal warfare on deliberate political mendacity and its dissemination in the press. To facilitate the creation of a German national press we demand:*

    (a) that all editors of, and contributors to newspapers appearing in the German language must be members of the nation;

    (b) that no non-German newspapers may appear without the express permission of the State. They must not be printed in the German language;

    (c) that non-Germans shall be prohibited by law from participating financially in or influencing German newspapers, and that the penalty for contravening such a law shall be the suppression of

any such newspaper, and the immediate deportation of the non-Germans involved.

The publishing of papers which are not conducive to the national welfare must be forbidden. We demand the legal prosecution of all those tendencies in art and literature which corrupt our national life, and the suppression of cultural events which violate this demand.

24. *We demand freedom for all religious denominations in the State, provided they do not threaten its existence nor offend the moral feelings of the German race.*

The Party, as such, stands for positive Christianity, but does not commit itself to any particular denomination. It combats the Jewish-materialistic spirit within and without us, and is convinced that our nation can achieve permanent health only from within on the basis of the principle: The common interest before self-interest.

25. *To put the whole of this programme into effect, we demand the creation of a strong central state power for the Reich; the unconditional authority of the political central Parliament over the entire Reich and its organisations; and the formation of Corporations based on estate and occupation for the purpose of carrying out the general legislation passed by the Reich in the various German states.*

The leaders of the Party promise to work ruthlessly – if need be to sacrifice their very lives – to translate this programme into action.'

The notices which advertised the *Hofbräuhaus* meeting contained an abridged version of the twenty-five points. The posters and leaflets were designed in accordance with the principles which Hitler had already laid down in dealing with propaganda in general. Hitler had an innate understanding of the communication process and the posters and leaflets were produced in a form which would appeal to the masses. Hitler recorded with pride that the text was concise and definite and employed absolutely dogmatic form of expression. Hitler and his team distributed these posters and leaflets with a dogged energy and waited for the effect they would produce.

Hitler had an intuitive flair for effective mass communication. In the pages of 'Mein Kampf', he expanded upon the mechanics of effective propaganda and why he had settled upon the colour red for the DAP promotional materials despite the fact that this was the colour of his political enemies whom Hitler in typical fashion sought to antagonise:

'For our principal colour we chose red, as it has an exciting effect on the eye and was therefore calculated to arouse the attention of our opponents and irritate them. Thus they would have to take notice of us, whether they liked it or not, and would not forget us.'

It had been announced that the crucial meeting would begin at 7.30 P.M. on 19 February 1920, a quarter-of-an-hour before the opening time Hitler recalled how he had walked through the main hall of the *Hofbräuhaus* on the Platz in Munich. He described how his heart was nearly bursting with joy as he noted that the great hall was filled to overflowing. Nearly 2,000 people were packed into the big hall, and to Hitler's delight he noted that many of those present were exactly the target audience which the party had always sought to reach. Another lesson in the power of advertising had been delivered and Hitler was a willing student.

On a more sinister note Hitler recorded that more than half the audience consisted of a belligerent faction who seemed to be communists or independents and who were obviously there to break up the meeting, however events transpired otherwise. When the first speaker had finished without incident, Hitler got up to speak. After just a few minutes Hitler was met with a hailstorm of interruptions and a series of violent encounters broke out in the body of the hall. Hitler's handful of loyal war comrades supported by some new followers (who would later become the fearsome SA), immediately grappled with the disturbers and soon restored order. It was a brief but significant skirmish. Hitler was an advocate of political violence, with this the very first of his political battles won, Hitler was able to continue with his speech. In the pages of '*Mein Kampf*', Hitler proudly recorded that after half an hour the applause began to drown the interruptions and the organisations from the remaining left wingers. According to Hitler's version of events, their interruptions gradually ceased and applause took their place. Hitler sensed that the time had now come to explain the twenty-five points and he proceeded to expand upon them, point after point, explaining every nuance to the assembled mass gathered in the hall. Sensing that the momentum was beginning to build, Hitler urged the crowd to voice their own collective judgment on each point. Under the mesmeric spell of Adolf Hitler the reactions from the crowd gathered in intensity as one point after another was accepted with ever increasing enthusiasm. When the last point was reached he had before him a hall full of people united by what Hitler described as 'a new conviction, a new faith and a new will.'

Nearly four hours had passed when the hall began to clear. As the masses streamed towards the exits, crammed shoulder to shoulder, shoving and pushing, Hitler knew that his movement had now set down roots among the German people. Hitler, employing a measure of prescience, prophesied that this was a movement 'which would never pass into oblivion'. He was to be proved right, but for all the wrong reasons. 24 February 1920 was, for Hitler, the beginning of his envisaged Thousand Year Reich and despite his supposed aversion to *völkisch* influences he excitedly noted his bombastic interpretation in the pages of '*Mein Kampf*':

'A fire was enkindled from whose glowing heat the sword would be fashioned which would restore freedom to the German Siegfried and bring back life to the German nation. Beside the revival which I then foresaw, I also felt that the Goddess of Vengeance was now getting ready to redress the treason of 9 November, 1918.'

As the hall slowly emptied, Hitler watched in satisfaction. The movement was now on the march. Although Drexler was still chairman of the DAP, Hitler was now the real star and the driving force behind the movement. In March 1920, Hitler advocated that the party should enlarge its name. Hitler advocated that the name of the party should be expanded from the manageable *Deutsche Arbeiterpartei* (German Workers' Party) to the cumbersome *Nationalsozialistische Deutsche Arbeiterpartei* (National Socialist German Workers' Party). Hitler, as always, would have his way and on 1 April 1920 the party became known as the National Socialist German Workers' Party changing it's acronym from DAP to NSDAP. The term Nazi was ultimately coined for short hand usage, although it appears that the name only began to appear from the Thirties onwards.

On the surface, the adoption of the word 'socialist' was a strange move as Hitler had always been hostile to many socialist ideas. There were however a number of items on the list of twenty-five points concerning profit sharing, education and health care which fitted a socialist agenda. However, Hitler could by no stretch of the imagination be described as a socialist. He was a right wing ultra-nationalist and staunch anti-Semite. These traits were combined with an intense and lingering hatred for the *Dolchstoss* politicians, the 'November Criminals', whom he considered had dishonoured Germany by signing the Versailles Treaty and were now bent on exploiting local grievances against a weak federal government. Nonetheless Hitler was sufficiently astute to recognise that socialism was an increasingly popular political philosophy in Germany and was a vote winner which could potentially provide a key to power. This was reflected in the growth in the German Social Democrat Party (SDP), then the largest political party in Germany.

Hitler therefore attempted to claim the term socialist as his own and in the process he attempted to redefine socialism by placing the word 'National' before it to create a new compound word *Nationalsozialiste*. Hitler tempered any suggestion that he had genuine socialist pretensions by the claim he was only in favour of equality for those who had 'German blood'. His own personal agenda however always remained nationalist and racist and despite the incorporation of the word socialist the right wing doctrine which underpinned the party remained crystal clear to all. The racist and anti-Semitic aspects of the twenty-five points took precedence over the genuinely socialist ideas surrounding profit sharing, health care and education. Hitler had to go to great lengths to explain the change to his own followers and in his speeches he was compelled to expand at length on what social actually meant in the context of the party:

"National' and 'Social' are two identical conceptions. It was only the Jew who succeeded, through falsifying the social idea and turning it into Marxism, not only in divorcing the social idea from the national, but in actually representing them as utterly contradictory. That aim he has in fact achieved. At the founding of this Movement we formed the decision that we would give expression to this idea of ours of the identity of the two conceptions: despite all warnings, on the basis of what we had come to believe, on the basis of the sincerity of our will, we christened it 'National Socialist.' We said to ourselves that to be 'national' means above everything to act with a boundless and all-embracing love for the people and, if necessary, even to die for it. And similarly to be 'social' means so to build up the state and the community of the people that every individual acts in the interest of the community of the people and must be to such an extent convinced of the goodness, of the honourable straightforwardness of this community of the people as to be ready to die for it.' [29]

The addition of the word socialist did nothing to dilute Hitler's extremist agenda and under the strident political programme outlined in the twenty-five points, Jews and other 'aliens' would lose their rights of citizenship, and immigration of non-Germans should be brought to an end. The proof of Hitler's true intent can easily be traced in the post 1933 actions of the NSDAP.

Otto Strasser met Hitler for the first time in October 1920, and in the pages of his 1940 polemic entitled 'Hitler and I', recorded the first meeting and first political argument that he and Hitler had entered into:

"'Come and have lunch with us tomorrow and meet General Ludendorff and Adolf Hitler… I insist on your coming, it's very important."

---

29. Text of Hitler speech given in Munich 12 April 1922.

These words, spoken by my brother Gregor, came to me over the telephone at Deggendorf in Bavaria, where I was spending my holidays with my parents in October, 1920. Gregor sensed my hesitation, and he was aware of my mistrust of Hitler and his propaganda, but he insisted. My acceptance of his invitation was a turning-point in my life, affecting my whole future.

What young German officer would not have leapt at the chance of meeting General Ludendorff? In the chaotic state that Germany was in then, what young German could have had so little curiosity as not to want to see for himself what Adolf Hitler was like? For the youth of Germany, eager to create a new future, was then starting to rally round him.

My brother's invitation came to me at a crucial moment. Not long before I had left the Socialist Party, and I was still searching for my way.

My eldest brother Paul had become a Benedictine, my younger brother Anton was at boarding-school, and Gregor, my senior by five years, and my sister were both married. Next day's outing therefore promised to be a welcome change, and I looked forward to breathing a little fresh air. It is about sixty miles from Deggendorf to Landshut, in Lower Bavaria, where Gregor was living with his young wife. I took an early train, and walked from the station under a clear autumn sky. Gregor kept a chemist's shop in the high street, and it was a meeting place for all the notables of the town. I expected to be early, but I noticed that the iron shutters were down, and a beautiful car was standing in front of the house. General Ludendorff and Hitler must have come from Munich by road, and they had arrived before me.

Gregor quickly introduced us. I was first impressed with Ludendorff. He had heavy features and a firm double chin. There was something compelling about the way he gazed at you from under his bushy brows, and in spite of his civilian clothes he looked every inch a general. One sensed his will-power immediately. His companion, who wore a blue suit, seemed to be trying to occupy as small a place upon his chair as possible. He appeared to be trying to shelter under the redoubtable general's wing. What shall I say of Adolf Hitler's personal appearance? It was then entirely unfamiliar. He was a man of thirty-one, with regular features and a stubbly moustache. His face was not yet lined with thought. The pouches that were later to appear under his eyes were scarcely visible. That face that has since become familiar to the whole world had not yet assumed its true significance. Hitler was a young man like other young men. His pallor indicated lack of fresh air and physical exercise.

We went in to lunch. Ludendorff kept his inquisitorial eye upon me.

"Your brother has spoken to me about you," he said. "How many years' service have you done?"

"Four-and-a-half years, sir," I replied. I was the youngest Bavarian volunteer. I served for three years in the ranks, and for a year and a half as second-lieutenant and lieutenant. I was in the army from 2 August 1914, until 30 June 1919, and was twice wounded.'

"Bravo," said Ludendorff. Raising his clear green glass, which rested on a massive stem, he offered to drink with each of us. We all naturally responded to his gesture, but to my astonishment I noticed that Hitler's glass contained nothing but water.

"Herr Hitler is a teetotaler," Gregor explained, with a host's smile. "He is also a vegetarian," he added, with a glance almost of apprehension at his wife. The roast had just been brought in.

"Herr Hitler will not offend me by refusing my cooking," my little sister-in-law said calmly, but at the same time challengingly.

An instinctive dislike of the guest who had been thrust on her was perceptible in her eyes and her whole attitude.

Else never approved of her husband's intimacy with Adolf Hitler. She tolerated him during the years that followed without ever daring to express her revulsion aloud. But her hostility to Hitler never changed. That day Adolf Hitler ate meat. I do not think he has done so since. Ludendorff pursued his inquiries about my military career. "And how did you come to be recommended for the Order of Max-Joseph?'"

The decoration to which the general referred was an extremely rare one, of which I was deprived by the ending of the war. I had been recommended for it as a consequence of a deed of arms recorded in the Golden Book of the First Regiment of Bavarian Light Artillery, a crack regiment in which I was proud of having served. Bubbling over with youthful pride and enthusiasm, I described the incident to General Ludendorff, while Adolf Hitler, suddenly embarrassed at having been no more than a corporal and having no military exploits of his own to boast about, enclosed himself in a hostile silence.

On several occasions when Ludendorff spoke to him he answered with a "Yes, your Excellency", or "Exactly your Excellency". His manner was both obsequious and sullen. Gregor, who had been an officer too, but was already on very close terms with Hitler, felt uncomfortable. The harmony of his lunch party seemed to be imperilled, and the plans that he had built on it appeared to be vanishing into thin air. Gregor, as leader of the Nationalist ex-service men of Bavaria had incorporated his followers in the National-Socialist movement that spring. He had founded the first provincial branch of the Party, and was thus Hitler's first Geuleiter. Thus, both as host and as politician, the turn the luncheon was taking was naturally displeasing to him. With his innate organizing gifts and the authority that the chemist shares with the doctor and the priest in the provinces, he had succeeded in converting the distrustful and uncouth Bavarians to Hitler's cause. Was he to fail with his own brother? We went into the sitting-room, a dark room with heavy oak furniture. The general, reclining in a leather armchair, pondered, a cigar between his lips. Hitler could not keep still, but kept pacing up and down with lowered head, no doubt meditating his revenge.

He suddenly turned and made a frontal attack upon me.

"Herr Strasser," he said, "I do not understand how it is possible for a loyal ex-officer like you to have been a Red leader during the Kapp Putsch in March." He must have heard the story from my brother. At last he was upon his own ground.

"My 'Reds', Herr Hitler," I replied, "acted in support of the legal Government of the country. They were not rebels, as you seem to imply, *but patriots, who were trying to check the rebellious followers of a few reactionary generals."*

Hitler gradually worked up to a high state of excitement.

"No," he replied, "one must not be satisfied with the letter, one must try to penetrate to the spirit. The Kapp Putsch was necessary, though it was ineffectively carried out. The 'Versailles Government' must be overthrown." Never did I hear Hitler talk of the 'Weimar Republic'. He always spoke of the 'Versailles Government', and always used the phrase with profound contempt. I found myself in a somewhat difficult position. Had I been alone with Hitler, I should have replied with my usual vehemence. But Ludendorff was present, and Ludendorff's role during the famous putsch had not been at all clear. He had been in the Unter den Linden in Berlin at the very hour of Erhardt's victorious entry. Was he a chance spectator or a secret accomplice? I have never found out.

"The reactionaries," I said, "exploited the political ignorance of a lot of patriotic officers. During the War Kapp was hand-in-glove with Tirpitz, the Prussian reactionaries, the Junkers, heavy industry, Thyssen and Krupp. The Kapp Putsch was no more or less than an attempted cou d'etat."

Ludendorff, whose thoughts had seemed to be elsewhere, then intervened and took my part "He is right," he said. "The Kapp Putsch was senseless. One must start by gaining the people, in order to be able to dispense with force." Hitler immediately became outwardly docile and obsequious.

"'Yes, your Excellency," he said sonorously. Then he continued in a monotonous voice:

"That is the object of my movement. I wish to inflame the people to the idea of revenge. Only the people and its total fanaticism can make us win the next war.'"

I was shocked by this idea and opposed it vigorously. "There is no question of revenge and there is no question of war,'" I replied. "'Our Socialism must be national in order to establish a new order in Germany and not to set out on a new policy of conquests.'"

"Yes," said Gregor, who had been listening very seriously, "from the Right we shall take nationalism, which has so disastrously allied itself with capitalism, and from the Left we shall take socialism, which has made such an unhappy union with internationalism. Thus we shall form the National-Socialism which will be the motive force of a new Germany and a new Europe."

"And," I continued, "the emphasis in this amalgamation must be on the socialism. Don't you call your movement Nationalsozialist in a single word, Herr Hitler? German grammar tells us that in compound words of this kind the first part serves to qualify the second, which is the essential part."

I then proceeded to quote some quite undeniable examples to illustrate this feature of the German language, which is very rich in compounds of this kind. I saw Hitler flush, and a vertical line appeared on his forehead, intersecting a horizontal line.

"But perhaps your Baltic adviser, Herr Rosenberg, is too ignorant of the German language to appreciate the nuance," I added somewhat maliciously.

Hitler suddenly lost patience and struck the table furiously with his fist. "Enough of this hair-splitting,'" he exclaimed. He then made an effort to regain his self-control, and with a half-serious, half-mocking smile, turned to my brother Gregor and said: "I am afraid I shall never get on well with this intellectual brother of yours."

I then witnessed one of those exhibitions of rhetorical acrobatics for which Hitler was to become famous. Side-stepping an argument on a level at which his elementary-standard intelligence could not follow me, he launched out into a violent anti-Semitic tirade, completely evading the issue. "Playing about with ideas like that is quite useless," he said, once more addressing himself to me.

"What I am talking about is reality, and reality is Jewry. Look at the Communist Jew who was Marx and the capitalist Jew who is Rathenau. All evil comes from the Jews, who pollute the world. Ever since I have got to know them, ever since I have come to understand them, I have been unable to meet a man in the street without

wondering whether he was a Jew or not. Jews control the Social-Democratic Press. They conceal their fiendish devices behind a mask of reformist ideals. Their aim is the destruction of the nation and the obliteration of the differences between races. Jews lead the workers and talk of improving their lot; in reality they aim at enslaving them, and killing their patriotism and their honour in order to establish the international dictatorship of Jewry. What they cannot achieve by persuasion they will try to achieve by force. Their organization is flawless, they have their fingers in every pie. They have their agents in all the Ministries, and they even pull strings in the highest places in the land; and they have the support of their co-religionists all over the world; they are an ulcer leading to the downfall of nations and individuals."

The more persuasive Hitler tried to be, the more critical did I become. He paused for breath and saw me smile. "You do not know the Jews, Herr Hitler, and permit me to tell you that you over-estimate them," I replied. The Jew, you see, is above all adaptable. He exploits existing possibilities, but creates nothing. He makes use of socialism, he utilizes capitalism, he would even exploit National- Socialism if you gave him the chance. He adapts himself to circumstances with a suppleness of which, apart from him, only the Chinese is capable. Marx invented nothing. Socialism has always had three sides. Marx, in collaboration with the good German Engels, studied its economic side, the Italian Mazzini examined its national and religious implications, and Bakunin, a Russian, developed its Nihilist side, from which Bolshevism was born. Thus you see that socialism was not of Jewish origin at all.'

"Certainly not," Ludendorff agreed. "The old economic principles are out-of-date. No regeneration is possible apart from National-Socialism properly understood. That alone can cause prosperity to return to our country. I wish to give the German people a touch of the whip to pull them together and make them capable of crushing France."

"You still stress the nationalist side. Once more you misunderstand

the principle of the thing. I certainly don't approve of the Treaty of
Versailles, but the idea of fighting France seems stupid to me. The day
will come when the two countries will have to unite to fight Russian
Bolshevism."

Hitler made an impatient gesture. I suddenly thought of the Red
Terror in Munich, when I, an ex-officer just come out of hospital,
joined the force of General von Epp to fight the Bolsheviks in Bavaria.
Where was Hitler that day? In what corner of Munich was the soldier
skulking who should have been fighting in our ranks? As though
divining my thoughts, he came over to me, tapped me familiarly on
the shoulder and summoned up all his charm. "After all," he said, "I
would still rather be hanged on a Communist gibbet than become a
German Minister by the grace of France."

Ludendorff rose to say good-bye, and Hitler followed him.

"Well?" said my brother when he returned after accompanying the
two men to the door.

"I liked Ludendorff," I said. "He's not brilliant, like Conrad von
Hotzendorf, the unrecognized genius who was generalissimo of the
Austro-Hungarian armies, but he is a man. As for Hitler, I thought
him too servile towards the general, too quick in argument and in the
art of isolating his opponent. He has no political convictions, he has
the eloquence of a loud-speaker."

"Perhaps," said Gregor, "his corporal's stripes are pinned to his
body. All the same there's something about him. He has a magnetic
quality which it is difficult to resist. What fine things we could do if
we could use him to express your ideas, employing Ludendorff's energy
and my own organizing ability to carry them out."'

In 1920, Hitler's immediate concern was to distance the party
from esoteric aspects of the *völkisch* movement which were growing in
influence and had adopted a range of increasingly bizarre ideas dredged
up from Germany's mythology and revived folk memories of her ancient
past. As well as their strange behaviour Hitler also despised the timidity
of the *völkisch* leaders who were content to hide behind quasi-masonic
secret societies. He claims he did not set much store on the friendship

of people who did not succeed in getting disliked by their enemies. Therefore, he considered the friendship of such people as not only worthless but even dangerous to his young movement:

'That was the principal reason why we first called ourselves a party. We hoped that by giving ourselves such a name we might scare away a whole host of völkisch dreamers. And that was the reason also why we named our Party, the National Socialist German Workers' Party. It was not without good reason that when we laid down a clearly defined programme for the new movement we excluded the word völkisch from it. The concept underlying the term völkisch cannot serve as the basis of a movement, because it is too indefinite and general in its application.'

Not content with his lengthy exposition, Hitler kept on railing at great length against the *völkisch* influences. On page after page of *'Mein Kampf'* he vents his spleen against the *völkisch* fringe. Hitler clearly had a major issue with those who went around beating the big drum for the *völkisch* idea. His long and incoherent rant against the *völkisch* movement demonstrates that by 1924, the whole concept had clearly become a major irritant to Hitler. The followers of the esoteric Germanic mystics had by then formed new 'mystical' orders including the New Templars. According to Hitler the full name of the new party was designed to keep away the unorthodox champions of the *völkisch* movement:

'... those heroes whose weapon is the sword of the spirit and all those whining poltroons who take refuge behind their so-called 'intelligence' as if it were a kind of shield.'

Hitler had formed a bond with Deitrich Eckart, a man who was able to express similar ideas to his own, but much more cogently and elegantly. With Eckart to guide him Hitler was sufficiently confident that the philosophical under-currents could be expressed succinctly. He now felt safe to expound upon his belief that the *völkisch* fringe was entirely out of harmony with the spirit of the new German nation and he deeply resented those he perceived as harping on about far-off and forgotten nomenclature which he reckoned belonged to the ancient

Germanic times and had no distinct association with his age or party. Hitler correctly identified the fact that this habit of borrowing words from the dead past tended to mislead potential members into thinking that the external trappings of vocabulary were the most important feature of a movement as opposed to the policies of the current day:

'At that time, and subsequently, I had to warn followers repeatedly against these wandering scholars who were peddling Germanic folk-lore and who never accomplished anything positive or practical, except to cultivate their own superabundant self-conceit. It is typical of such persons that they rant about ancient Teutonic heroes of the dim and distant ages, stone axes, battle spears and shields, whereas in reality they themselves are the woefullest poltroons imaginable. For those very same people who brandish Teutonic tin swords that have been fashioned carefully according to ancient models and wear padded bear-skins, with the horns of oxen mounted over their bearded faces, proclaim that all contemporary conflicts must be decided by the weapons of the mind alone. And thus they skedaddle when the first communist cudgel appears. Posterity will have little occasion to write a new epic on these heroic gladiators.'

Hitler certainly did have the rational ability to detect the fundamental flaws in the more whimsical fringes of the *völkisch* scene but, as always, he took his justifiable prejudice against the *völkisch* movement to a new and more paranoid level. He announced that he had sensed the malign possibility of serving Jewish interests by the reverence which some sections of the population accorded to the Germanic *völkisch* movement:

'... but the Jew finds it to his own interest to treat these folk-lore comedians with respect and to prefer them to real men who are fighting to establish a German State.'

Hitler claimed that he had seen too much of the *völkisch* mystics not to feel a profound contempt for what he described as their 'miserable play-acting'. To the masses of the nation he noted that they were a justified object of ridicule, however he was not about to give up easily on the topic and ranted on that these 'comedians' appeared to him to be extremely proud of themselves notwithstanding what he perceived as their 'complete fecklessness', which Hitler, with a typical flourish of unfounded justification, described as 'an established fact'. In this way Hitler felt that the *völkisch* fringe were making themselves a veritable nuisance by deluding many 'sincere and honest patriots', for whom the past was worthy of honour.

Hitler's ill humour with the *völkisch* tag did not extend to the most popular right wing newspaper of the day. In December 1920, with the help of Eckart and a personal loan which Anton Drexler subscribed for, the NSDAP scraped together the finance to acquire the *'Völkischer Beobachter'*. This right wing newspaper, owned by Rudolf Freiheur von Sebottendorff, had formerly been the *'Münchener Beobachter'* and was now destined to become the main organ of the party.

In 1918, the paper had been acquired by the Thule Society and in August 1919 was renamed *'Völkischer Beobachter'*. The NSDAP purchased the paper in December 1920, largely on the initiative of Dietrich Eckart, who became the first editor. Later, in 1921, Hitler acquired all shares in the company, making him the sole owner of the publication. Despite his hatred of what the *völkisch* movement had become Hitler did nothing to change the name of the paper. We must assume that while he went to some lengths to exclude the word *völkisch* from his party he was always content to have it associated with his newspaper. This was typical of the type of contradiction which Hitler created throughout his life, he often sought to have more than one horse running in a race and notwithstanding his seemingly unbridled prejudice he was content to allow the title of this key publication to remain unchanged as *'Völkischer Beobachter'*. It would appear he was only too aware of the power of the *völkisch* ideas at the ballot box and was happy to benefit from that by association.

Initially the paper appeared twice weekly; but at the beginning of 1923, it became a daily paper, and at the end of August in the same year it began to appear in the large broadsheet format giving the paper an up-market veneer which was certainly not justified by the tone of its contents. For twenty-five years the *'Völkischer Beobachter'* formed part of the official public face of the Nazi party. The paper quickly became dubbed as the 'fighting paper of the National Socialist movement of Greater Germany' (*Kampfblatt der nationalsozialistischen Bewegung Grossdeutschlands*).

In 1921, Hitler immersed himself in the running of the paper, but as a complete novice in publishing, he soon learned many commercial lessons for which, by his own admission, he had to pay dearly. By Hitler's paranoid reasoning the number of papers in Jewish hands meant there was at that time only one important newspaper that defended the cause of the German people. For Hitler this was a matter for grave concern and the '*Völkischer Beobachter*' was the only popular organ which championed his views.

Hitler soon discovered that the new acquisition had all the correct journalistic qualities, but it was soon clear that Freiher von Sebottendorff hadn't sold the paper for purely altruistic reasons. Commercially, the paper was a disaster just waiting to happen. Hitler soon recognised that he was out of his depth and conceded its management as a business concern was simply impossible. Hitler, for once, recognised that the scale of the problem was beyond his limited experience and sought to alter matters as promptly as he could. Financial disaster loomed and Lucky Linzer now needed some of his trademark good luck, and as frequently happened, luck was on his side. It appeared in the shape of a chance meeting with a former Great War colleague. In 1914, in the trenches of the Great War, Hitler recollected how he had made the acquaintance of Max Amann, who was then his superior. Amann had a great deal of entrepreneurial flare and would later become the general business Director of the Party. During four years in the War, Hitler had abundant opportunities to observe what he later described as the unusual ability, diligence and the rigorous conscientiousness of his future collaborator:

'In the summer of 1921, I applied to my old regimental comrade, whom I met one day by chance, and asked him to become business manager of the movement. At that time the movement was passing through a grave crisis and I had reason to be dissatisfied with several

of our officials, with one of whom I had a very bitter experience. Amann then held a good situation in which there were also good prospects for him. After long hesitation he agreed to my request, but only on condition that he must not be at the mercy of incompetent committees. He must be responsible to one master, and only one. It is to the inestimable credit of this first business manager of the party, whose commercial knowledge is extensive and profound, that he brought order and probity into the various offices of the party. Since that time these have remained exemplary and cannot be equalled or excelled in this by any other branches of the movement. But, as often happens in life, great ability provokes envy and disfavour. That had also to be expected in this case and borne patiently.'

Without the entrepreneurial skills of Amann to call upon, the acquisition of the *'Völkischer Beobachter'* could well have resulted in financial meltdown which would have signified the end of the NSDAP, but ownership of the paper was essential to everything that Hitler envisaged and was especially important for a number of well thought out reasons. When he entered the DAP, Hitler at once took charge of the propaganda function. From his experience in the Great War, he correctly believed the most important political activity was the control and influence of the press. He understood the power of the press and had railed against it at length during the Great War.[30] His overriding objective was to spread the new ideas among as many people as possible, as fast as possible, and a tame newspaper was one obvious way to achieve that end.

Propaganda was to become synonymous with the National Socialist movement, but it is the bedrock on which every political party and regimes and institutions of every political hue are founded. The terrible crimes of the Nazi regime understandably overshadow the fact that Hitler was first and foremost a formidable politician. His fearsome oratorical skills made him a communicator par excellence and his studies in art and design contributed to his powerful record as propagandist,

---

30. *'Mein Kampf'*: Murphy translation 1938, Coda Books Electronic Edition 2011.

the like of which the world had not yet witnessed. Long before Goebbels came on the scene, Hitler had formed a highly credible and practical understanding of the mechanics of mass communication and advertising and he instinctively understood how eye catching graphic design could be effectively harnessed to shape public opinion. It is an uncomfortable truth, but many of the tactics practised by today's politicians which are now so commonplace, were developed and road tested by Adolf Hitler.

As director of propaganda for the party, Hitler took care to shape the output of the *'Völkischer Beobachter'* very carefully. Under the editorship of the talented Deitrich Eckart, the lively and combative style of the paper was neatly dovetailed to conform to the cohesive style and form which Hitler gave to all the early propaganda. Hitler was therefore able to claim with some satisfaction that it was due to the effect of his propaganda that within a short period of time hundreds of thousands of citizens became convinced in their hearts that the policies of the NSDAP were somehow right for Germany.

Hitler's innate understanding of the power of imagery soon led him to the conclusion that the major disadvantage for the party lay in the fact that members of the party possessed no unifying outward symbol of membership which linked them together. Hitler soon set to work on the problem and immediately recalled from his youth the psychological impact of the red-black-gold symbols of 1848 were to the *Deututscher Schulverein* (German Schools Association) to which Hitler had once belonged. His understanding of the power of a political symbol arose not just from a sentimental point of view. In Berlin, after the War, Hitler was present at a mass-demonstration of Marxists in front of the Royal Palace and in the *Lustgarten*. He described how the sea of red flags, red armlets and red flowers was sufficient to give that huge assembly of about 120,000 people an outward appearance of strength. Hitler recorded that by 1920 he was able to feel and understand how easily the man in the street succumbs to the hypnotic magic of such a grandiose piece of theatrical presentation.

The problem for Hitler was that his party inclined towards the right, the natural province of the bourgeoisie, which as a group neither possessed nor stood for any easily digestible *weltanschauung*. Hitler refers to this group – the 'bourgeoisie' – as the natural pool of supporters for the nationalist cause. A better translation might be obtained by the substitution of the word conservative for 'bourgeoisie' as Hitler was referring to their outlook on the world rather than their economic status. He noted that the conservatives had no rallying banner and simply sported the black-white-red colours of the second German Reich and eschewed the Black-Red-Gold design which was chosen as the flag of the German Republic founded at Weimar in 1919. Hitler reasoned that this new Reich was morticed together without the aid of the conservatives and the flag itself was born of the post war events and was therefore merely a State flag possessing no importance in the sense of any particular ideological mission.

Hitler noted that up until 1920, in opposition to the Marxists, there was no flag that would have represented a rallying point for a consolidated resistance to them. For even if the political elements of the German bourgeoisie were loath to accept the suddenly discovered black, red and gold colours as their symbol, after the year 1918 they nevertheless were incapable of counteracting this with a future programme of their own.

To Hitler's way of thinking the conservatives were likely to warm to a return to the values of the Second Reich, hence the resurrection of the black, white and red colours of the old German war flag. It was obvious to Hitler however, that the symbol of a régime which had been overthrown by the Marxists under inglorious circumstances was not now worthy to serve as a banner under which Marxism was to be crushed. However much many Germans may have loved and revered those old colours, that flag was now tainted by failure and Hitler appreciated that it had little value for the struggle of the future.

Hitler adopted the standpoint that it was actually a lucky development for the German nation that it had lost its old flag, the National Socialists recognised that hoisting the old colours would not symbolise their new aims:

'For we had no wish to resurrect from the dead the old Reich which had been ruined through its own blunders, but to build up a new state.'

Hitler subscribed to the view that the new movement which was fighting Marxism along these new lines must display on its banner the symbol of the new State. The question of the new flag was an important issue and one which could not easily be resolved. Suggestions poured in from all quarters, but Hitler would not be rushed as he knew that a really striking emblem might be the first stimulus which could cause an awakening interest in his movement.

For this reason Hitler declined all suggestions from various quarters for identifying the movement by means of a predominantly white flag like that of the old state. He reasoned that white is not a colour capable of attracting and focusing public attention. For him it was a colour suitable only for 'young women's associations' and not at all appropriate for a movement that stands for reform in a revolutionary period. Hitler tells us that black was also suggested and he considered it certainly well-suited to the times, but embodying no significance to empress the will behind the National Socialist movement and again incapable of attracting attention.

White and blue was discarded, despite what Hitler called its admirable aesthetic appeal, as being the colours, depending on the hue, of either Bavaria or Prussia, and generally speaking, with these colours it would have been difficult to attract attention to the movement. The same applied to black and white. Hitler also recalled that black, red and gold did not enter the question at all as they were associated with the Weimar Republic.

Hitler finally settled on a combination of black, white and red as, in his view, the effectiveness of these three colours was far superior to all the others and formed, in his opinion, the most strikingly harmonious combination to be found. Hitler was always for keeping the old black-white-red colours, because as a soldier he regarded them as his most sacred possession and also he claimed that in their aesthetic effect, they conformed more than anything else to his personal taste. Accordingly he claimed he had to discard all the innumerable suggestions and designs which had been proposed for the new movement, among which were many that had incorporated the swastika into the old colours. Hitler claimed that, as leader of the party, he was unwilling to make public his own self created and highly favoured design, on the grounds that it was possible that someone else could come forward with a design just as good, if not better, than his own. Somewhat predictably Hitler eventually decided that his own design was the best all along and the time had come to reveal his masterpiece to a waiting world:

'After innumerable trials I decided upon a final form, a flag of red material with a white disc bearing in its centre a black swastika. After many trials I obtained the correct proportions between the dimensions of the flag and of the white central disc, as well as that of the swastika. And this is how it has remained ever since.'

The new flag appeared in public in the midsummer of 1920. It suited the new movement admirably, both being new and innovative. Not a soul had seen this flag before its unveiling and Hitler recorded that its effect at that time was something akin to that of a blazing torch. Hitler recalled how he experienced an almost a boyish delight when one of the ladies of the party who had been entrusted with the making of the flag finally handed it over for the first time. A few months later the party in Munich was in possession of six of these flags.

Hitler was ecstatic over his latest creation, not only because it incorporated what he termed 'those revered colours' expressive of a homage to what Hitler called the 'glorious past'. The key to the design obviously lay in the visually arresting Swastika design. For Hitler, this *völkisch* symbol was also an eloquent visual expression of the will behind the movement. For a modern readership it has become synonymous with evil on such an unimaginable scale that it is almost impossible to approach this icon of the twentieth century with any measure of objectivity as a piece of graphic design. We have to be satisfied with the fact that, by any objective measure, the new symbol satisfied all the criteria which surrounded its creation. It was eye catching, interesting and dynamic and from the outset, Hitler was prone to boasting over the qualities of what is now universally recognised as a symbol of unbridled malevolence:

> 'We National Socialists regarded our flag as being the embodiment of our party programme. The red expressed the social thought underlying the movement. White the national thought. And the swastika signified the mission allotted to us – the struggle for the victory of Aryan mankind and at the same time the triumph of the ideal of creative work which is in itself and always will be anti-Semitic.'

As soon as the new symbol was unveiled, Hitler immediately ordered the corresponding armlets for the small squad of men who kept order at meetings. The steadily increasing strength of the hall guards over the next few months and years was a main factor in popularising the new symbol. Two years later, when the small squads of hall guards had grown into the feared *Sturm Abteilung* (SA) (Storm Detachments), Hitler deemed it necessary to give this aggressive organisation a particular standard of its own. He therefore designed a neo-classical banner topped with gold which harked back to the Roman legions. Hitler entrusted the execution of this new piece of political paraphernalia to an old party comrade, Herr Gahr, who was a goldsmith. This peculiar standard became the distinctive token of the SA and it was to become featured in huge numbers as the National Socialist party mushroomed, spreading fear throughout Germany.

Up to the middle of 1921, the intense activity of creating and issuing propaganda and gathering in new followers to the NSDAP was sufficient to fully occupy Hitler and was of immense value to the movement. However, in the summer of that year, a number of events transpired which were to radically alter the make up of the party and lead to the radical shake up of the party and the introduction of absolute dictatorship; this was the concept of the *Führer* principle. In Hitler's bland choice of words the events of 1921 seem fairly innocuous:

> 'An attempt made by a group of patriotic visionaries, supported by the chairman of the party at that time, to take over the direction of the party led to the break up of this little intrigue and, by a unanimous vote at a general meeting, entrusted the entire direction of the party

to my own hands. At the same time a new statute was passed which invested sole responsibility in the chairman of the movement, abolished the system of resolutions in committee and in its stead introduced the principle of division of labour which since that time has worked excellently.'

As always, the truth is somewhat different from the highly glossed version which Hitler presents in *'Mein Kampf'*. The NSDAP was very much centred on Bavaria and in Munich in particular. Hitler was growing increasingly concerned over the attempts by a number of his colleagues led by Anton Drexler to achieve an understanding with other *völkisch* groups which would provide a national platform. Among these were the DSP. Drexler, as leader of the NSDAP, entered into talks on the understandable basis that a merger of two parties who held almost identical views would result in a larger movement with greater power and influence. Given the similarity of the view points held by both parties, a compromise was easily achievable.

In forming this reasonable and rational view, Drexler and his supporters grossly underestimated the power of Adolf Hitler. Hitler had not changed since the day when his form teacher formed the view that he was autocratic, bad tempered and self opinionated and twenty years later he was no less combative, unreasonable and belligerent. He did not believe that the party could progress by compromise, he saw political battles purely in terms of an aggressive struggle to the death. Parties on the left were there to be destroyed by political violence, while those on the right were to be subsumed into the NSDAP. In Hitler's harsh world of social-Darwinist politics, there was no possibility of compromise or agreement. Hitler, after all had clearly spelled out his principles:

'We shall meet violence with violence in our own defence.'

The ultimatum offered by Hitler to his political rivals would become all too familiar, the simple choice was surrender to the will of Hitler and NSDAP or be destroyed in a campaign of political annihilation; there was no other alternative. Infuriated by the possibility of a merger with the DSP, Hitler tendered his resignation, only to withdraw the threat once the merger talks collapsed. Assuming that the danger of a potential merger had passed Hitler left for a fund-raising trip to Berlin with Eckart, their mission was once again to find funding for the ailing '*Völkischer Beobachter*'. While he was away Hitler learned of a plot to merge the NSDAP with the *Deutsche Werkgemeinschaft*, led by Dr Otto Dickel, a talented speaker who posed an unwelcome threat to Hitler's pre-eminence. In a fit of towering rage Hitler took action and resigned from the party on 11 July 1921. This move appears to have been unpremeditated and could easily have resulted in the end of his own political aspirations. However, the prospect of the NSDAP without Hitler, or even worse, Hitler as the leader of a rival party, was too much for the fledgling NSDAP to countenance. In an effort to appease Hitler and bring him back into the party, merger talks were summarily abandoned and Drexler was tasked with coaxing Hitler back into the fold. When Drexler's overtures failed Deitrich Eckart was entrusted with the job of bringing the star speaker back, but Hitler had other ideas.

Hitler demanded that, as the price for his return, he should be made full party President with absolute dictatorial powers. This demand was one of a number of conditions stipulated by Hitler which together marked the introduction if the infamous *Führerprinzip* or leader principle. The hand of Eckart can be clearly traced in the demands, but there is a great deal of Hitler's own thought at work here too. If Hitler was to have his way, the concept of democracy must be abandoned as far as the NSDAP were concerned, in future Hitler's word was to be absolute law. It was to be decreed that the party would forever be based in Munich. From now onwards it was accepted that only Hitler could make decisions on behalf of the party. He also demanded the end of all merger talks. The party would from now on be shaped entirely according to Hitler's vision, only his word would carry any weight, he alone was the leader and everyone else was relegated to the position of follower.

Despite the radical nature of his proposals, which were totally unique in party politics, Hitler managed to secure his own way. Hitler rejoined the party as member No. 3680 on 26 July 1921. The *Führer* principle had now been accepted; there was no turning back. Hitler had his first taste of absolute power:

'From 1 August 1921 onwards I undertook this internal reorganisation of the party and was supported by a number of excellent men. I refused to countenance that kind of folly and after a short time I ceased to appear at the meetings of the committee. I did nothing else except attend to my own department of propaganda and I did not permit any of the others to poke their heads into my activities. Conversely, I did not interfere in the affairs of others.

When the new statute was approved and I was appointed as president, I had the necessary authority in my hands and also the corresponding right to make short shrift of all that nonsense. In the place of decisions by the majority vote of the committee, the principle of absolute responsibility was introduced.'

On the surface, Hitler's disdain for the process of democracy is merely another perverse aspect of his unique view on life. However, in a small measure of mitigation, it should be borne in mind that Hitler's only experience of democracy in action had been gained during his visits to the Austrian *Reichsrat* in 1908 and 1909. The chamber was then *the elected parliament of Cisleithania*, still subordinate to the Emperor Franz Josef I, but presiding over the legislative process in Cisleithania. As we have seen, Hitler visited the *Reichsrat* as an impoverished young man and there could hardly have been a worse example of democracy in action.

That bizarre and uncontrollable institution provided an extremely peculiar and totally unpalatable version of democracy. As we have seen, any one of ten official languages could be employed in a single debate, but no interpretation service was provided and no limit was imposed on the length of speeches. The result was that almost the entire chamber could sit in uncomprehending ignorance while a speaker droned on in Ruthenian or Polish. We should bear in mind that Hitler was in the habit of frequently attending the Austrian Parliament at a time when fights and juvenile antics were common place. These strange and unbecoming practices therefore informed his view of democracy and democratic institutions.

Hitler was present at a time when the technique of the filibuster was regularly employed by various members of the *Reichsrat* in an effort to disrupt the genuine workings of the parliament. Their opponents in their turn were inclined to attempt to disrupt these frustrating but technically legal proceedings by, among other things, turning up playing children's musical instruments and whirling wooden rattles to create an impenetrable cacophony. The behaviour of both sides was, on occasion, so childish and unconstructive that Hitler's answer was to turn his back on democracy altogether. With the *Reichsrat* as a model, Hitler grew into a genuine opponent of what he perceived to be democracy in action. Taking into account the background of his personal experience, we can begin to understand his reasoning:

> '*In any case, a movement which must fight against the absurdity of parliamentary institutions must be immune from this sort of thing. Only thus will it have the requisite strength to carry on the struggle.*'[31]

It was at this unfortunate juncture that Hitler met the man who, with the exception of Dietrich Eckart, would do more to shape his views than any other individual. Julius Streicher was a bullheaded political rough house and rabble rouser from Nuremberg. He was a fanatical anti-Semite who would go on to publish '*Der Stürmer*', the notorious anti-Semitic journal which would later form Hitler's favourite reading. The meeting between Hitler and Streicher is often overlooked and it provides a very plausible explanation for the problem which has vexed historians. During his Vienna period, Hitler undoubtedly held strongly anti-Semitic views in the mould of Schönerer or Wolf. The reasons are less clear why Hitler developed from a mainstream anti-Semite to a full blown dyed-in-the-wool vicious ultra anti-Semite capable of sanctioning mass murder on an unimaginable scale. In 1920, Hitler had fallen under the influence of Eckart who was a fierce anti-Semite. Eckart was Hitler's mentor and it is certain that he wielded a great deal of influence. The entrance of Julius Streicher brought a rougher edge and may hold the final clue to the final transformation from Hitler as a

---

31. Ibid.

committed opponent of Jewry into fully fledged anti-Semite and arch enemy of the Jews.

Streicher prided himself on his self-imposed reputation as 'the number one Jew baiter', and as such his legacy is viewed with disdain. His career and the faux pornographic rantings of his publications are so odious that many serious historians are understandably reluctant to immerse themselves in the Streicher mire. As a result Streicher is marginalised and relegated to the status of a fringe demagogue. This was not the case from Hitler's perspective. Streicher had a major influence on Hitler and he is one of the few Nazi era figures to be accorded a glowing personal testimonial in the pages of *'Mein Kampf'*. Hitler was grateful to Streicher for his willingness to submit to Hitler's growing influence and merge into the NSDAP a significant proportion of the *Deutsche Werkgemeinschaft*, a Nuremberg based nationalist umbrella movement, complete with its own newspaper, the *Deutscher Volkswille*. This unexpected development gave Hitler a foothold outside of Munich and provided a taste of similar successes to come. It was not to prove a smooth transition as Nuremberg would soon become the scene of tedious in-fighting between Streicher and his great rival Walther Kellerbauer, but the merger provided the first rung on the bridge to the north and began the process of expanding the party beyond its Munich roots. From that point onwards Streicher was a frequent and welcome visitor in Munich and he played a prominent role in the growth of the NSDAP. By virtue of his prominent position Streicher also had a large part to play in the concomitant entrenchment of anti-Semitic policies. By 1921, Hitler was surrounded by virulent anti-Semites who could deliver their message in the high flown tones of Eckart or in the vicious language of the gutter dwelling Streicher. The result was that the anti-Semitic aspects of party policy became increasingly prominent and ultimately took on the same importance as the nationalist elements as it became ingrained at the centre of the party's agenda.

By 1921, after eighteen months under Hitler's influence, the business quarters of the NSDAP had become too small, so the party machine decamped to a new place in the Cornelius Strasse. Again, the party office was located in a restaurant, but instead of one room, the growing band of party functionaries now had three smaller rooms and one large room with great windows. At that time this appeared a wonderful thing to Hitler and his band of political warriors. The NSDAP headquarters remained there until the end of November 1923.

According to Hitler, one source of frustration for the NSDAP at the time was the close political fraternisation that he perceived to exist in Bavaria between the Bavarian government, the Marxists and the ruling Centre Party which together served to act against the interests of the nationalist movement. The political party that held power in Bavaria at the time was the Bavarian People's Party, the BVP, which was affiliated with the Centre Party at national level. The BVP did its best to counteract the effect which the growing Nazi propaganda was having on opposition supporters. According to Hitler, the Centrists now used their influence to take definite steps to halt the growth of the NSDAP. He was convinced that the instruments of the state were now being mobilised in a variety of seemingly innocuous measures employed against the NSDAP. Hitler saw enemies everywhere and claimed that if the police could find no legitimate grounds for prohibiting the display of NSDAP placards, then they might offer spurious excuses such as that they were disturbing the traffic in the streets. The results were effective and in 1921, there were over 30 instances of NSDAP advertising and pamphlets being banned.[32] It was by such questionable means, Hitler argued, that the German National People's Party calmed the anxieties of their 'Red' allies by completely prohibiting those placards which proclaimed the NSDAP message. For Hitler, these minor persecutions were sufficient to prove that national officials were involved in a series of seemingly arbitrary actions which nonetheless served to cloak a concerted campaign against the NSDAP. Hitler noted with relief that, as the nationalist spirit gradually gained a deeper hold on the people, the Government was gradually forced to follow public feeling and the campaign gave way to active support. However, the NSDAP certainly

32. Ian Kershaw: 'Hitler 1889-1936: Hubris' p. 176.

did not have things their own way and large and powerful elements within the Government authorities did everything in their power to hamper the spread of right wing nationalism.

Hitler singled out for praise two officials whom he considered to have acted against the prevailing tide of hostility towards the nationalist cause.

These were Ernst Pöhner who was Chief of Police at the time and was assisted by his loyal counsellor Dr. Frick, his Chief Executive official. These were the only men among the higher officials who according to Hitler:

> 'Had the courage to place the interests of their country before their own interests in holding on to their jobs.'

Of those officials in senior positions, Ernst Pöhner was identified as a bitter thorn in the side of the centrists attempting to block the progress of the NSDAP. There is no question over Pöhner and Frick's National Socialist credentials as both were later implicated in the Beer Hall Putsch and Frick stood trial along with Hitler.

Hitler was prepared to accept that at the next level down the minor officials working against the NSDAP did not act from political motivation; in his opinion, they simply conformed to the wishes of the Government, so as to secure their daily bread for themselves. In Hitler's opinion, only Pöhner and his collaborator, Dr. Frick, had fought against the tide and actively backed the NSDAP cause and fought to overturn the bans on party literature. With the support of the few officials whom he could count on, Hitler was all the time gathering support inside the government. Outside he was also gaining new adherents for the party, but there were many in Munich who saw the dangers which lay ahead and who remained steadfastly opposed to Hitler and the NSDAP. Among them was Alexander Moritz Frey who, like Hitler, had survived the war. He was now trying to eke out a living as a writer. Moritz Frey's account is likely to be coloured by his absolute dislike of Hitler and all he stood for, but there is no reason to doubt his description of the occasional meetings with Hitler and his entourage during this period:

'We ran into each other sometimes in Café Heck, one of the three Hofgarten cafés. Hitler would sit there together with a half dozen confidants. He always greeted me hastily, the blood rising quickly in his face, probably because of his antipathy towards me. He sent his Max Amann over to me. He was supposed to win me over to the movement. 'Hitler will make it, believe me, Frey, he will make it. And you will regret it if you don't listen to me,' he told me.... He tried several times, inviting me to large Nazi rallies... I made it unmistakably clear to him that I did not share the Nazi outlook. He knew that I was published in democratic and social-democratic periodicals, and he harshly condemned my 'service in the pay of the Jewish press'. I took my leave of him with just as much energy.'*

Opposition to Hitler came from many quarters and he was not surprised to discover that even among the *völkisch* movement, his popularity was by no means assured. In some quarters Hitler and his followers were despised for their lack of intellectual rigour. For once, Hitler was justified in his suspicions that intellectuals looked down upon him and his movement. The enthusiastic recourse to violence coupled with the mob mentality provoked their justified derision:

'They reproached us bitterly not only for what they called our crude worship of the cudgel but also because, according to them, we had no intellectual forces on our side. These charlatans did not think for a moment that a Demosthenes could be reduced to silence at a mass-meeting by fifty idiots who had come there to shout him down and use their fists against his supporters. The innate cowardice of the pen-and-ink charlatan prevents him from exposing himself to such a danger, for he always works in safe retirement and never dares to make a noise or come forward in public.'

One of the many who were drawn to the National Socialist cause at this juncture was Kurt Ludecke. Ludecke, who was later to write an account of his life with Hitler, was a colourful character to say the least. Having been invalided out of the army in 1916 on mental health grounds, Ludecke recovered sufficiently to begin a highly successful career as an international businessman. He appears to have been an inveterate deal maker, a mover and shaker with an easy charm which allowed him to access many different social circles. He also appears to have lived life to the full and had an uncanny knack for getting himself into high profile scrapes, including being branded as a spy by the French government. For many years the larger than life aspects of Ludecke's 1938 volume 'I Knew Hitler' were dismissed as being too imaginative to be true, however in recent years Ludecke has been rehabilitated somewhat and is now seen as a highly credible source by many formerly sceptical historians. Ludecke had befriended Count Reventlow who was an influential figure in *völkisch* circles and in August 1922, Reventlow provided the introduction to Adolf Hitler which would change the course of Ludecke's life for ever. Ludecke's extensive account of hearing Hitler speak is an excellent source in that it provides a comprehensive insight into the circumstances which prevailed in Germany at the time that Hitler was first harbouring thoughts of seizing power by force.

'The final struggle for supremacy among the many would-be dictators had begun; the process of pitiless elimination of the weak was under way. It was deeds, not words, that counted now.

Reventlow suggested that I go with him to Munich, where the political situation was taking on even deeper colour. He had said that he would introduce me to General Ludendorff, and now he began to talk also of Dr. Pittinger and of one Adolf Hitler. I had heard that there was an agitator of that name; but, ill-advised by the teacher, I had not tried to meet him. Munich was still the city of charm, but with each visit I found its political aspect more absorbing. The contrast with Berlin was marked; one was the Mecca of Marxists and Jews, the other the citadel of their enemies.

When Reventlow introduced me to Dr. Pittinger, I was warmly received into the circle of his friends. Here were Colonel Stockhausen, his chief of staff; Count von Soden, the 'chief du cabinet' of Crown Prince Rupprecht; Kahr, the ex-minister; and Poehner, the former police-president. I met many others of their group, and learned much about them, partly through Reventlow's sarcastic tongue. When they proposed appointing me liaison officer for the Bund Bayern und Reich between Bavaria and the North, I joined. But it was faute de mieux, for I could not escape a vague apprehension that somewhere, in either its personnel or its platform, the Bund was too weak for action.

The drastic new laws were threatening the sovereignty of Bavaria, and relations between Berlin and Munich were strained. Within Bavaria itself, two chief political interests were clashing: the Centrist Bavarian Peoples' Party, ready to secede from the Reich if necessary, and the Nationalist völkisch element, opposed to any secession. The latter had used Munich, safely so far, as a base for their campaign against Berlin. The Bavarian Government, which was Centrist, was now in the quandary of choosing between surrendering its sovereignty to Berlin or risking an alliance with the völkisch Nationalists, which was also against their own interests. Finally they yielded to Berlin, making Bavaria, like the rest of Germany, a hunting-ground for Berlin police seeking the extradition of National activists. The wave of indignation that surged through the land reached its climax in a huge mass demonstration of protest in Munich on 11 August 1922, under the sponsorship of the 'Vaeterlandische Verbaende', which was in effect a holding company loosely co-ordinating all the patriotic societies, large and small, and including at that time the Nazi Party – the National Socialist German Workers' Party.

This was the greatest mass demonstration Munich had ever seen. It was one of incalculable historical importance, for on that day a little-known figure stepped into the light as a recognised public speaker of extraordinary power. This was a man who until then had literally been snubbed by the higher-ups in the patriotic societies. Now, because of his growing local importance and for the sake of a united front, he had been invited to appear as one of two speakers on a programme in which all were taking part. Adolf Hitler was scheduled to speak last. I t needed no clairvoyance to see that here was a man who knew how to seize his opportunity. Red placards announced in huge black letters that he was to appear. Many who read them had never even heard his name. Here were inflammatory slogans: 'Versailles: Germany's Ruin... Republic of the People or State of the Jews?... International

Solidarity: A Jewish World Swindle... Down with the November Criminals... The National Socialist Movement Must Conquer....

And every one of his placards ended with the blunt phrase: "Jews Not Admitted."[33] The great mass demonstration in Munich against the Law for the Protection of the Republic. It took place in the late summer of 1922, all patriotic societies, including the National Socialist Movement, were represented. Ludecke went on to recollect the day on which he first heard Hitler speak to the assembled masses who were there in support of the various conservative parties and movements which together constituted the Vaeterlandische Verbaende. It was a bright summer day. The Reds had tried their best to break up the Nazi columns marching through the city, comprising Storm Troopers followed by sections of the Party. Soon the assailants were in flight, bruised and beaten, and it had been demonstrated for the first time that Nationalists as well as Reds had the right to march in formation through the streets of Munich, and that the Nazis were determined to maintain this right.

The 'Patriotic Societies' had assembled without bands and without flags. But when the Nazis marched into the Koenigsplatz with banners flying, their bands playing stirring German marches, they were greeted with tremendous cheers. An excited, expectant crowd was now filling the beautiful square to the last inch and overflowing into surrounding streets. There were well over a hundred thousand.

The first speaker, little Dr. Buckeley, harangued this mass in true political fashion. At last he relinquished the platform, and Hitler faced the multitude. Reventlow had seen to it that we were near the speakers' stand. I was close enough to see Hitler's face, watch every change in his expression, hear every word he said.

When the man stepped forward on the platform, there was almost no applause. He stood silent for a moment. Then he began to speak, quietly and ingratiatingly at first. Before long his voice had risen to a hoarse shriek that gave an extraordinary effect of an intensity of

---

33. Kurt Ludecke: 'I Knew Hitler' Coda Books Electronic Edition 2011.

feeling. There were many high-pitched, rasping notes – Reventlow had told me that his throat had been affected by war-gas – but despite its strident tone, his diction had a distinctly Austrian turn, softer and pleasanter than the German.

Critically I studied this slight, pale man, his brown hair parted on one side and falling again and again over his sweating brow. Threatening and beseeching, with small, pleading hands and flaming, steel-blue eyes, he had the look of a fanatic. Presently my critical faculty was swept away. Leaning from the tribune as if he were trying to impel his inner self into the consciousness of all these thousands, he was holding the masses, and me with them, under a hypnotic spell by the sheer force of his conviction. He urged the revival of German honour and manhood with a blast of words that seemed to cleanse. "Bavaria is now the most German land in Germany!" he shouted, to roaring applause. Then, plunging into sarcasm, he indicted the leaders in Berlin as 'November Criminals', daring to put into words thoughts that Germans were now almost afraid to think and certainly to voice.

It was clear that Hitler was feeling the exaltation of the emotional response now surging up toward him from his thousands of hearers. His voice rising to passionate climaxes, he finished his speech with an anthem of hate against the 'Novemberlings' and a pledge of undying love for the Fatherland. "Germany must be free!" was his final defiant slogan. Then two last words that were like the sting of a lash:

'Deutschland Erwache!' (Awake, Germany!) There was thunderous applause. Then the masses took a solemn oath "to save Germany in Bavaria from Bolshevism".'[34]

Hitler was not averse to becoming personally involved in the crude tactics which his middle class opponents despised but which had such a galvanising effect on men like Ludecke. On 14 September 1921, Hitler led a delegation of brawlers intent of breaking up a meeting of the *Bayernbund* due to be addressed by his arch political opponent Otto

---

34. Ibid.

Bellerstedt whom Hitler described as his greatest political rival. Hitler's supporters disrupted the events and demanded that Hitler should be allowed to speak. The hall was plunged into darkness and a number of *Bayerbund* supporters were seriously injured in the ensuing melee. Hitler was clearly the ring leader and Bellerstedt successfully pressed charges against him. Hitler now found himself sentenced to a month's imprisonment in Stadelheim prison. He served his time behind bars between 24 June and 27 July 1922.

Hitler bided his time and in 1934, Bellerstedt became one of the unsung victims of the night of the long knives when he was arrested and taken to Dachau prison camp where he appears to have been summarily executed.

- CHAPTER 14 -
THE GROWTH OF
THE NSDAP

HITLER'S ENTHUSIASM FOR political violence was perverse and rather juvenile. Like an overgrown school bully he adored rough house violence. This immature love of violent behaviour dovetailed perfectly with the party concepts of honour, sacrifice, duty and blind obedience. Despite the fact that he had ended up in jail in 1922 for his part in encouraging violence, the lesson was totally lost on Hitler and he sought to justify the application of political violence in the pages of *'Mein Kampf'* with the scoundrel's claim that actions such as those which had led to his imprisonment were a necessary form of 'self defence'. He argued that the simplest follower who had the courage to stand on the table in a beer-hall where his enemies were gathered and defend his position against them achieved more than most political theorists. Hitler pathetically opined that the brawler by his actions would at least convert one or two people to believe in the movement.

With his innate love of violence and love of all things militaristic, it was no surprise that Hitler embraced paramilitary activity. It should be borne in mind that in the early twenties each side of the struggle was equally guilty of resorting to violent means, the rival parties on the left such as the *Kommunischte Partei Deutschlands* (KPD) frequently marched fully armed and Hitler was determined to fight fire with fire. His military mania would soon witness the growth of the SA, which in time would become his own private army. As a lowly corporal, Hitler had not experienced full military command, but he recognised that a campaign backed by organised violence would require a body of men organised along military lines. In this he was ably assisted by the activities of the omnipresent Ernst Röhm an amazing networker, homosexual hedonist and ceaseless activist whose senior connections in the army allowed him access to weapons and gained him the nickname 'the machine gun king'. The lingering spectre of the *Freikorps* hovered around the political scene in the early twenties and their influence is often understated. These large bodies of well-armed and under-employed young men cast a malign pall of potential violence over all forms of political activity. The Weimar Republic and the various state governments were constantly in a state of fear over the potential for an armed coup at any moment.

The *Freikorps* provided a pool of ready manpower for other connected purposes. A permanent group of party members who would serve as the *Saalschutz Abteilung* (hall defence detachment) for the DAP were initially gathered around Emil Maurice; they had stuck together after the February 1920 flare up preceding Hitler's reading of the twenty-five points at the *Hofbräuhaus*. To begin with there was little organisation or structure to this group who were originally called the *Ordnertruppen* or Order Troops. More than a year later, on 3 August 1921, Hitler redefined the group as the *Turn und Sportabteilung* (Gymnastic and Sports Division) of the party, he did so in order to disguise the true nature of the organisation and avoid trouble with the authorities who were on their guard for a possible *putsch* by the forces of the extreme right and left. It was by now well recognised as an appropriate, even necessary, organ of the party. The future SA developed by organising and formalising the groups of ex-soldiers and beer hall brawlers who were to protect gatherings of the Nazi Party from disruptions from Social Democrats and Communists.

The small band of rough heads assembled to do the party's dirty work soon grew into the fearsome *Sturm Abteilungen* (Storm Detachments) and as it expanded the leadership of the SA passed from Emil Maurice to the young Hans Ulrich Klintzsch. Klintzsch had been a naval officer and a member of the Ehrhardt Brigade of Kapp Putsch fame and was, at the time of his assumption of SA command, a member of the notorious *Organisation Consul* (OC). The National Socialists under Hitler were now taking advantage of the more professional management and organisational techniques of the experienced volunteers with military backgrounds.

Under their popular leader, the future *Stabschef* Ernst Röhm, the SA grew in importance within the Nazi power structure, initially growing in size to thousands of members. In 1922, the Nazi Party created a youth section, the *Jugendbund*, for young men between the ages of 14 and 18 years.

The swastika arm bands initially distributed would have been enough to distinguish the SA from the rank and file, but it was not enough for Hitler or his followers. Their mind set was formed by their years of military service and the inevitable result was the impetus for the creation of a uniformed paramilitary force. The SA felt at home in uniform and were quick to adopt military style uniforms. A large consignment of surplus tropical uniforms from the war were made available at a knock down price and they were eagerly snapped up as the uniform of the SA. In December 1922, the hated Brown Shirts led by Ernst Röhm made their first appearance on the pages of history. The SA were eventually to become too big for Hitler's liking, but in the early days of the movement Hitler needed a strike force who could intimidate and outfight the forces of the left and initially, at least, he was delighted with the work of Röhm and his followers:

'How those young men did their job! Like a swarm of hornets they tackled disturbers at our meetings, regardless of superiority of numbers, however great, indifferent to wounds and bloodshed, inspired with the great idea of blazing a trail for the sacred mission of our movement.'

As early as the summer of 1920, the organisation of squads of men as hall guards, ostensibly created for the purpose of maintaining order at NSDAP meetings, was gradually assuming definite shape. In a climate of genuine political violence it was essential for an extremist party to be able to defend itself amidst the dog-eat-dog world of post war politics. By the spring of 1921, this body of men numbered around 1,000 and were sectioned off into squads of one hundred, which in turn were sub-divided into smaller groups.

The urgency for the growth of the SA was understandable, violence was now a frequent occurrence at meetings as Hitler's opponents led by the KPD became increasingly hostile towards the burgeoning NSDAP. As the number of the meetings steadily increased the NSDAP still frequently met in the Munich *Hofbräuhaus*, but they also met with increasing frequency in the large meeting halls throughout the city. In the autumn and winter of 1920-1921, meetings in new venues such as the *Bürgerbräu* and Munich *Kindlbräu* had assumed much larger proportions and even the large meetings of the NSDAP were routinely overcrowded with the result that the police were compelled to close and bar the doors long before proceedings commenced.

The increasing public interest taken in these meetings, particularly during the latter half of 1920, compelled the NSDAP to hold two meetings a week. Hitler recalled how eager crowds gathered round NSDAP posters as soon as they were unveiled. With a hyperbolic flourish he also claimed that the large meeting halls in the town were always filled to bursting as tens of thousands of people, 'who had been led astray' by the teachings of Marxism, found their way into the NSDAP fold.

At last the party was on the map and Hitler had achieved one of his early goals. The party was by no means the largest, but it was at least being spoken about. Hitler noted with pride that the words 'National Socialist' had become common property and at last signified a definite party programme. The circle of supporters and members was constantly increasing, so that in the winter of 1920-21, the NSDAP were beginning to be taken seriously, at least in Munich. No other conservative party was able to hold large scale mass demonstrations. The cavernous Munich Kindl Hall, which held 5,000 people, was on more than one occasion overcrowded and up till then there was only one other hall, the Krone Circus Hall, into which the NSDAP had not ventured.

Hitler took delight in the ability of his strong arm teams to control increasing levels of violence associated with the NSDAP meetings. He also drew personal satisfaction from the increasing scale of the meetings. The combination of growing public support and the occasional display of physical strength were the two elements which Hitler prized most as his party grew and prospered.

The beer hall brawls and mass meetings were important to Hitler at a personal level. In the autobiographical sections of *'Mein Kampf'* he records, with obvious pride, a detailed description of four key events which took place during 1921 and 1922. In this respect *'Mein Kampf'* provides us a pointer to the things that mattered most to Hitler the man and, as such, they provide a unique insight into his inner world. He gives a surprisingly detailed account of the fights, squabbles and rallies which were important to him. On the surface these events are not of enormous significance in themselves and, in the case of the *Schaalsclacht*, the tawdry events which to Hitler seem tumultuous appear to a modern audience as insignificant and petty.

It is only as a result of the large amount of space which Hitler accords to these relatively minor events in *'Mein Kampf'* that we are alerted to the factors which preoccupied his mind at the time. Had these key events not been highlighted at such length in his book they might otherwise have been overlooked and we would have lost a rare insight into the workings of Hitler's mind.

The initial Circus Krone meeting, held in November 1921, was the first of four events which held great significance for Hitler. In retrospect it fades into insignificance as part of a procession of such events, but we know from *'Mein Kampf'* that Hitler considered this mass meeting to be his first real personal triumph. It is worth revisiting the events in detail in order to appreciate the weight that Hitler himself attached to otherwise insignificant events.

At the end of January 1921, there were new problems for Germany which led to increased anxiety throughout the country. The main source for concern was the Paris Agreement, by which Germany pledged herself to pay the unbelievable sum of a hundred million gold Marks. The agreement was due to be confirmed by the allies who had issued the London Ultimatum. To mark the beginning of a popular protest an old-established Munich working committee, representative of various conservative groups, deemed it advisable to call for a public meeting of protest. As a firm opponent of anything connected with Versailles Hitler was anxious that the meeting should be held as soon as possible, but as the days wore on without an announcement Hitler records that he became increasingly nervous and restless as he felt that a lot of time was being wasted and nothing undertaken.

To Hitler's extreme frustration, the organisers continued to dither. Finally a meeting was suggested in the König Platz, but this was turned down by the organising committee as some members feared the proceedings might be wrecked by Red elements. An alternative suggestion was for a demonstration in front of the sacred Feldherrn Hall, which even the forces of reaction would hesitate to profane by violent acts, but this too came to nothing. Finally a combined meeting in the Munich Kindl Hall was suggested and agreed in principle. Meanwhile, day after day had gone by; the big parties had entirely ignored the terrible event, and the working committee could not decide on a definite date for holding the demonstration.

On Tuesday, 1 February 1921, Hitler became increasingly agitated and put forward an urgent demand for a final decision. He was put off until Wednesday, 2 February 1921. On that day Hitler again demanded to be told clearly if and when the meeting was to take place. The reply was again uncertain and evasive, the committee would only vouchsafe that it was 'intended' to arrange a demonstration the following week. At that Hitler lost all patience and in a characteristic fit of pique decided to take matters into his own hands. His gambler's mentality came to the fore and as *Führer* of the NSDAP he resolved to conduct a demonstration of protest on his own initiative. At noon on Wednesday 2 February 1921, Hitler tells us that he sprang into a frenzy of action and hurriedly dictated the text of the poster and at the same time hired the Krone Circus Hall for the next day, Thursday 3 February 1921. In those days this was a highly questionable undertaking. Not only because of the uncertainty of filling that vast hall, but also because of the risk of the meeting being wrecked by left wing opponents.

Numerically the growing squad of hall guards was up to the task of policing the *Hofbräuhaus*, but was not strong enough for such a vast hall as the *Zirkus Krone*. Hitler was also uncertain about what to do in case the meeting was broken up as tactically: policing a huge circus building was a different proposition from an ordinary meeting hall. Hitler acknowledged the riskiness of the venture and noted that one thing was certain: a failure would destroy the forward momentum which was being built and would throw the NSDAP back into reverse for a long time to come. Hitler knew that if just one meeting was wrecked his playground bully tactics would be exposed and his party's prestige as the proponent of the application superior force would be seriously injured. The floodgates would be opened and his opponents would be encouraged to repeat their success.

To compound the uncertainty Hitler had allowed only one day in which to post the bills advertising the meeting. This was the day of the meeting itself, Thursday 3 February 1921. To add spice to the gamble it rained on the morning of that day and there was genuine reason to fear that many people would prefer to remain at home rather than hurry to a meeting through rain and snow, especially when there was likely to be violence and bloodshed.

In a rare glimpse of self doubt Hitler recorded in *'Mein Kampf'* how, on that Thursday morning, he was suddenly struck with fear that in the short timescale which he had allowed the hall might not be filled to anything like capacity. He admitted that such a failure would have made him look ridiculous in the eyes of the working committee and his many opponents. However, Hitler was never one to give in easily and faced with the prospect of public humiliation his fear of failure spurred him on to even greater efforts. As the rain turned to sleet Hitler redoubled his efforts and immediately dictated various leaflets, had them printed and distributed that same afternoon.

Hitler knew that it was now a matter of urgent necessity to deliver the message by all means available, and he was sufficiently astute to realise that with time running out extraordinary measures were required. In desperation he resorted to copying the tactics of the Marxist parties which he so despised. Two lorries were hastily hired and were draped as much as possible in red, each had the new NSDAP flag hoisted on it and was then filled with fifteen or twenty members from the party. As the day wore on a desperate series of increasingly frantic orders were given to all available members to canvas the streets as thoroughly and rapidly as possible, to distribute every last leaflet and cajole as many members of the public as possible to attend the mass meeting to be held that very evening. Hitler had stolen the promotional device from his Marxist rivals and he vainly boasted that this was the first time that lorries had driven through the streets bearing flags which were not actually manned by Marxists.

Despite all his best efforts, initially things appeared to have gone badly wrong for Hitler. At 7 P.M. only a few had gathered in the circus hall. In an agony of self doubt Hitler sat at home waiting by the telephone. It must be presumed that if the event was to prove a failure Hitler intended to avoid the personal embarrassment by hiding at home. Hitler records that he was being kept informed by telephone every ten minutes and in an unusual bout of frankness admits that he was becoming uneasy. He knew full well that in the usual scheme of things by seven or a quarter past NSDAP meeting halls were already half filled; sometimes even packed to bursting with the police struggling to maintain order from those still struggling to gain admission. In their anxiety those reporting to Hitler had entirely forgotten to take into account the huge dimensions of this new meeting place. A thousand people in the *Hofbräuhaus* was quite an impressive sight, but the same number in the *Zirkus* building was simply swallowed up by the sheer scale of the venue. In reality there were far more supporters in attendance than the reports suggested. Shortly afterwards Hitler received more hopeful reports and at a quarter to eight he was informed that the hall was three-quarters filled, with huge crowds still lined up at the pay boxes. It was then that Hitler finally left for the meeting. Hitler arrived at the *Zirkus* building at two minutes past eight. There was still a crowd of people outside, partly inquisitive people and many opponents who obviously did not wish to make a contribution to nationalist funds by paying the admission money. According to Hitler they preferred to wait outside and hope for interesting developments for developments.

When Hitler finally entered the great hall of the *Zirkus Krone* he records that he felt the same joy he had felt a year previously at the first meeting in the Munich *Hofbräu* Banquet Hall. It was not until he had forced his way through the solid wall of people and reached the platform that he perceived the full measure of his triumph, at which point the feelings of success became overwhelming. To Hitler's delight he saw that the hall was packed to its limits. More than 5,600 tickets had been sold and, allowing for the unemployed, poor students and the NSDAP's own detachments of men for keeping order, Hitler estimated that a crowd of about 6,500 must have been present.

Rising to the occasion and fuelled by a raging sense of euphoria Hitler began to speak. His theme was 'Future or Downfall' and he recalls how he was filled with joy as he spoke for about two and a half hours. From the speaker's platform Hitler had the feeling after the first half-hour that the meeting was going to be a big success. Hitler's speeches typically built very slowly from an almost quiet speaking voice to a manic intensity over the course of a speech which tended to last between two and three hours. After the first hour of the speech Hitler recalled that he was already being received by spontaneous outbreaks of applause, but in a departure from the norm after the second hour this died down to a solemn stillness which Hitler boasted would be forever remembered by all those present. According to his own account nothing broke this imposing silence and only when the last word had been spoken did the meeting give vent to its feelings by spontaneously singing the national anthem. It was a momentous occasion for Hitler, a political breakthrough and a vindication of his increasing belief in his own judgment.

> *'I watched the scene during the next twenty minutes, as the vast hall slowly emptied itself, and only then did I leave the platform, a happy man, and made my way home.'*

The events of 3 February 1921 were one of a series of gambles which informed the growing conviction in Adolf Hitler that he had the ability to make marginal judgment calls. Once again Lucky Linzer had ridden his luck.

A famous series of photographs were taken of the occasion of the first meeting in the Krone Circus Hall. Entitled *'Hitler Spright'* (Hitler speaks) the wide shot of the huge crowd bears mute testimony to Hitler's version of events. For Hitler, occupying the centre of his own universe, the meeting had enormous significance.

Hitler's own description of the events is mirrored in the description provided for us by Kurt Ludecke who in the pages of 'I Knew Hitler' left his own description of a Hitler speech delivered in the fervent hot house atmosphere of *Zirkus Krone*.

'Hitler evidently combined the practical and the spiritual. Counting apparently on the effect of his address in the afternoon, he had arranged for the evening a Nazi meeting in the Zirkus Krone.

The term 'Nazi' had been only slightly known up to the hour of his address. Nazi – a sound of a sort that is common in Bavarian speech – is a contraction of the first word of the title of Hitler's party, the 'Nationalsozialistische Deutsche Arbeiter-Partei.' Now we were hearing these syllables wherever we went in Munich. Reventlow and I found the Zirkus so jammed that there was scarcely room for a pin to drop. Around the platform was grouped a guard of SA – the 'Sturmabteilung,' husky fellows who looked ready to cope with any situation. I could see the need of them, for it was apparent that the Nazis, more than any others in those days, were daring to assail the Jews, the Communists, the bourgeois round-heads, denouncing what they believed evil. More Storm Troopers encircled the arena and flanked the aisle leading to the tribune. All of them wore red arm-bands bearing the now famous symbol – a black swastika in a white circle.

We were shown to seats reserved for us within a few feet of the platform. In a moment, the expectant murmur of the throng hushed, then ceased. Hitler was entering.

It took courage to risk a second address that day, but the experience of the Koenigsplatz was repeated with even greater intensity, if that was possible. Standing under his own banners, addressing his own followers, Hitler was even more outspoken, flaying the 'system' with that fury of invective of which he is a master and disclosing an extraordinary talent for conveying the most complicated matters in plastic, popular form, comprehensible to anyone.

Again his power was inescapable, gripping and swaying me as it did every one within those walls. Again I had the sensation of surrendering my being to his leadership. When he stopped speaking, his chest still heaving with emotion, there was a moment of dead silence, then a storm of cheers.

Count Reventlow introduced me to Hitler, still perspiring, dishevelled in his dirty trench-coat, his hair plastered against his brow, his face pale, his nostrils distended. Looking closely at him for a long moment, I did not need to wonder where he found the reserves of character and courage that were enabling him to forge ahead of the other leaders. Everything dwelt behind his eyes. We shook hands, and it was arranged that I was to meet him at Nazi headquarters on the following afternoon.

Then his men gathered round him, and the Count and I left. The Zirkus Krone had set the seal on my conversion.'

Ludecke may have been won over but the wider world cared somewhat less and after all of his efforts Hitler was outraged when the Munich press reproduced the photographs but reported the meeting as having been merely 'nationalist' in character. He was incensed by the fact that they omitted all mention of the NSDAP as promoters of the event.

Despite his frustrations over the lack of anticipated press coverage Hitler sensed that his movement had, for the first time, developed beyond the dimensions of the myriad of tiny *völkisch* parties which littered the Munich scene. At a personal level however Adolf Hitler was clearly as mesmeric as he was in public and we are fortunate to have this insight into a personal interview with Hitler from the pages of Ludecke's 'I Knew Hitler'.

'At three the next afternoon, I stepped into the open door of what had once been a little Kaffeehaus in the Komeliusstrasse, in the poorer section of the city. This was Nazi headquarters. There was a show-window displaying Nazi literature, a large room with a reception corner barred off by a wooden rail, a counter where members paid their dues, a few tables and chairs. That was all, except for two

smaller rooms beyond. Hitler took me into one of these and closed the door behind us.

At once I offered myself to him and to his cause without reservation. As frankly as I had talked to Reventlow, I told him the story of my life, dwelling especially upon years during and after the war when I had felt myself baffled at every turn. Hitler listened closely, studying me keenly, now and then rising from his chair and pacing the floor. I was impressed again by his obvious indifference to his personal appearance; but again I saw that the whole man was concentrated in his eyes, his clear, straightforward, domineering, bright blue eyes. When I mentioned my appointment in the Bund Bayern und Reich he frowned, but approved my suggestion that it might be wise to maintain the connection for a while, to remain vigilant and learn what was going on. When I rose to leave, it was after seven; we had been talking for over four hours. Solemnly clasping hands, we sealed the pact. I had given him my soul.'

It was clear to Ludecke and thousands like him who had fallen under Hitler's spell that the NSDAP was on the rise and could no longer be ignored. With his gambler's instincts now running unchecked Hitler seized the opportunity and, in an effort to dispel any doubt that the meeting was merely an isolated success, he immediately arranged for another meeting at the *Zirkus Krone* in the following week. The follow up meeting witnessed the same success as the original. Once more the vast hall was overflowing with people. Hitler knew he was on a roll and seized the moment and decided to hold a third meeting during the following week, which also proved a similar success. His speeches were now beginning to form a coherent pattern which struck a rich chord with the conservative and *völkisch* elements. Kurt Ludecke provides a clear impression of how this heady mix of policy and oratory was being received throughout Bavaria.

'Hitler had unfolded a practical programme which would demand the utmost of my strength and ability. I must come down out of the clouds and prepare for intelligent action. Hitler had accepted me with definite interest; but just the same I was today merely one among less

than a thousand inscribed members. Tomorrow would I be helping
him to lead, or would I be merely one of those who were led, losing
my identity more and more each day as new recruits rallied under the
swastika banner?

The Party was young, well-founded; nothing could prevent it from
growing, and I was resolved to grow with it. The strength and will
were there; I needed only knowledge and opportunity. During the
ensuing weeks I was diligent in learning the ropes, studying the inside
structure of the Party, meeting people, reading pertinent literature,
discharging whatever duties were given me, and publicising the Nazi
cause and the personality of Hitler wherever I could.'

Following these initial successes, early in 1921, Hitler records how
he increased NSDAP activity in Munich still further. Mass meetings
were routinely held once a week, but during some weeks two meetings
were held. During midsummer and autumn this increased to three.
The NSDAP met regularly at the Circus Hall and it gave Hitler great
satisfaction to see that every meeting brought the same measure of
success. Ludecke too recorded the phenomenal success of Hitler as a
public speaker:

'I do not know how to describe the emotions that swept over me
as I heard this man. His words were like a sacrament. When he spoke
of the disgrace of Germany, I felt ready to spring on any enemy. His
appeal to German manhood was like a call to arms, the gospel he
preached a sacred truth. He seemed another Luther. I forgot everything
but the man; then, glancing round, I saw that his magnetism was
holding these thousands as one.

Of course I was ripe for this experience. I was a man of thirty-two,
weary of disgust and disillusionment, a wanderer seeking a cause;
a patriot without a channel for his patriotism, a yearner after the
heroic without a hero. The intense will of the man, the passion of his
sincerity seemed to flow from him into me. I experienced an exaltation
that could be likened only to religious conversion. I felt sure that no
one who had heard Hitler that afternoon could doubt that he was
the man of destiny, the vitalising force in the future of Germany. The

masses who had streamed into the Koenigsplatz with a stern sense of national humiliation seemed to be going forth renewed. The bands struck up, the thousands began to move away. I knew my search was ended. I had found myself, my leader, and my cause.'

The result of the mass meetings was reflected in an ever-increasing number of supporters and members who now flocked to the party. Naturally, such success was deeply resented by Hitler's opponents. Plans were soon laid by left wing elements to put a definite end to Hitler's activities. Hitler knew that an orchestrated attack would come sooner or later but he did not believe that smaller venues such as the *Hofbräuhaus* in Munich were suitable for the interruptive tactics of his adversaries. He feared such a thing would eventually happen in one of the bigger halls, especially that of the Krone Circus, but on this point his judgement proved flawed. The first attempt to overthrow the NSDAP by force was actually mounted in the *Hofbräuhaus* and an extended description of this otherwise insignificant political skirmish is given at length in *'Mein Kampf'*. Hitler was inordinately proud of the second of the four events during the period 1921-1922, which he singled out as being of special significance to the development of National Socialism and its methods.

On 4 November 1921 Hitler was due to speak at one of the smaller NSDAP meetings which still occasionally took place in the Munich *Hofbräuhaus*. In order to carry out this direct action Hitler's left wing adversaries had resolved to send to the meeting a body of workmen employed in certain 'Red' factories: they were charged with breaking up the meeting by force. News eventually leaked out of a planned attack, but the warning was received very late in the day. Hitler and his cronies should have received the news sooner but it transpired that, on that particular day, the NSDAP had given up its old business office in the *Sternecker Gasse* and had moved into other quarters which were not yet in functioning order. The telephone arrangements had been cut off by the former tenants and had not yet been reinstalled. As a result the numerous attempts made that day to inform Hitler by telephone of the planned intervention did not reach their target until very late in the day.

According to Hitler's account the news only arrived on the evening of 4 November between 6 P.M. and 7 P.M.. Hitler therefore had confirmation that the *Hofbräuhaus* meeting would be targeted, but there was very little he could do about it.

In the pages of *'Mein Kampf'* Hitler tells how he used these fraught circumstances to build a self congratulatory word picture which attempts to raise a mundane beer hall brawl into an epic moment full of portent and significance for the future. According to Hitler's self laudatory account of the proceedings the result of the late warning was that, on this crucial evening, the SA were not present in strong force at that particular meeting. There was in fact only one squad scheduled to be present which did not consist of the usual one hundred men, but, as fate would have it, was limited to just forty-six. The NSDAP communications network of telephone connections were not yet sufficiently organised to be able to give the alarm in the course of a mere hour or so. As a result a sufficiently powerful force of order troops to deal with the situation could not be called together. In any event it is unlikely that they would have been summoned. Hitler was aware that there had been frequent similar false alarms concerning red interventions which had not materialised and took the decision to carry on regardless.

When Hitler arrived in the entrance hall of the *Hofbräuhaus* at 7:45 P.M. that evening he swiftly understood that he had made a serious mistake, there could be no doubt as to what his opponents intended. The hall was already full to overflowing and the police had been forced to bar the entrances. Hitler's adversaries were fully prepared and had taken the precaution of arriving very early. They were therefore ensconced in the hall, which left a large body of NSDAP followers locked outside. The small bodyguard awaited Hitler at the entrance. In a moment of pure theatre Hitler claims to have had the doors leading to the principal hall closed and then paused to make a dramatic exhortation to his bodyguard of forty-six men. He claims that in this short speech he made it clear to his 'boys' that perhaps on that evening, for the first time, they would have to show their unbending and unbreakable loyalty to Hitler and the movement and that not one should leave the hall unless carried out dead. He added that he would remain in the hall come what may and that he did not believe that one of them would abandon him, and that if he saw any one of them act the coward he would personally tear off his armlet and badge from any offender. Hitler now demanded of them that despite their limited numbers they should act aggressively if the slightest attempt to sabotage the meeting were made and that they must remember that the best defence is always attack.

Hitler records that his pep talk was greeted with a triple *'Heil'* which sounded more hoarse and violent than usual. Safe in the knowledge that he had the necessary muscle behind him Hitler advanced through the hall. With the practised eye of a trench warfare veteran he swiftly noted where his opponents sat closely huddled together:

'Innumerable faces glowing with hatred and rage were fixed on me, while others with sneering grimaces shouted at me together. Now they would 'Finish with us. We must look out for our entrails. Today they would smash in our faces once and for all.' And there were other expressions of an equally elegant character. They knew that they were there in superior numbers and they acted accordingly.'

Despite the unpromising outlook Hitler was able to open the meeting; and began to speak. In *'Mein Kampf'* he records how, in the hall of the *Hofbräuhaus*, he stood always at the side, away from the entry and on top of a beer table. Hitler was therefore speaking right in the midst of the audience. Perhaps this circumstance was responsible for creating a certain feeling and a sense of agreement which he felt was missing elsewhere.

Hitler recalled his nervousness on realising that in front of him, and especially towards his left, there were only opponents. He describes them as mostly robust youths and men from the hotbeds of left wing politics; the Maffei Factory, Kustermann's, and from the factories on the Isar.

According to Hitler's description, along the right-hand wall of the hall they were thickly massed quite close to the table from which he would make his speech. Hitler watched apprehensively as his opponents began to order litre mugs of beer, one after the other, and to stow the empty mugs under the table until whole batteries of ammunition were collected. Hitler soon realized that the threat was real, and there was no way this meeting could possibly end peacefully.

In spite of continuing interjections, Hitler was able to speak for about an hour and a half. He soon felt comfortable as if he were master of the situation. Even the ringleaders of the disturbers appeared to be convinced that Hitler had mastered the situation; the evidence for this comes from Hitler's one sided account where we are told that they steadily became more uneasy, often left the hall, only to return and speak to their men in what appeared to the watching Hitler to be an obviously nervous manner.

In a rare moment of candour Hitler records that he made, what he describes as a small psychological error which he committed in replying to a verbal interruption. Hitler claims that he recognised that he had made the mistake the moment the words had left his mouth. Despite his ability to record so much else of the evening, he does not enlighten us as to the exact nature of the faux pas which gave the signal for the outbreak of violence, all we know is that Hitler, faced with one heckler too many, lost his composure.

Hitler recorded that there were a few furious outbursts and suddenly a man jumped on a seat and shouted 'Liberty!' At that signal mayhem broke out in the hall. In a few moments the hall was filled with a yelling and shrieking mob. The heavy glass beer-mugs flew through the air and exploded into vicious shards of glass on impact. Amid the uproar one heard the crash of chair legs, the crashing of mugs, groans and yells and screams. Hitler maintained his place:

'It was a mad spectacle. I stood where I was and could observe my boys doing their duty, every one of them. There I had the chance of seeing how rough a conservative meeting could be. The dance had hardly begun when my Storm Troops, as they were called from that day onwards, launched their attack. Like wolves they threw themselves on the enemy again and again in parties of eight or ten and began steadily to thrash them out of the hall. After five minutes I could see hardly one of them that was not streaming with blood. Then I realised what kind of men many of them were, above all my brave Maurice and Hess,

who is my private secretary today, and many others who, even though
seriously wounded, attacked again and again as long as they could
stand on their feet. Twenty minutes long the pandemonium continued.
Then the opponents, who had numbered seven or eight hundred, had
been driven from the hall or hurled out headlong by my men, who had
not numbered fifty. Only in the left corner a big crowd still stood out
against our men and put up a bitter fight. Then two pistol shots rang
out from the entrance to the hall in the direction of the platform and
now a wild din of shooting broke out from all sides. One's heart almost
rejoiced at this spectacle which recalled memories of the War.'

The last sentence of Hitler's description speaks volumes about the man. It is hard to comprehend the perverse sentiment which is being expressed, but it is there in black and white. The increase in adrenalin combined with the noise of gun fire acts almost like an aphrodisiac on Hitler. In his fevered description of the beer hall brawl Hitler displays a passionate longing for violence, and he openly celebrates and rejoices an episode of violence which, for good reason, the rest of humanity seeks to avoid. Any man who commits to print a description of how his heart 'rejoiced' at the spectacle of gunfire and mob violence and provides the frankly astonishing revelation that these events recalled for him his happy memories of the War, must surely be dismissed on the obvious grounds that he is clearly deranged. In common with all too many passages in *'Mein Kampf'* this astonishing reference is a clear pointer to the mindset of Adolf Hitler, but it too was sadly overlooked as the firebrand was swept to power in the horse trading which followed the 1933 election.

Hitler proudly records that the disruption in the hall lasted about twenty-five minutes and adds with obvious satisfaction that, by the end of the violence, the hall looked as if a bomb had been exploded there. Many of the brawlers had to be bandaged and others taken away, but crucially the NSDAP remained masters of the situation. Hermann Essen, who was chairman of the meeting, announced: 'The meeting will continue. The speaker shall proceed,' and Hitler went on with his speech.

When Hitler had finally finished speaking and the chairman had declared the meeting at an end an excited police officer rushed in, waved his hands and declared: 'The meeting is dissolved.'

Hitler had learned a real lesson concerning the need to be prepared for political violence, but he alone saw the true meaning as a lesson in anti-Semitic terms. On November 9, 1921, just five days after the incident which was henceforth known as 'Die Saalschlacht' (The Battle of the Hall) Adolf Hitler addressed a gathering of SA men. He had already begun to associate the brawl with the Jews:

'For us there are only two possibilities: either we remain German or we come under the thumb of the Jews. This latter must not occur; even if we are small, we are a force. A well-organised group can conquer a strong enemy. If you stick close together and keep bringing in new people, we will be victorious over the Jews.'

The *Sturm Abteilung* now had its name and Hitler began to shape the development of his fearsome new weapon. He steadfastly forbade all participation in secret societies, and took care that they should not be allowed to develop in such a direction. It was Hitler who insisted that the training of the SA must not be organised from the military standpoint but from the most practical position for party purposes. He saw to it that its members should undergo a good physical training, however; pride of place was not given to military drill, but rather to the practice of combative sports. Hitler considered boxing and jujitsu more important to the realities of a political dog fight than some kind of mediocre training in rifle-shooting and drill. Under the stern eye of Ernst Röhm the SA troopers were groomed to develop a high level bodily efficiency which would help develop in the individual a conviction of his own superiority over his opponents and would give him confidence in his own powers. Hitler agreed with Röhm that the SA troopers must also develop that athletic agility which could be employed as a defensive weapon in the service of the Movement.

In order to safeguard the Storm Detachment against any tendency towards secrecy, Hitler decreed it must be uniformed so that its members could immediately be recognised by everybody. The large number of its effectives also served as an outward display of public strength and visibly demonstrated the gathering power of the movement to the whole community.

Hitler had practical knowledge of the arcane secret societies spreading through Germany and he wished to avoid the pitfalls which secrecy brought with it. The members of the Storm Detachment were therefore absolutely forbidden to hold secret gatherings and were ordered to march and go about their grim business as publicly as possible. In order to keep at bay all temptations towards finding an outlet for their activities in secret conspiracies, from the very beginning Hitler was careful to indoctrinate the minds of the SA with the principles of the NSDAP movement and focus the members of the SA so thoroughly to the task of bringing about the establishment of a new National Socialist People's State. Hitler seems to have been remarkably successful in his objective. He claims that the strategic struggle against the Weimar Republic was thus placed on a higher plane separating his men ideologically from the level of petty revenge and small conspiracies which occupied similar organisations. For Hitler, the struggle of the SA with its relentless round of petty bar room brawls was elevated to the level of a spiritual struggle on behalf of an NSDAP *weltanschauung*, and he seems to have been able to take the SA with him on that fanciful journey which envisaged the destruction of Marxism in all its shapes and forms.

From Hitler's point of view it was vital that the form of organisation adopted by the SA, as well as its uniform and equipment, had to follow different models from those of the old Army. The Roman model of the century was therefore adopted with *Abteilungen* divided into units of one hundred. As the tasks they had to perform were different from those faced by true paramilitary groups such as, for example, the *Freikorps* the SA had to be specially suited to the requirements of the party. The SA, as it was now known, developed swiftly along the lines which Hitler had decreed. By the midsummer of 1922, the party controlled six of these formations which consisted of a hundred men each. By the late autumn of 1922, these formations received their distinctive brown shirted uniforms.

In 'Mein Kampf' Hitler pin pointed two further events which he declared were of supreme importance for the subsequent development of the SA. The first of these was a great mass demonstration against the Law for the Protection of the Republic. This demonstration was held in the late summer of 1922, on the Königsplatz in Munich, it was a cooperative event staged by all the right wing patriotic societies. The National Socialist Movement also participated in the demonstration and this was the demonstration described by Ludecke. The march-past of the NSDAP, in serried ranks, was led by all six Munich companies of a hundred men each, followed by the political sections of the Party. Two bands marched with them and a phalanx of fifteen of the new swastika flags fluttered above the marchers.

In recalling the events of the day for 'Mein Kampf' Hitler missed none of the detail of the event and identified the importance and growing power of these emblems. It was a lesson in political theatre which was not missed on him. Hitler noted the fact that when the National Socialists arrived at the great square it was already half full, but no flag of any description was flying. The entry of the NSDAP with the military pomp of its massed banners aroused unbounded enthusiasm in the assembled forces of conservatism.

Hitler was one of the speakers who addressed that mass of about sixty thousand people. The demonstration was an overwhelming success; especially because it was proved that, for the first time, nationalist Munich could march on the streets, in spite of the threats of the Reds. Hitler recalled that members of the organisation for the defence of the Red Republic endeavoured to hinder the marching columns, but they were scattered by the companies of the SA within a few minutes and sent off with 'bleeding skulls'. For Hitler this minor skirmish was a triumph comparable to the *Schaalsclacht*. The National Socialist Movement had demonstrated for the first time that it was not prepared to be confined to the beer halls, in future it was determined to exercise the right to march on the streets and thus take this monopoly away from the forces of the left.

The additional result of that day for Hitler was the incontestable proof that the SA was the correct vehicle, both from the psychological viewpoint and as to the manner in which this body was organised ready for violence. The effortless manner in which they had imposed themselves on the left wing agitators during the demonstration had a huge effect on recruitment and enlistment progressed so rapidly that within a few weeks the number of Munich companies of a hundred men had doubled.

- CHAPTER 15 -

THE EXPANSION OF THE SA

THE NEXT MAIN development in the chain of four significant violent events as identified by Hitler in *'Mein Kampf'* was the expedition to Coburg held in October 1922. A number of conservative societies had resolved to hold a German Day at Coburg and Hitler and the SA were invited to take part. This invitation was only received at 11 A.M., but with the developing communication network it arrived in time for Hitler to pull together an impressive force.

Within an hour the arrangements for the participation in the German Congress were ready. Hitler was able to call upon eight hundred men of the SA to accompany him. These were divided into about fourteen companies and had to be brought by special train from Munich to Coburg. Coburg had only just voted by plebiscite to be annexed to Bavaria and the purpose of the day was to celebrate that event which was deeply resented by the parties on the left. Corresponding orders were given to other groups of the National Socialist SA detachments which had meanwhile been formed in various other localities to join the train en-route.

Hitler claims that this was the first time that such a special train ran in Germany. *'At all the stations where the new members of the SA joined us our train caused a sensation.'* Hitler noted with satisfaction that many citizens outside Munich had never seen the new NSDAP flag and it made a very great impression.

As the NSDAP delegation arrived at the station in Coburg they were received by a deputation of the organising committee of the German Day. To Hitler's extreme frustration they immediately announced that their plans had been curtailed following a series of negotiations intended to avoid political violence. A compromise had been reached at the urging of local trades unions that the SA should not enter the town with their flags unfurled and their forty-two strong band playing. It had also been agreed that the NSDAP should not march with closed ranks. Hitler did not feel that his party was bound by the compromise and immediately rejected these unmilitary conditions. He did not fail to declare before the gentlemen who had arranged this 'day' how astonished he was at the idea of their negotiating with such people and coming to an agreement with them. Hitler, in typical combative fashion, immediately announced that the Storm Troops would indeed march into the town as planned in company formation, with all flags flying and the band playing.

According to Hitler's self serving account of the events in Coburg, as soon as the SA came out into the station yard, they were met by a growling and yelling mob of several thousand, that shouted: 'Assassins', 'Bandits', 'Robbers', 'Criminals'. We are told that the SA for once comported itself with a model example of order and restraint. The companies fell into formation on the square in front of the station and at first took no notice of the insults hurled at them by the mob. The police were anxious and possibly uncertain over how to control the situation. As a result they did not pilot the SA to the quarters assigned to them on the outskirts of Coburg, a city quite unknown to the marchers, but for some inexplicable reason directed them to the *Hofbräuhaus* Keller in the centre of the town.

All along the route of the march the tumult raised by the accompanying counter demonstration steadily increased. Scarcely had the last SA company entered the courtyard of the *Hofbräuhaus* when the huge mass made a rush to get in after them, shouting madly. In order to prevent this, the police closed the gates. The SA were trapped at bay by the fury of the populace. Seeing the position was untenable Hitler claims he seized the initiative and called the Storm Detachment to attention and then asked the police to open the gates immediately. After a good deal of hesitation, the police consented. The SA now marched back along the same route as they had come, in the direction of their quarters; the route was now blocked and the SA had no option but to make a stand against the crowd. As their cries and yells all along the route had failed to disturb the equanimity of the SA companies, the crowd took to throwing stones and other missiles:

'*That brought our patience to an end. For ten minutes long, blows fell right and left, like a devastating shower of hail. Fifteen minutes later there were no more Reds to be seen in the street. The collisions which took place when the night came on were more serious. Patrols of the Storm Detachment had discovered National Socialists who had been attacked singly and were in an atrocious state. Thereupon we made short work of the opponents. By the following morning the Red Terror, under which Coburg had been suffering for years, was definitely smashed.*'

Hitler now learned that, at half-past one that day, there was to be a 'great popular demonstration', at which it was hoped that the workers of the whole district would turn up. Hitler was determined finally to crush what he perceived as this 'Red Terror' and so he summoned the SA to meet at midday. Their number had now increased to 1,500 and Hitler decided to march with these men to the Coburg Festival and to deliberately provoke his opponents by crossing the big square where the Red demonstration was to take place. Hitler wanted to see if they would attempt to assault us again. When the SA entered the square they found that instead of the ten thousand that had been advertised, there were only a few hundred people present. As the SA approached they remained silent for the most part, and some ran away. Only at certain points along the route some bodies of Reds, who had arrived from outside the city and had not yet come to know the SA, attempted to start an altercation: a few fisticuffs were enough to put them to flight.

Hitler claimed that one could see how the population, which had for such a long time been so wretchedly intimidated, slowly woke up and recovered their courage. They now welcomed the SA openly, and in the evening, on the return march, spontaneous shouts of jubilation broke out at several points along the route.

At the station there was a brief stand off as railway employees informed Hitler that all of a sudden the NSDAP train would not move. Thereupon Hitler had some of the ringleaders rounded up and told that if this were the case he would have all the 'Red Party' hostages arrested and taken aboard and that the SA would drive the train themselves with the hostages aboard. Faced with the prospect of sudden death the workers gave in and the train departed punctually and the SA arrived next morning in Munich safe and sound.

Hitler prided himself that the Coburg outing for the first time since 1914 had produced the equality of all citizens before the law. As far as Hitler was concerned at first it was not possible fully to estimate the importance of the consequences which resulted from that day. The victorious Storm Troops had their confidence in themselves considerably reinforced and also their faith in the sagacity of their leaders. Hitler's contemporaries began to pay special attention and for the first time many recognised the National Socialist Movement as an organisation that carried the seeds of a movement which was capable of seriously challenging the Marxist movement.

According to Hitler only the democrats lamented the fact that the SA were prepared to hit back with fists and sticks at a brutal assault, rather than respond with pacifist chants. Hitler prided himself on the fact that in Coburg itself at least some of the Marxist workers learned from the blows of National Socialist fists that these workers were also capable of fighting for their ideals. The Storm Detachment itself benefited most from the Coburg events. It grew so quickly in numbers that the Party Congress in January 1923, amounted to six thousand men who participated in the ceremony of consecrating the flags and hailed the first companies which were fully clad in their new uniform.

The experience of Coburg proved for Hitler the necessity of having distinctive uniform for the Storm Detachment, not only for the purpose of strengthening the *esprit de corps*, but also to avoid confusion and minimise the danger of not recognising one's opponent in a squabble. Up to that time they had merely worn the armlet, but now the tunic and the well-known cap were added.

The Coburg experience also had another important result. Hitler was now at peak confidence and determined to break the Red grip in all those localities where for many years it had prevented nationalist parties from holding their meetings. Hitler was now determined to restore the right of 'free assembly'. From that time onwards he brought his battalions together in such places and little by little the Red citadels of Bavaria, one after another, fell before the National Socialist propaganda. The Storm Troops became more and more adept at their job. They increasingly lost all semblance of an aimless and lifeless defence movement and came out into the light as an active militant organisation, fighting for the establishment of a new National Socialist German state.

- CHAPTER 16 -
THE BEER HALL PUTSCH

THE YEAR 1923 was to prove a momentous time for Hitler. It was largely shaped by the course of two major events. The onset of hyperinflation was one of the most significant events in the history of Germany and its aftershock still resonates today. Less well known, but equally important at the time, was the French military occupation of the Ruhr. The German nation could have overcome the economic problems, but when French troops occupied the Ruhr, the industrial heart of Germany was pierced and the blow galvanised resistance across the entire political spectrum.

This paralysing blow to Germany's economy and the equally damaging wound to her national pride united the German people once more. The outpouring of national indignation was to prove fertile ground for Hitler. French forces alighted on the fact that Germany had failed to deliver some 135,000 metres of promised telegraph poles and 24 million Gold Marks worth of coal. Although 14 million Gold Marks worth had been delivered this was not enough to satisfy the aggrieved French government and the mighty industrial heartland of Germany was seized by the French army. We can only imagine the frustration and anger which seethed through Hitler's tortured brain.

For once Hitler was not alone in his rage and turmoil, the workers of the Ruhr declared a general strike and, with the help of the army, sabotage and guerrilla warfare actions were organised. The French countered with arrests, deportations and even death sentences, but the strike held firm and industry in the Ruhr was completely paralysed.

The French-led strangulation of Germany's industrial economy hastened the final plunge of the Mark. Following the damaging effects of the Versailles treaty the currency was already on shaky ground. On the news of the occupation of the Ruhr, the Mark swiftly fell to a new rate of 18,000 to the dollar; by 1 July 1923, it had dropped like a stone to a new level of 160,000 to the dollar; by August a dollar was worth a million Marks. By November 1923, when Hitler undertook his ill fated Beer Hall Putsch, the situation had spiralled totally out of control. It took four billion Marks to buy a dollar, and thereafter numbers became virtually meaningless as the figures escalated daily. Eventually even trillions of Marks could not purchase a single dollar, the German currency had become utterly worthless and could no longer be exchanged at any price. The effects were felt inside the nationalist movement as the cover price of 'Der Sturmer' rose from 350 Marks early in 1923, to a staggering one and a half billion Marks by October 1923. With price rises of this magnitude numbers had become meaningless and the life savings of whole segments of German society were wiped out overnight; as a result the German people lost faith in the economic structure of German society. Many blamed the Democratic Republic, which had surrendered to the allies and cravenly accepted the burden of reparations. It did not go unnoticed that while whole swathes of German society were financially ruined, the government continued with its policy of deliberately allowing the Mark to tumble. It was obvious to many that the ruinous economic policy was still pursued in order to use the mechanism of inflation to free the state from its massive public debts, and above all to escape from paying reparations.

Throughout 1923, the presses continued to churn out worthless Marks and the domestic self immolation of Germany's currency enabled German heavy industry to wipe out its indebtedness by paying its obligations in trillions upon trillions of totally worthless Marks. This cynical ploy wiped out the rich and poor alike inside Germany, but more importantly it wiped out the crippling war debts and left Germany as a whole financially unencumbered by Versailles. The German people knew they were bankrupt, and they experienced the terrible hardship and hunger brought on by the economic meltdown. In their misery and despair they laid the blame squarely at the door of the Republic.

As an arch enemy of the Weimar Republic, Adolf Hitler sensed that his time was coming and he was able to seize upon the economic chaos to push home an early claim for the introduction of a dictatorship:

'*The government calmly goes on printing these scraps of paper because, if it stopped, that would be the end of the government, because once the printing presses stopped – and that is the prerequisite for the stabilisation of the Mark – the swindle would at once be brought to light... Believe me, our misery will increase. The scoundrel will get by. The reason: because the State itself has become the biggest swindler and crook. A robbers' state!... If the horrified people notice that they can starve on billions, they must arrive at this conclusion: we will no longer submit to a State which is built on the swindling idea of the majority. We want a dictatorship...*'

There is no doubting the fact that the miseries brought about by hyperinflation were leading millions of Germans toward the conclusion that the democratic process had become derailed. Hitler was ready and waiting to lead them on the downward path towards dictatorship and increasing numbers of the German populace were only too willing to follow. Hitler had begun to sense that the miserable conditions of 1923 might create an opportunity to overthrow the Republic and he was prepared to use force if necessary. With this in mind Hitler switched the training policy of the SA. During 1923, the force abandoned its focus on street fighting techniques. Bare fists and clubs were no longer enough, the SA was now being trained in weapons handling and tactics along the *Freikorps* model.

The NSDAP, though it was growing daily in numbers, was still a comparatively small movement and it was far from matching the influence of the BVP as the main political party in Bavaria. Outside of Bavaria the NSDAP was still almost entirely unknown. Julius Streicher's assistance had extended the party's influence as far as Nuremberg, but Hamburg, Hannover, Cologne and Berlin were still foreign territories where the name of Adolf Hitler was still unknown. There was no earthly prospect that such a small party could hope to overthrow the Republic. Such a momentous event would require a miracle. Hitler sensed that amidst the increasing unrest of 1923, there might just be a chance to twist the Federal structure to suit his ambitions. Bavaria was increasingly out of step with the rest of Weimar Germany and Adolf Hitler hoped that he might just be able to harness the support of the Bavarian government, the participation of the newly militarised SA and the assistance of the *Reichswehr* units stationed in Bavaria. If he could organise these disparate elements then, just as his hero Mussolini had done with his famous march on Rome in 1922, Hitler might lead a triumphant march on Berlin which would topple the traitors of the Weimar Republic. In reality Mussolini's insignificant force had faltered well short of Rome and he had been fortunate to be invited to form a government, but the myth of a successful march by his hero had become entrenched in Hitler's imagination.

For once the popular current was flowing towards Hitler's nationalist goal, the French occupation of the Ruhr bolstered the forces of nationalism, but at this juncture he chose to swim against the nationalist tide. The groundswell of nationalist sentiment in 1923 actually complicated Hitler's task of defeating the Weimar government. The national mood of outrage had the effect of unifying the German people and they fell behind the Republican government in Berlin which had at last chosen to openly defy France. This was the last thing Hitler needed. His aim was to abolish the Weimar Republic and he was prepared to follow any route to his goal of establishing a dictatorship. Against a strong current of public opinion Hitler pursued his familiar line:

> *'Down with the traitors of the Fatherland, down with the November Criminals!'*

Throughout the early part of 1923, Hitler dedicated himself to making preparations for the possibility of an armed struggle. In February, due largely to the organisational talents of Ernst Röhm, four of the armed 'patriotic leagues' of Bavaria joined with the NSDAP to form the so-called *'Arbeitsgemeinschaft der Vaterlaendischen Kampfverbaende'* (Working Union of the Fatherland Fighting Leagues) and the unified force came under the political leadership of Hitler. The armed patriotic leagues were the left-over remnants of the *Freikorps* who had overcome their leftist adversaries during the White counter revolution which threw the soviets out of Munich. The occupation of the Ruhr district, which did not come as a surprise to Hitler and his associates, gave him grounds for hoping that Germany would at last abandon its policy of submission and give the defensive associations a definite task to fulfil. The SA which now numbered several thousand robust and vigorous young men, was just one part of the *Kampfbund* and Hitler recognised that it could not be excluded from the possibility of having to perform in the national service. During the spring and summer of 1923, the SA was completely transformed into a fighting military organisation ready to move at a moment's notice.

They were now straining at the leash to engage the French army in the Ruhr or to come to grips with the Reds. However the initial attempts were to prove deeply frustrating and embarrassing for Hitler. Writing in 'Hitler and I' Otto Strasser recalled the first abortive attempt, which took place on 1 May 1923, to galvanise these new forces into action:

> *"'Orders have come from Munich. It's for to-night!' Heinrich Himmler, my brother's adjutant, stood to attention in Gregor's office, breathless with excitement.*
>
> *"Orders from Hitler?"*
>
> *"Yes."*
>
> *For weeks past, and more particularly during the last few days of April, 1923, Hitler had been declaring at numerous meetings that rather than allow the Red demonstrations to take place on 1 May the Reds would have to trample over his dead body. The time for action seemed to have come. The various formations of the Right were about to make a forcible reply to recent Communist risings.*
>
> *Orders came from headquarters to the villages of Lower Bavaria, and throughout 30 April rapid and mysterious preparations were made in the little town of Landshut. Gregor's patriotic ex-soldiers, for the past three years they had been Nazi stormtroopers, joyfully equipped themselves for the conquest of a new Germany. Scarcely a house but contained hidden arms, lovingly caressed by impatient hands, waiting for the great day of the Revolution.*

A number of old lorries had been put at the disposal of the insurgents. At nightfall the men of Landshut marched off, wearing the famous field-grey which had been worn by millions during the Great War. The lorries, lit only by lanterns, set out along the flat road that crosses the plain from Dachau to the neighbourhood of Munich. My brother Gregor commanded this little army of three thousand men. There was something eerie about the strange convoy as it made its way through the moonless night. Suddenly the silence was shattered by the violent blowing of motor horns. The landscape was lit up by the headlights of a number of fast police-cars, which rapidly overtook Gregor's slow-moving convoy.

"Schuppos! Police!" murmured Gregor's men.

The police lieutenant ordered Gregor's lorry to stop. The two leaders stood face to face.

"Good heavens!" exclaimed Gregor. "Where did you spring from?"

"From Landshut, like you," replied Lieutenant Georg Hofler, his brother-in-law. On leaving the army Georg Hofler had joined the police department, and he was now chief of police at Landshut.

"But where are you going?" said Gregor.

"To Munich, like you."

"Are you with us or against us?"

"I don't know. We shall be given our orders at Munich."

For a moment Gregor and Georg Hofler stared at each other, undecided. One was a blond giant with muscles of steel, the other thinner and more delicate, but with a bronzed face stamped with courage and resolution.

"Well, we shall see tomorrow," Gregor philosophically remarked.

"Good luck!" replied Hofler, shaking hands with him.

The police cars started off again in a trail of dust, and the lorries full of stormtroopers pursued their way more sedately behind them. This nocturnal encounter was the first comic scene in a farce which has often been described to me by Gregor and my brother-in-law.

"It was a dress rehearsal," Gregor assured me in his description of the events of 1 May, and when I told him that in my opinion the principal actor, Hitler, ought to have been hissed from the stage, he shrugged his shoulders, as though to say "You'll never understand him".

Gregor continued his way through the night, tormented by the thought that either Hitler was in league with the Government, and the schuppos had been sent to Munich to support the putsch, in which case the revolution would be more stultified than ever, or the secret was out, in which case the insurgents, deprived of the trump card of surprise, would all be under lock and key that same night.

However, the convoy reached Munich without further incident. At the big Munich parade ground of Oberwiesenfeld the junction of the three paramilitary formations duly took place. The stormtroopers, commanded by Goering, were there in force, and they were joined by Dr. Weber's Oberland Freikorps and the Reichsbanner led by Captain Heiss. The coup was to be attempted under the auspices of General Ludendorff, the political leadership was Adolf Hitler's and the military command was in the hands of Lieutenant- Colonel Kriebel.

The junction was effected at 8 A.M. A hot sun, worthy of July, played upon twenty thousand steel helmets and twenty thousand threadbare uniforms, dating from the War. The only detachment that yet wore brown shirts was that of the Munich stormtroopers, led by Lieutenant Rossbach. Brown shirts were much disliked by Adolf Hitler, but Lieutenant Rossbach, who was also the Reich youth organizer, had caused his recruits to adopt them.

All Adolf Hitler's men were there, including Hermann Goering in a uniform which had grown much too tight for him, Frick, Hess and Streicher, Gregor Strasser and his inseparable Himmler – all the big and little actors in the Hitlerian drama, those destined to play leading roles, those destined to remain in obscurity, those destined to be ruthlessly obliterated.

8 A.M. passed, and then 9 A.M. and 10 A.M. Adolf Hitler stood with puckered brows. From time to time he raised his heavy steel helmet to wipe the sweat from his forelock.

Time passed and the agreed signal did not come. At 11 A.M. a Reichswehr detachment appeared on the horizon, flanked right and left by men in the green police uniform. The demonstrators of the Oberwiesenfeld were rapidly surrounded. The police were under the command of Lieutenant Georg Hofler. Among the military officers was Captain Roehm. Like a maniac, Hitler made for Captain Roehm. His eyes were flashing, and he was almost foaming at the mouth.

"Have you betrayed us?" he angrily demanded.

But Roehm was not frightened of Hitler, whom he still regarded as a corporal belonging to the 7th Division, commanded by his friend General von Epp.

"What is happening?" Hitler repeated.

"The time is not yet ripe. The Government and the Reichswehr are tolerating the Red First of May demonstrations. North Germany is not yet ready," Captain Roehm coldly replied. Hitler looked into his eyes, then lowered his head.

"The time is not yet ripe," he was explaining to his followers a few moments later.

Gregor and Kriebel, however, still favoured action, and would have liked to have fired on the Reichswehr, but Hitler, taciturn and glowering, refused all day to yield to the most intrepid counsels.

Surrounded by the forces of the law, the proud insurgents of the early morning were unable to go home until after dark. The Red demonstrations passed off without incident, and the Nazis were covered with ridicule. The humiliating memory of the Oberwiesenfeld defeat was never effaced from Hitler's mind. The rancour he nourished against Roehm was born that day.

Sleeplessly, night and day, Hitler prepared the Nazi Party's revenge. The setting up of a Red government in Saxo-Thuringia helped to throw oil on the flames. This time Roehm seemed to have made up his mind, and General von Epp rallied to the side of the plotters

The Government, suddenly alarmed at the progress of Communism in the North, now tried to isolate Southern Germany. It wished to avert a civil war, which would have been the inevitable consequence of a

Nazi coup attempted on a nation-wide scale. On 26 September, von Kahr, a man with an iron hand, was appointed State Commissioner for Bavaria, von Epp was removed from the active list and replaced by General von Lossow, and soldiers were made to take the oath, not to the Reich but to Bavaria only. Ludendorff was forbidden to enter or remain in Munich. Ludendorff and Epp were furious. Roehm, who saw his influence at an end, was livid. Hitler could scarcely restrain his rage, and Gregor, who always favoured the bolder course, counselled action at the earliest opportunity. In his opinion it was necessary to coerce the new Bavarian authorities into rallying to the insurgents of the Right and marching with them and their men against Communist Prussia and the North.'

In September 1923, an even stronger paramilitary group was established under the name of the *'Deutscher Kampfbund'* (German Fighting Union), it included the battle hardened *Oberland* League, a *Freikorps* unit which had successfully fought against Polish regular troops and the *Reichskriegsflagge*, a conservative veterans association some 4,000 strong. This new organisation sprang from a great mass meeting held at Nuremberg on 2 September 1923, to celebrate the anniversary of the German defeat of France at Sedan in 1870. Most of the nationalist and militaristic groups in southern Germany were represented. Hitler gave a characteristically animated speech full of venom directed against the 'November Criminals'. He received an ovation after a violent speech against the national government. The objectives of the new *Kampfbund* were openly stated: the overthrow of the Republic and the tearing up of the Treaty of Versailles. The *Reichskriegsflagge* came under the leadership of the ubiquitous Ernst Röhm. In an uncharacteristically charitable move Hitler had agreed to share power as one of three leaders of the *Kampfbund*. The military leader of the *Kampfbund* was Hermann Kriebel, its adjutant was Röhm and its political leader was Hitler.

By the autumn of 1923, relations between the Weimar Republic and the state of Bavaria reached a point of crisis. Under mounting pressure from France, Gustav Stresemann, the Weimar chancellor, caved in and announced the end of passive resistance in the Ruhr. He also ordered the resumption of German reparation payments. The Bavarian state government took a much more bullish line and was in no mood to accept such a solution. In Berlin it was feared that Bavaria might secede from the Reich and form a South German Union with Austria. Hitler did not demure and in 1923 he was, at least temporarily, prepared to sacrifice his *Grossdeutschland* principles in order to attain power. The Bavarian cabinet would not follow the Berlin line and proclaimed its own state of emergency and named the conservative Gustav von Kahr as state commissioner with dictatorial powers. General Otto von Lossow, commander of the *Reichswehr* in Bavaria, and Colonel Hans von Seisser, the head of the state police, sided with the Bavarian Government, together they formed the triumvirate of provincial leadership. A new and important connection was the fact that Ernst Röhm was a staff officer subordinate to Lt. General Otto von Lossow the commander of *Wehrkreis VII*, the *Reichswehr* military region which covered Bavaria.

As tension mounted, a state of emergency was proclaimed throughout Germany, but Kahr refused to recognise that it had any application in Bavaria. He refused point blank to carry out orders from Berlin. At this juncture the national government demanded the suppression of Hitler's newspaper, the *'Völkischer Beobachter'*. The closure was ordered from Berlin because of its increasingly vitriolic attacks on the Republic. On 5 October 1923, Kahr finally ordered the paper to close for ten days but contemptuously refused to follow further instructions and allowed the paper to resume publication unhindered. To compound his defiance of the constitution, Kahr forced the officers and men of the *Reichswehr* to take a special oath of allegiance to the new Bavarian government.

Berlin was now faced with both a political and a military rebellion which the commander of the *Reichswehr*, General von Seeckt, was charged with the responsibility of suppressing. He issued a warning to the Bavarian triumvirate and to Hitler that any *putsch* on their part would be opposed by force. Hitler however had begun to believe that the chaotic conditions of 1923, had created an ideal opportunity to overthrow the Republic which would not recur. It was too late to draw back, his rabid followers were demanding action.

Hitler's S.A and *Kampfbund* commanders were most anxious to enter the fray and urged him to strike at once. Hitler must have been concerned that, if the government gained much more time and began to succeed in restoring unity and tranquility, his own opportunity would also be lost. The NSDAP was still much too small for independent action and Hitler realised that somehow he would have to contrive to put Kahr, Lossow and Seisser in a position where they would have to agree to act with him. Hitler soon began to toy with the idea of using coercion and decided to kidnap the triumvirate and force them to use their power at his bidding. At this point a brief notice appeared in the press that Kahr would address a meeting of business organisations at Munich's *Bürgerbraukeller*, a large beer hall on the outskirts of the city.

The meeting was scheduled to take place on 8 November 1923, word soon spread that General von Lossow, Colonel von Seisser and other notables would be present. Afraid that von Kahr was going to define the struggle without him, Hitler decided to act and 'coax these people into complicity'.

The *Bürgerbraukeller* meeting provided the opportunity to round up all three members of the triumvirate and, at pistol point, cajole them into joining the NSDAP in carrying out the revolution which Hitler envisaged would culminate in a march on Berlin and the overthrow of the Weimar Republic.

With typical impetuosity Hitler had decided to act and had left little room for manoeuvre as the force of events began to carry all before them. Everything now had to be done at a reckless pace. The *putsch* was confirmed and planned on the evening of 7 November in a hasty session in Kreibel's apartment. The decision left very little time for accurate planning and preparation and the seeds of disaster were already sewn. Success required clear communication to a large number of senior figures. Lack of time meant that not all members were notified or properly briefed. For the purpose of communicating, the party used two pieces of paper; one coloured red meaning 'the real thing' and the other white signifying a practice run. The leadership chose to keep the subterfuge running and chose to pass the white tag out, thus leading to much confusion and lack of coordination on the day of the *putsch*. Hitler had at last decided to act. Recalling his thoughts thirteen years later after he had achieved his goal, he told his old followers, assembled at the *Bürgerbraukeller* to celebrate the anniversary of the *putsch*:

'I can calmly say that it was the rashest decision of my life. When I think back on it today, I grow dizzy... If today you saw one of our squads from the year 1923, marching by, you would ask, 'What workhouse have they escaped from?'... But fate meant well with us. It did not permit an action to succeed which, if it had succeeded, would in the end have inevitably crashed as a result of the movement's inner immaturity...'

The storm troopers were hastily alerted for duty at the big beer hall on the evening of 8 November 1923. By a huge coincidence, which seems almost too good to be true, Alexander Moritz Frey claims that he met Hitler on the night before the *putsch* i.e. 7 November. Moritz Frey recalls the forlorn figure of Hitler wandering around on his own in a deranged state. Why they should meet on this night of all nights and why Hitler should be wandering around in this manner rather than plotting with Röhm and Kriebel stretches our credibility too far but Moritz Frey is absolutely certain of the date:

'As fate would have it, I met Hitler on the evening before his putsch in the Bürgerbraukeller. It was in Maximilianstrasse again and incredibly nobody appeared to recognise Hitler, at least not the majority of the passers-by. He was alone, prowling along in the manner of a predator before it leaps, imagining its prey, he didn't see his surroundings; the evil, fanatical stare was directed into the empty air, which meant he was walking along in the abundance of his demoniacal visions. He was walking along, not wearing a hat, his permanently oily, shimmering black hair was combed very precisely, and he was wearing a yellow raincoat.'

The coincidence seems just too large and we should take this claim with a large pinch of salt as it is far more likely that on the night of 7 November 1923, rather than wandering aimlessly round the streets of

Munich Hitler would be bunkered down with his cronies planning the most important events of his life. It is also unlikely that Hitler would walk the streets unaccompanied by Ulrich Graf, the former wrestler who was his personal bodyguard. Hitler was impetuous and hot headed, but he was not a fool, and he knew full well that a military operation of this type needed a great deal of careful planning and communication. The Moritz Frey description goes too far in describing Hitler's inner thoughts, it smacks of conjecture and should therefore be treated with care.

The *putsch* was finally unleashed on the night of 8 November 1923. About 8:45 P.M. on the evening of 8 November, after Kahr had been speaking for half an hour to some 3,000 well refreshed captains of Munich industry, the S.A. troops suddenly surrounded the *Bürgerbraukeller*. Hitler at the head of a phalanx of around 20 of his closest associates pushed forward into the hall. At Hitler's shoulder marched Hermann Göring, Alfred Rosenberg, Rudolf Hess, Ernst Hanfstaengl, Ulrich Graf, Johann Aigner, Adolf Lenk, Max Amann, Scheubner-Richter, Wilhelm Adam. Not present were Julius Streicher and Ernst Röhm.

Ernst Röhm was waiting with his *Reichskriegsflagge Freikorps* in the *Löwenbräukeller*, another beer hall, and he was tasked with the objective of seizing key buildings throughout the city in order to bring the police and the army into line with the *putschists*. At the same time, other co-conspirators under Gerhard Rossbach were to mobilise the students of a nearby Officers Infantry school to seize other objectives. Communications were difficult and Hitler was receiving only sketchy reports of what was happening elsewhere. Röhm had been given a key role to play but on the night his objectives were too numerous and widespread, and it was his bodged efforts which would lead to the *putsch* unravelling over the course of the next 24 hours.

Back in the *Bürgerbrauhaus*, in order to ensure that the assembled hall knew Hitler meant business, a detachment of his SA men mounted a machine gun in the entrance and trained the weapon on the crowd. To complete the impression Hitler jumped up on a table and, with a melodramatic flourish, fired a revolver shot into the ceiling. Naturally this commotion caused Kahr to paused in mid speech. As the audience strained to view the cause of the disturbance Hitler made his way to the platform. A police major tried to stop him, but Hitler was not found wanting in his moment of action. He was resolutely focused on his goal and he menacingly pointed the pistol at the policeman who seeing the murderous intent in Hitler's eyes sensibly stepped back and allowed Hitler to push on towards the stage. Kahr, looking 'pale and confused' stepped back, and Hitler took his place.

Hitler began his address in an uncharacteristically fierce tone of voice:

'The national revolution has begun! This building is occupied by 600 heavily armed men. No one may leave the hall. Unless there is immediate quiet I shall have a machine gun posted in the gallery. The Bavarian and Reich governments have been removed and a provisional national government has been formed. The army and the police are marching on the city under the swastika banner.'

Hitler had launched another of his impetuous gambles. This time he was operating on a scale far larger than any previous ventures. He knew that there was no truth in his claims, but in the shock and general confusion which accompanied his dramatic entrance there was no objective point of reference and no one in the hall knew for sure what was happening. Hitler's revolver certainly was real, the bullet he had fired was real. The storm troopers with their rifles and machine gun appeared to vindicate Hitler's claim. Hitler now ordered Kahr, Lossow and Seisser to follow him to a private room offstage. The room had been specially rented by Rudolf Hess for the precise purpose of thrashing out a compromise agreement.

Escorted off the stage by menacing SA men, the three highest officials of Bavaria did Hitler's bidding and trooped off at gun point while the crowd looked on in astonishment. The departure of both the bemused triumvirate and Hitler created a vacuum in the hall, the energy levels dropped and the mood in the hall swiftly changed to one of increasing resentment. Many in the crowd were sitting on beer-swollen bladders and as they were refused permission to attend the lavatories, their discomfort contributed to a change in mood. As the hiatus dragged on the crowd began to grow more sullen and difficult. Eventually Hermann Göring felt it necessary to step on to the rostrum and quiet them with a pep talk. It was not one of Göring's better offerings as he began:

'*There is nothing to fear, you've no cause to grumble. You've got your beer!*'

Göring went on to inform the restless crowd that in the next room a new government was being formed. He neglected to inform the crowd that the deal was actually being concluded under coercion, at the point of Adolf Hitler's revolver, but in any event the crowd was clearly not buying the Göring line.

They would have had even less reason to believe Göring's version of events if they had been afforded a glimpse into the meeting room where things were not progressing at all well. As soon Hitler had herded his prisoners into the adjoining room, he told them, 'No one leaves this room alive without my permission.' He then grandiosely informed them they would all have key jobs either in the Bavarian government or in the Reich government which he would be forming along with Ludendorff. Again Hitler was taking a huge risk: Ludendorff was as yet completely unaware of what was being done in his name.

Hitler now dispatched Heinz Pernet (Ludendorff's stepson) along with Johann Aigner and Scheubner-Richter to urge Ludendorff to come to the beer hall. His personal prestige was being harnessed to give the whole enterprise credibility and if there was to be any prospect of success it was now essential that the renowned general should appear in the beer-house at once.

Although the great war hero later claimed to have known nothing of the planned *putsch*, he had consistently lent his prestige to conservative revolutionary movements and it is likely that he was fully briefed on 7 November along with the other senior figures. Hitler had been cultivating Ludendorff as a potential ally for some time, but he seems to have made a huge leap in the assumption that Ludendorff would perform any service which Hitler required. Behind the scenes Hitler now began his efforts to convert the triumvirate to get behind his new vision for Germany. The three prisoners at first refused even to speak to Hitler. In his typical belligerent fashion the highly agitated Hitler continued to harangue them with one of his trademark monologues. The triumvirate still did not answer. Their continued silence unnerved Hitler. Finally he waved his gun at them and tried his best to bully his audience into submission:

'I have four shots in my pistol! Three for my collaborators, if they abandon me. The last bullet for myself! If I am not victorious by tomorrow afternoon, I shall be a dead man!'

Hitler knew he was getting nowhere with his plan. Not one of the three men who held the power of the Bavarian state agreed to join him, even at pistol point. Hitler became irritated by von Kahr and summoned Ernst Pöhner, Friedrich Weber and Hermann Kriebel to stand in for him while he returned to the auditorium to make a speech (as he had promised some fifteen minutes earlier). Flanked by Rudolf Hess and Adolf Lenk, Hitler returned to the auditorium to make an extemporaneous speech that changed the mood of the hall almost within seconds. Mounting the tribune, he faced the sullen crowd and announced that the members of the triumvirate in the next room were about to join him in forming a new national government:

'I propose that the direction of policy be taken over by me... Ludendorff will take over the leadership of the German national army.'

Dr. Karl Alexander von Mueller, a professor of modern history and political science at the University of Munich and a supporter of von Kahr, was an eyewitness. He reported the events:

'Hitler started quietly reminding the audience that his move was not directed against von Kahr. I cannot remember in my entire life such a change in the attitude of a crowd in a few minutes, almost a few seconds... Hitler had turned them inside out, as one turns a glove inside out, with a few sentences. It had almost something of hocus-pocus, or magic about it.'

Hitler concluded his short speech with a demand:

'Outside are Kahr, Lossow and Seisser. They are struggling hard to reach a decision. May I say to them that you will stand behind them?'

The audience now roared its approval. Hitler was now in full flow and he finished with triumphant flourish:

'You can see that what motivates us is neither self-conceit or self-interest, but only a burning desire to join the battle in this grave eleventh hour for our German Fatherland... One last thing I can tell you. Either the German revolution begins tonight and the morrow will find us in Germany a true nationalist government, or it will find us dead by dawn!'

Not for the first time and certainly not for the last. Hitler had spun a masterful lie, and it had worked. When the gathering heard that von Kahr, General von Lossow and Police Chief von Seisser were actively considering joining Hitler (as opposed to the reality that they were stone-walling him) the mood in the hall abruptly changed. There were loud cheers. The sound of the cheers could well have been self prophesying as they must have impressed the three men still locked up in the little side room.

To cap matters in Hitler's favour General Ludendorff now appeared in full military uniform looking for all the world as if he had been expected all along. He spoke scarcely a word to the brash young man, but Hitler had other priorities, all he required was that Ludendorff lend his famous name to the undertaking and win over the three wavering Bavarian leaders. Ludendorff proceeded to do as requested by Hitler. He informed the triumvirate that events had clearly moved on and it was now a question of joining a great national cause. Awed by the attention of the generalissimo, the trio appeared to give in. Yet another Hitler gamble had seemingly paid off. Ludendorff's timely arrival had saved Hitler and once more his brinksmanship had been rewarded with success. Overjoyed at his lucky break Hitler seized the moment and led the others back to the platform, where each made a brief speech and swore loyalty to each other and to the new regime. The crowd leaped on chairs and tables in a delirium of enthusiasm, and Hitler beamed with joy as public handshakes were exchanged among the speakers. The meeting began to break up. Then news came of a clash between Röhm's storm troopers and regular troops at the army engineers' barracks. Secure in the belief that he had struck a genuine bargain with the triumvirate Hitler made a fateful decision to drive to the scene and settle the matter personally, leaving Ludendorff in charge of the beer hall.

Hitler's decision to leave Ludendorff in charge turned out to be a fatal error. Lossow, Kahr and Seisser asked for permission to leave the hall and Ludendorff accepted their word of honour that they would continue as promised. The three had no intention of doing any such thing. Soon news of the coup went out to Berlin, and orders came back to the army in Bavaria to suppress the *putsch*. As soon as he was free from the beer hall von Kahr ordered placards posted throughout Munich proclaiming:

> 'The declarations extorted from myself, General von Lossow and Colonel von Seisser at the point of a revolver are null and void.'

The triumph which earlier in the evening had seemed to Hitler so near and so easily won was rapidly fading into chaos. The night was marked by confusion and unrest among government officials, armed forces and police units, and individuals deciding where their loyalties lay. In the expectation that he would be busy forming a new government Hitler hastily appointed Julius Streicher as head of NSDAP propaganda. Streicher bustled off into the night to begin his work which commenced next morning with a trademark speech in Marineplatz outside the town hall. Throughout that fateful night units of the *Kampfbund* were scurrying around to arm themselves from secret caches, and seizing buildings. At around 3 A.M., the first casualties of the *putsch* occurred when the local garrison of the *Reichswehr* spotted Röhm's men coming out of the beer hall. They were ambushed while trying to reach the *Reichswehr* barracks and had to fall back. In the meantime, the *Reichswehr* officers put the whole garrison on alert and called for reinforcements. Hitler had planned a *putsch*, not a civil war. Despite his feverish excitement he realized that he lacked the strength to overcome the police and the army. He had wanted to make a revolution with the armed forces, not against them. In the early morning, Hitler ordered the seizure of the Munich city council as hostages. He further sent the communications officer of the *Kampfbund*, Max Neunzert, to enlist the aid of Crown Prince

Rupprecht of Bavaria to mediate between von Kahr and the *putschists*. Neunzert failed in the mission.

Ludendorff now proposed a plan that might still bring victory and avoid bloodshed. He was supremely confident that German soldiers, even German police – who were mostly ex-soldiers – would never dare to fire on the legendary commander who had led them to great victories on both the Eastern and the Western fronts. Ludendorff now proposed that he and Hitler would march with their followers to the centre of the city and take it over. Not only would the police and the army not dare to oppose him; he was certain they would join him and fight under his orders. Hitler agreed. There seemed no other way out. At this moment, Ludendorff cried out, *'Wir marschieren!'* (We will march!), and Hitler's men marched out with no apparent plan of where to go. Toward 11 A.M. on 9 November Hitler and Ludendorff led a column of some 3,000 *Kampfbund* members out of the gardens of the *Buergerbraukeller* toward the centre of Munich. It was not a very formidable armed force, but Ludendorff, who had commanded millions of Germany's finest troops, apparently thought it sufficient for his purposes.

On a bridge a few hundred yards north of the beer cellar the rebels met their first obstacle: a detachment of armed police barred the route. Göring sprang forward and threatened, if the police fired on his men, to shoot a number of hostages he claimed to have at the rear of his column. Whether Göring was bluffing or not, the police commander apparently believed he was not, and let the column cross the bridge. Outside the city hall the populace was in ferment. Julius Streicher was making an impassioned speech to a vast crowd which filled the square.

There was no need to add to the chaos and, on the spur of the moment, Ludendorff decided to lead the marchers to the Bavarian Defence Ministry which had become the scene of a stand-off between the *Reichswehr* and the *Kampfbund*. As the marchers neared their objective at the War Ministry, they learned that Röhm and his storm troopers were surrounded by soldiers of the *Reichswehr*. Neither side had fired a shot. Röhm and his men were all ex-soldiers, and they had many wartime comrades on the other side of the barbed wire. Neither side had any heart for killing and Ludendorff hoped that the arrival of the SA in military array would convert the *Reichswehr* to the cause.

To reach the War Ministry and free Röhm, Hitler and Ludendorff now led their column through the narrow *Residenzstrasse*. At the end of the gully-like street a detachment of police about 100 strong, armed with carbines, blocked the way. They were in a strategic spot, and this time they did not give way. Under the command of State Police Senior Lieutenant Baron Michael von Godin they held their nerve and refused to allow the marchers to pass. Facing the police were, in the vanguard four NSDAP flag bearers followed by Adolf Lenk and Kurt Neubauer, Ludendorff's servant. Behind those two came more flag bearers then the NSDAP leadership in two rows. Hitler was in the centre, slouch hat in hand, the collar of his trench coat turned up against the cold. To his left in civilian clothes, a green felt hat and a loose loden coat was Ludendorff. To Hitler's right was the *Kampfbund* leader Scheubner-Richter. To his right came Alfred Rosenberg. On either side of these men were Ulrich Graf, Hermann Kriebel, Friedrich Weber, Julius Streicher, Hermann Göring and Wilhelm Brückner. Behind these came the second string of Heinz Pernet, Johann Aigner (Scheubner-Richter's servant), Gottfried Feder, Theodor von der Pfordten, Wilhelm Kolb, Rolf Reiner, Hans Streck and Heinrich Bennecke, Brückner's adjutant. Behind this row marched the *Stosstrupp*, the SA, the Infantry School and the men of the *Freikorps Oberländer*.

At this tense juncture Hitler's personal bodyguard, Ulrich Graf, stepped forward and shouted 'Don't shoot! His excellency Ludendorff is coming.' There was nevertheless an outbreak of gunfire. Fourteen demonstrators and four police officers were killed. (Two SA troopers had been killed earlier at the War Ministry). The quick thinking Graf shielded Hitler with his body, Graf instantly received several bullet wounds, and almost certainly saved Hitler's life. Incredibly Graf recovered from his injuries and went on to become a senior SS officer.

Which side fired first has never been established. At any rate a shot was fired, and in the next instant a volley of shots rang out from both sides. The police detachment being static and with rifles aimed at point blank range were able to discharge a volley of devastating force into the body of the marchers. The explosive force of the discharge at such short range was shocking and demoralising. The blast hit marchers at murderously short range and they were physically rocked back on their heels.

Despite the ferocity of the initial fusillade the superior mass of the SA could easily have won the day. However, in their biggest challenge to date, the SA leaders were found severely wanting. A swift charge by 3,000 resolute fighting men would undoubtedly have overcome the small police detachment, but at this vital juncture resolute leadership was found wanting. Stunned into inactivity and lacking in resolve all courage deserted the SA men. For all the rhetoric of Hitler and his henchmen there was no courageous leader prepared to overcome the inertia in order to seize the moment. At that precise moment a hero was required to lift up the fallen banner, rally the troops and charge on into the face of danger. The shock and power of the police volley produced a total leadership failure which spelled, in that brief moment, the doom of Hitler's hopes. For all their high flown oratory not one of the National Socialist leadership could master the moment. Battles are lost or won in split second when morale crumbles on one side or other. The National Socialists lost their most crucial battle to date as soon as the first bodies fell and Scheubner-Richter was killed; while Göring went down with a wound in his thigh and Hitler too was injured, the rest were found wanting.

Many in the National Socialist hierarchy were highly decorated military and *Freikorps* veterans but not one of Streicher, Frick, Hess, Rosenberg, Kriebel and Weber had the courage and the wit to lead by example and turn the situation around. All were there and most had the requisite military experience, any one of them could have provided the missing leadership impetus. However, no one individual had the courage take the initiative and rally the troops. Within a minute the firing stopped, but the street was already littered with bodies. Fourteen *Kampfbund* men and four state policemen were dead or dying, many more wounded and the rest, including Hitler who had suffered a dislocated shoulder, now lay on the pavement to save their lives.

There was one exception and, had his example been followed, the day might have had a different ending. Ludendorff did not fling himself to the ground, standing erect and proud in the best soldierly tradition, he marched calmly and resolutely onwards; he carried on between the muzzles of the police guns where he was arrested and swiftly released on his officer's word of honour. He must have seemed a lonely and bizarre figure. Not one SA trooper followed him. Not even Hitler. In fact, according to the testimony of one of his own followers, which was supported by several other witnesses. Hitler 'was the first to get up and turn back,' leaving his dead and wounded comrades lying in the street. Rather than lead an attempt to relieve Ludendorff and Röhm he allowed himself to be hustled into a waiting motorcar and was spirited off to the country home of Ernst Haenfstengl, where, two days later, he was arrested. Otto Strasser was not an eye witness to the events but he certainly heard of the events first hand from those who were present and his published account certainly accords with those who were there on the day:

'At midday it was decided that there should be a 'propaganda march' through the city. By this time Munich was full of military and police. The procession set out with Hitler and Ludendorff at its head, and the armed stormtroopers marched in the rear. Hitler, optimistically believing that he had the crowd with him, did not believe there would be any fighting. Actually it was immaterial whether the crowd were with him or not. However loudly it cheered the propagandists in the Marienplatz, however intensely it desired the blood of the 'criminals of 1918', what counted that day was the attitude of the police.

When Hitler's men debouched upon the Feldherrnhalle, the police opened fire. What followed is among the most disgraceful episodes in post-War history.

While Ludendorff, with head high, marched steadily forward towards the police cordon that was firing upon his men, Hitler, whom Ulrich Graf protected with his body, flung himself flat on the ground.

All the versions that say anything else are false. Hitler flung himself ignominiously to the ground. In the melee that followed thirteen

*Nazis were killed and many were wounded, among them Hermann
Goering. Arrests began immediately, but Hitler, the leader of the
movement, showed a clean pair of heels. He was whisked away in a
private car.*

*After the affray my brother Gregor, at the head of his men, was
able to gain the road to Landshut. On the march home a Reichswehr
detachment challenged and stopped them. Colonel Erhardt came
forward as intermediary, and advised Gregor to surrender.*

"Make way or I fire," Gregor replied.

*The Reichswehr no doubt decided that enough blood had been
spilled that day. Gregor and his men were able to reach their homes
without further hindrance.'*

Rather surprisingly the *putsch* failed to drive a wedge between Hitler
and Ludendorff. When the skirmish broke out at the Odeonsplatz and
Hitler fled, Ludendorff continued to march undaunted into the muzzles
of the police rifles. Despite having good grounds to extinguish their
relationship Ludendorff later became a frequent visitor calling on Hitler
in Landsberg prison.

Despite the poor performance of the SA on this crucial day the first
NSDAP martyrs were created and the dismal events of the day were
re-engineered to represent a triumph of courage and imbued with a
veneer of noble sacrifice and became hallowed in NSDAP mythology.
One legend which was allowed to grow from the ashes of defeat was the
concept of the *Blutfahne* (the Blood Flag). On 9 November the company
flag of the *5th Munich Sturm Abteilung Company* was being carried by
Heinrich Trambauer and was dropped to the ground when Trambauer
was wounded in the shock of the police volley. The flag was stained with
the blood of the NSDAP dead primarily from party member Andreas
Bauriedl who fell on top of the flag when he was shot and killed. The
Blood Flag reappeared in 1925, in the possession of Kurt Eggers. It
was remounted on an elaborate black pole with a special unique wreath
flag top, the pole also contained a dedication plate listing the names of
those killed in the Munich Putsch, whose blood was also claimed to be
on the flag. The flag became a sacred relic and was borne, after 1925,

at the party rallies by SS *Sturmbannführer* Jacob Grimminger. One of the most visible uses of the flag was by Adolf Hitler, who at the annual party rallies at Nuremberg, staged a new consecration ritual in which he touched new Nazi banners with the *Blutfahne*, thus 'sanctifying' the new flags with the old.

Hitler fled Munich to the house of Ernst 'Putzi' Hanfstaengl the loyal National Socialist devotee who had done much to introduce Hitler into Munich society. Ernst Hanfstaengl himself had briefly fled to Austria, while maddened with the pain of his injury Hitler had perversely sought refuge in Hanfstaengl's own home. Hitler adored Frau Hanfstaengl whom he worshipped as a model wife and mother. Perhaps it was this image of the perfect home in Uffing, just outside of Munich, which attracted Hitler like a wounded animal running hunted to its lair. It certainly was not a rational choice for a safe haven, Putzi Hanfstaengl had been conspicuously involved on the *putsch* and had been observed standing full square behind Hitler during the dramatic entrance to the beer hall. It was only a matter of time before the police came to his own house looking for him. It is possible that, in his shame and confusion, Hitler had taken a decision that he would not be taken alive.

Two days after the *putsch*, Hitler was arrested and charged with high treason. Hanfstaengl's wife, Helene, allegedly dissuaded Hitler from committing suicide, when the police came to the arrest him. Some of his fellow conspirators were arrested while others escaped to Austria. The Nazi Party headquarters were raided, and publication of the *'Völkischer Beobachter'* was banned.

Within a very short space of time Hitler and all of the key rebel leaders except Göring, Hanfstaengl and Hess were rounded up and jailed. The Nazi *putsch* had ended in a fiasco. Within days the party was dissolved and National Socialism, to all appearances, was dead. Its dictatorial leader had been seen to run away at the first hail of bullets, and for the time being was utterly discredited. His meteoric political career, it seemed, was now at an end. However in the long run as history now records, that career was merely interrupted, and as events would soon show, only for a matter of months. Hitler was shrewd enough to see that his trial, far from finishing his career, could potentially provide a new platform from which he could play the wounded martyr and at the same time project the National Socialist agenda to a much wider audience throughout Germany and beyond.

Hitler was well aware that the foreign correspondents of the world press as well as of the leading German newspapers were flocking to Munich to cover the trial, which began on 26 February 1924. By the time it had ended 24 days later Hitler had transformed a humiliating defeat into a political triumph. He was allowed the run of the court and using his skills as an orator and politician he made von Kahr, von Lossow and Seisser appear as traitors against the national cause and he impressed the German people with his eloquence and the fervour of his nationalist message, which was soon emblazoned on the front pages of the world's media.

The key defendants in the Beer Hall Putsch trial were Ludendorff, Hitler, Röhm, Wilhelm Frick, Heinz Pernet, Dr Freidriech Weber, Hermann Kriebel Wilhelm Bruckner and Robert Wagner. Although Ludendorff was easily the most famous of the prisoners in the dock it was Hitler who at once grabbed the limelight. From beginning to end he dominated the courtroom. The Bavarian minister of justice, an old friend and protector of the Nazi leader, had seen to it that the judiciary would be lenient. As we have seen, this was not the first time Hitler had been in trouble with the law. In an incident in September 1921, he and some SA had disrupted a meeting of the *Bayernbund*, and Hitler had ended up serving a little over a month of a three-month jail sentence in Stadelheim prison. Part of his sentence had been suspended subject to his continuing good behaviour. Presiding Judge Georg Neithardt was appointed judge in both Hitler cases and he took such a lenient approach that there remains a strong suggestion that Hitler received favourable treatment. Hitler was allowed by Neithardt to interrupt as often as he pleased, to cross-examine witnesses at will and speak on his own behalf at any time and at any length. His opening statement consumed four hours, but it was only the first of many long harangues.

Hitler's confidence in himself, and in the leniency of the court produced a confidence and a swagger which allowed him, without fear of any great consequence to make a number of self-incriminating speeches which are extraordinary coming from a man charged with high treason:

'I alone bear the responsibility. But I am not a criminal because of that. There is no such thing as high treason against the traitors of 1918. The army we have formed is growing from day to day. The hour will come when these rough companies will grow to battalions, the battalions to regiments, the regiments to divisions, that the old cockade will be taken from the mud, that the old flags will be taken from the mud, that the old flags will wave again, that there will be a reconciliation at the last great divine judgment which we are prepared to face. For it is not you, gentlemen, who pass judgment on us. That judgment is spoken by the eternal court of history. You may pronounce us guilty a thousand times over, but the goddess of the eternal court of history will smile and tear to tatters the brief of the state prosecutor and the sentence of this court. For she acquits us.'

When the verdict was delivered, Hitler was not actually acquitted as many observers had predicted he would be, only Ludendorff was actually acquitted. Hitler and the other accused were found guilty. Hitler was sentenced to five years' imprisonment in a fortress, but was knowingly assured by Presiding Judge Georg Neithardt that he would be eligible for parole after he had served six months. Given that he was already under suspended sentence and there was the blood of eighteen men on his hands, Hitler's new sentence was ridiculously light and the intention that he would serve only a part of it was clear from the judge's promise in open court. The *putsch*, though a fiasco, made Hitler a national figure and, in the eyes of many who had not previously even known his name, he was now a patriot and a hero.

There then followed the charade of Hitler's incarceration. It must be stressed that a term of 'imprisonment in a fortress' was a very different thing from being sent to prison. This was an honourable form of penalty which allowed the prisoner to maintain his honour, reputation and his dignity. That summer of 1924, serving his term in the old fortress-prison at Landsberg, Adolf Hitler was treated as an honoured guest. He enjoyed a suite of rooms with a day room which offered a splendid view of the Bavarian countryside.

He was free to exercise and socialise and could hold political meetings with his fellow internees. Visitors flocked to pay him homage and he was inundated with gifts. In 2006, the records from the former prison office at Landsberg Prison were uncovered and sold at auction at the Socialise Auction House in the Bavarian city of Fürth. The bundles of paper included 300 cards filled out by Hitler's visitors, as well as extensive correspondence from the prison management.

Some of the documents were previously unknown, one of the newly discovered document was the prison's 'intake book,' which contains an entry that reads: 'Hitler, Adolf.' Date of admission: April 1, 1924. Medical examination results: 'health, of moderate strength.' Height: 1.75 meters (5'9"). Weight: 77 kilograms (169 lbs). The names of the loyal followers who joined Hitler at Landsberg are listed on the same page: Friedrich Weber, Hermann Kriebel, Emil Maurice and his later deputy, Rudolf Hess.

Hitler began to receive visitors shortly after he was admitted to the prison. Erich Ludendorff visited Hitler several times. Hitler's other guests included 'Captain Röhm, Munich,' 'Councillor Dr. Frick, Munich' and 'Alfred Rosenberg, certified architect and writer, Munich,' the inner circle of leaders of the young Nazi Party at the time. Röhm, Frick and Rosenberg later became head of the SA, interior minister of the German Reich and the Nazis' chief ideologue, respectively. Other visitors could more readily be categorised as wealthy benefactors, like Helene Bechstein, the wife of a Berlin piano manufacturer, who shared Hitler's love for the music of Richard Wagner and who had assisted in the purchase of the *'Völkischer Beobachter'*. Another visitor, Hermine Hoffmann from Munich's Solln neighbourhood, was nicknamed 'Hitler's Mommy'. According to the documents, the attentive visitor and widow of a school principal also had securities sent to Hitler.

As an inmate, Hitler wanted for nothing. His wing on the second floor was nicknamed *'Feldherrenhügel'*, or 'the general's hill'. His confidant Ernst Hanfstaengl later recorded, after having visited Hitler, that he felt as if he had 'walked into a delicatessen. There was fruit and there were flowers, wine and other alcoholic beverages, ham, sausage, cake, boxes of chocolates and much more.' Despite having gained a significant amount of weight as a result of his lavish diet, Hitler apparently turned down Hanfstaengl's suggestion that he get some exercise.

Hitler had other ideas on his mind. He soon borrowed a typewriter and began to hammer out the opening pages of the book which would become *'Mein Kampf'*. Later he found it easier to dictate, to Rudolf Hess, and chapter after chapter of the book that was to become the bible of Nazism flowed out in an unstructured jumble of words.

Hitler initially wanted to call his book 'Four and a Half Years of Struggle Against Lies, Stupidity and Cowardice' but in a rare moment of cooperation with his advisors he shortened it to *'Mein Kampf'* (My Struggle). During the years of Nazi regime, few Germans felt secure without a copy in the house. Not every German who bought *'Mein Kampf'* necessarily read it and many in the Nazi hierarchy secretly boasted of never having read the book. *'Mein Kampf'* is generally disregarded as being unreadable. This is certainly not the case. While it certainly meanders on from subject to subject and displays little in the way of a coherent structure, there is enough of Hitler across the two volumes to repay careful study by any student of the period. Indeed it might be argued that had more Germans read it before 1933, and had foreign statesmen of the world taken the time to peruse it carefully while there was still time, both Germany and the world might have been saved from the catastrophe which befell the world in the twentieth century. For whatever other accusations can be made against Hitler, no one can accuse him of not putting down in writing exactly the kind of Germany he intended to make if he came to power. The blueprint of the Third Reich and of the barbaric New Order which Hitler inflicted on conquered Europe, is spelled out in all of its repellent detail.

Hitler's basic ideas and prejudices were formed in his early 20s and reinforced by his experiences in the Great War. He was full of a burning passion for German nationalism, a hatred for democracy, Marxism and the Jews, and maintained a certainty that Providence had chosen the

'Aryans,' especially the Germans, to be the master race. These views were cemented in place by his association with men like Eckart, Rosenberg and Streicher. In *'Mein Kampf'* he expanded his views and applied them to the problem of not only restoring Germany to a place in the sun but making a new kind of state, based on race, in which would be established the absolute dictatorship of the Leader – himself. He muses on the desirability of having 15,000 Jews subjected to poison gas, wistfully wishes that recalcitrant newspaper editors could have been hanged during the Great War, and waxes lyrical for page after page on the necessity for armed struggle.

Considerable editorial advice and pruning by three helpers could not prevent Hitler from meandering from one subject to another in *'Mein Kampf'*. He insisted on airing his thoughts at random on almost every conceivable subject, including culture, education, the theatre, movies, comics, art, literature, history, sex, marriage, prostitution and syphilis. Here in *'Mein Kampf'* was presented the outline of the Nazi idea of racial superiority, of the conception of the master race, on which the Third Reich and Hitler's New Order in Europe were based. Hitler saw the world as a social-Darwinist jungle where the fittest survived and the strongest ruled. These brutal ideas were set down in all their appalling crudeness as he sat in Landsberg prison dictating and dreaming of the Third Reich he would build on these shoddy foundations.

Instead of supporting the position that Hitler should serve his entire sentence as a political prisoner, the prison governor, *Oberregierungsrat* Leybold, became a staunch supporter, fighting for Hitler's early release. He wrote at length of Hitler's excellent prison behaviour and became his advocate. Leybold worked in combination with Hitler's lawyers to successfully achieve his early release. Somewhat surprisingly Hitler actually served a longer term than the six months which Judge Neithardt had projected. He actually served a little over nine months and at 10 A.M. on 20 December, 1924, he walked free form Landsberg. There is no question that Hitler's release was politically motivated as can be seen from the tone of the letter written by Leybold in support of Hitler's early release:

'As requested by the State Attorney's office, State Court I, Munich, I report as follows:

The political offender Adolf Hitler was consigned to the Fortress of Landsberg on 1 April, 1924. Up to the present date he has served five and a half months. By 1 October, he will have expiated his offences by ten and a half months' detention.

Hitler has shown himself to be an orderly, disciplined prisoner, not only in his own person, but also with reference to his fellow prisoners, among whom he has preserved good discipline. He is amenable, unassuming, and modest. He has never made exceptional demands, conducts himself in a uniformly quiet and reasonable manner, and has put up with the deprivations and restrictions of imprisonment very well. He has no personal vanity, is content with the prison diet, neither smokes nor drinks, and has exercised a helpful authority over other prisoners. As a man unused at any time to personal indulgences he has borne the loss of his freedom better than the married prisoners. He has no interest in women, and received the visits of women friends and followers without any particular enthusiasm but with the utmost politeness, and never allowed himself to be drawn into serious political discussions with them. He is invariably polite and has never insulted the prison officials.

At the beginning of his imprisonment he received a large number of visitors, but in the last few months he has discouraged them and withdrawn himself from political discussion. He writes very few letters, and for the most part they are letters of thanks. He is entirely taken up with the writing of his book, which is due to appear in the next few weeks. It consists of his autobiography together with his thoughts about the bourgeoisie, Jewry and Marxism, the German revolution and Bolshevism, and the National Socialist movement with the events leading up to November 8, 1923. He hopes the book will run into many editions, thus enabling him to fulfil his financial obligations and to defray the expenses incurred at the time of his trial.

Hitler will undoubtedly return to political life. He proposes to re-found and reanimate his movement, but in the future he proposes

313

not to run counter to the authorities, but to make use of all possible permissible means, short of a second bid for power, to attain his ends.

During his ten months under detention while awaiting trial and while under sentence, he has undoubtedly become more mature and calm. When he returns to freedom, he will do so without entertaining revengeful purposes against those in official positions who opposed him and frustrated him in November, 1923. He will not agitate against the government, nor will he wage war against other nationalist parties. He is completely convinced that a state cannot exist without internal order and firm government.

Adolf Hitler is undoubtedly a man of many-sided intelligence, particularly political intelligence, and possesses extraordinary will power and directness in his thinking.

In view of the above facts, I venture to say that his behaviour while under detention merits the grant of an early release. He is counting on the decision of the Court to suspend his sentence as from 1 October of this year, when he will have earned a probationary period after completing six months of his sentence from 1 April, 1924. In many of his letters Hitler anticipates that he will be released on 1 October.'

Adolf Hitler was not released on 1 October as he had hoped. He was, in fact, released on 20 December 1924. Hoffmann was on hand to take his picture and his chauffeur was ready to drive him away in a new Mercedes. His short stay in prison and had done little to extinguish the bitter strain of militant nationalism which Hitler espoused and had instead witnessed the creation of the Nazi bible. It was to prove a missed opportunity to extinguish the flame of National Socialism which over the next seventeen years would grow to envelop most of Europe.